Book 3 | Third Edition

Liam Ashe & Kieran McCarthy

Today's World

Leaving Certificate Geography
Elective 5, Options 7, 8 & 9

The Educational Company of Ireland

First published 2013
The Educational Company of Ireland
Ballymount Road
Walkinstown
Dublin 12
www.edco.ie

A member of the Smurfit Kappa Group plc

ISBN 978-1-84536-559-2

The paper used in this book comes from Managed Forests in Northern Europe For every tree felled, at least one new tree is planted

Editor: **Kristin Jensen**
Design: **Brosna Press**
Layout: **Design Image**
Illustrations: **Design Image, Maria Murray, Martyn Turner,
Paul Fitzgerald**
Indexer: **Eileen O'Neill**
Cover Design: **Graham Thew Design**
Cover Photography: © **Shutterstock.com: Pablo Scapinachis**

Acknowledgements
Brazilian Embassy
Central Statistics Office Ireland
Dublin Transport Authority
Frances Ashe
IDA Ireland
Ordnance Survey Ireland
Rose McCarthy
Shane McCarthy
Sustainable Energy Authority of Ireland
United Nations Development Programme

The authors wish to acknowledge their debt to Kristin Jensen
of Between the Lines Editing and Eimear O'Driscoll of the
Educational Company of Ireland. They also wish to thank
Declan Dempsey, Catriona Lehane, Emer Ryan and Martina
Harford of the Educational Company of Ireland.

Photograph Acknowledgements
Alamy
Connacht Tribune
Corbis
Dublin City Council
Educate Together
Emma O'Sullivan
European Photo Services (Peter Barrow)
European Union
Getty Images
Imagefile
Inpho Photography
© iStockphoto.com: Kulicki, LordRunar, nicoolay
John Herriott (Ireland Aerial Photography)
NASA
Photocall Ireland
Rob Kitchin
Robert Schwandl
Science Photo Library
© Shutterstock.com: Anna Omelchenko,
    guentermanaus, johnbraid, Martin Good, Mike
    Treglia, Nanisomova, Stubblefield Photography

Ordnance Survey *Ireland*
National Mapping Agency

Ordnance Survey maps and aerial photographs
reproduced from Ordnance Survey Ireland Permit
No. 8860
© Ordnance Survey Ireland/Government of
Ireland

Today's World 3

Contents

PREFACE

Today's World 3

Preface

This new edition of *Today's World 3* meets the demands of the Leaving Certificate geography syllabus at both Higher and Ordinary Levels. It covers the following units of the syllabus:

- Elective Unit 5 (The Human Environment)
- Optional Unit 7 (Geoecology)
- Optional Unit 8 (Culture and Identity)
- Optional Unit 9 (Atmosphere–Ocean Environment)

All students must study one elective unit. Three optional units (Higher Level students only) are also included in *Today's World 3*. This allows teachers and students to make choices within the syllabus (only one optional unit is required).

The material in this edition has been revised and updated. Special care has been taken with the text to ensure that it is easy to read and presented in an interesting way. The revised text remains in harmony with the requirements of the Leaving Certificate geography examination.

Today's World 3 uses full-colour photographs, illustrations, graphs, tables and cartoons throughout to illuminate the text.

A chapter on the study of Ordnance Survey maps and aerial photographs has been included in this edition. It will help students to develop the necessary skills to answer examination questions on Ordnance Survey maps and aerial photographs.

Human geography is rapidly changing. All of the major themes relating to population change over time and space, migration, settlement, urban functions, urban planning and urban problems are examined.

Up-to-date case studies are used in both the elective and optional units. Many of the case studies deal with recent events and developments. For instance, cultural issues surrounding migration, the food crisis in East Africa in 2011 and urban growth in Brazil are examined.

Case studies are linked to regions examined in *Today's World 1* where possible. There is also continuity between the settings and regions in *Today's World 1* and those in the elective and optional units in *Today's World 3*. For example, the biome studied in the geoecology unit in this book is the tropical rainforest biome and connects with Brazil, the subtropical region studied in *Today's World 1*.

Chapters in both the elective and optional units end with actual exam questions from Leaving Certificate papers from 2006 onwards.

The edcoDigital website supports an online version of this book. The website contains a great deal of supplementary material, including:

- PowerPoint presentations with diagrams, photographs and charts
- Relevant website links

A range of student exercises can be found at **www.edco.ie/todaysworld3**.

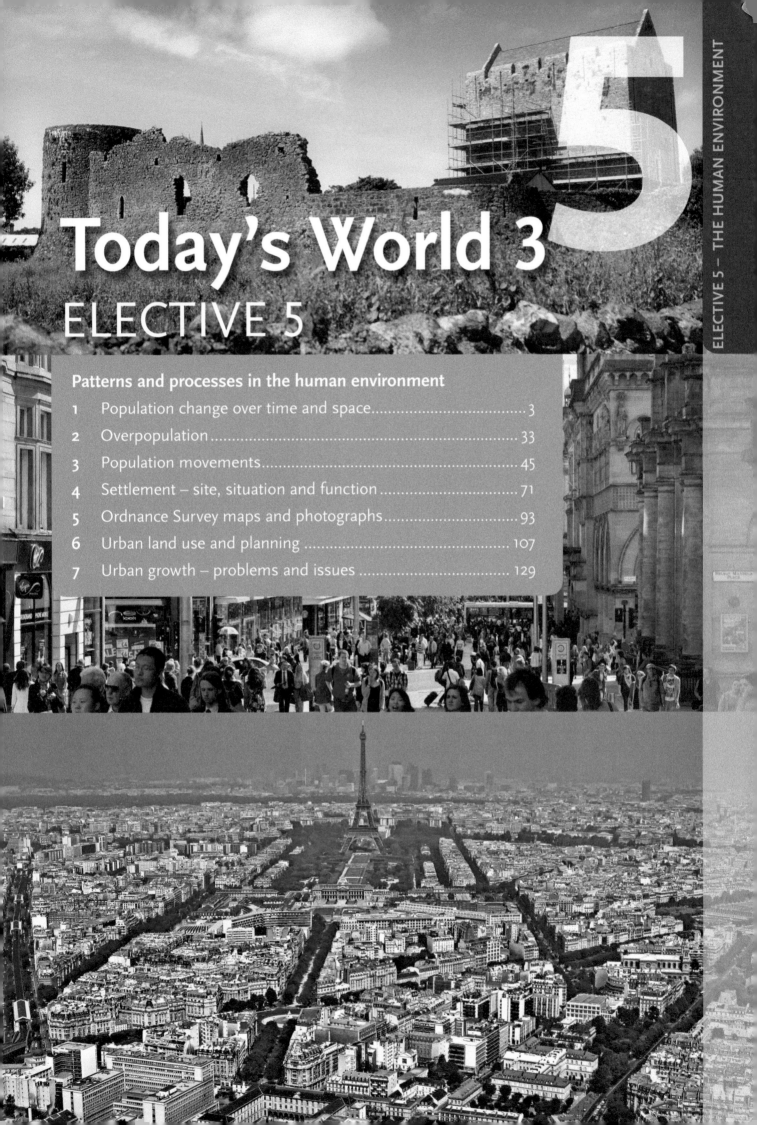

Today's World 3
ELECTIVE 5

Patterns and processes in the human environment

Population change over time and space

INTRODUCTION

Population characteristics change over time and space around the world.
Population characteristics include:

- population distribution and density
- population growth patterns
- fertility and mortality rates
- population structure.

POPULATION DISTRIBUTION

Population distribution describes the spread of a population across a region or country. We can say that the population is evenly or unevenly distributed in a county, province or country.

In the world as a whole, the population is unevenly distributed. Very few people live in regions that have **high altitudes**, that are **very dry**, that are **too wet** or **too cold**.

- Almost 90% of the population lives in the Northern Hemisphere.
- Most people in the Northern Hemisphere live between latitudes 20° and 60° because these middle latitudes have temperate climates.
- **Two-thirds** of the world's population lives in **one-tenth** of the land area of the globe. People have been attracted to floodplains such as the Nile, the Ganges and the rivers of China, where food can be grown on alluvial soils.

Learning objectives

After studying this chapter, you should be able to understand:

- that population distribution and density vary within countries
- that population growth can be measured using the population distribution model
- that fertility and mortality rates vary over time and from country to country
- that population pyramids vary between countries.

Link

The population of Brazil is unevenly distributed. See *Today's World 1*, page 364.

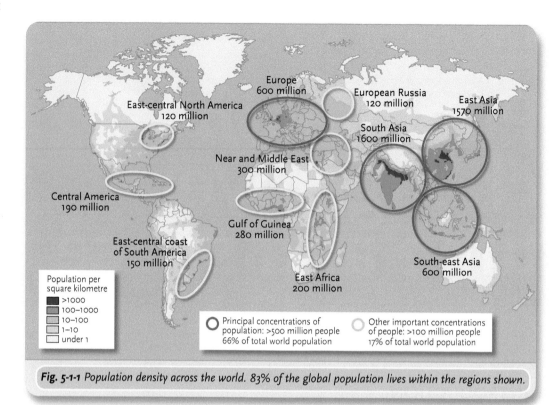

Fig. 5-1-1 *Population density across the world. 83% of the global population lives within the regions shown.*

Questions

1. Why are there variations in population density across South America?
2. Suggest two reasons for the very low densities in the higher latitudes of the Northern Hemisphere.
3. What is the total population in the three great regions of population in South and East Asia?
4. Name three highly populated countries in South-east Asia.

POPULATION DENSITY

Population density refers to the average number of people per square kilometre in a country or region. Population density maps show **the number of people per km²** in an area.

Calculating population density

The population density of a country is calculated by dividing the population by the number of km² in that country.

Example:

$$\frac{\text{Population of the Republic of Ireland}}{\text{The number of km}^2} = \frac{4,588,252}{70,283} = 65.28$$

This is the figure for the Republic of Ireland as a whole. However, population densities vary within Ireland. Some counties, such as those in the west, have a low population density, while Co. Dublin and surrounding counties have much higher densities.

County	Population	Area in km²	Density per km²
Galway	250,653	5,939	42
Dublin	1,273,069	921	1,382

Table 5-1-1 *County population density of Galway and Dublin, 2011.*

Now calculate the population densities for Kildare and Roscommon using the information below.

County	Population	Area in km²	Density per km²
Kildare	210,312	1,693	?
Roscommon	64,065	2,547	?

Table 5-1-2 County population of Kildare and Roscommon.

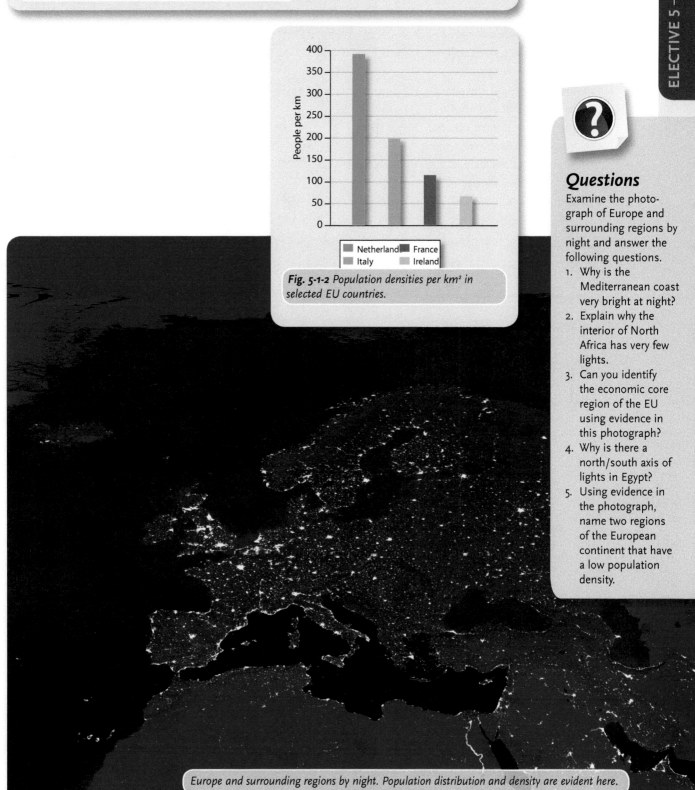

Fig. 5-1-2 Population densities per km² in selected EU countries.

Europe and surrounding regions by night. Population distribution and density are evident here.

Questions

Examine the photograph of Europe and surrounding regions by night and answer the following questions.

1. Why is the Mediterranean coast very bright at night?
2. Explain why the interior of North Africa has very few lights.
3. Can you identify the economic core region of the EU using evidence in this photograph?
4. Why is there a north/south axis of lights in Egypt?
5. Using evidence in the photograph, name two regions of the European continent that have a low population density.

Population density in Ireland

The population of Ireland is unevenly distributed. The 2011 population density map of the Republic of Ireland shows the stark contrast between eastern and western regions.

■ Large areas of the country have fewer than 10 people per km². Physical factors help to explain this. The mountains of west Mayo and Connemara and other counties of the west and south-west support very few people. Large areas of the Midlands have low densities because of boglands and marshy areas in the Shannon Basin.

Question
Explain two reasons for the low population densities in the mountains of the west of Ireland.

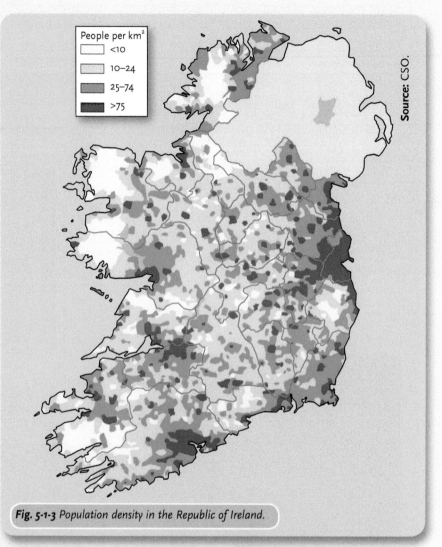

People per km²
<10
10–24
25–74
>75

Source: CSO.

Fig. 5-1-3 *Population density in the Republic of Ireland.*

Connemara, with the Twelve Pins in the left background.

- Many rural areas across the country have fewer than 25 people per km². This is due to the flight from the land, from rural to urban areas over time, because of the mechanisation of farming. The growth of manufacturing since the Lemass era of the 1960s and the creation of jobs in industrial estates in towns and cities accelerated this trend.

- Urban centres have the highest densities in the country. It is also evident that the districts surrounding urban centres have densities of more than 75 people per km². This is because people

live in surrounding villages and towns, where homes may be cheaper than in the nearby city. These areas are the commuter belts of nearby urban centres. Dublin's status as a primate city is evident. Almost the whole of Co. Dublin has densities of more than 75 people per km². This is because the opportunities in Dublin have encouraged inward migration from the provinces and from abroad.

- The commuter zone of the capital is also evident in Counties Louth, Meath, Kildare and the coast of Wicklow, where higher densities exist.

Questions

Examine Fig. 5-1-3 and answer these questions.

1. Why do certain parts of Co. Wicklow have a density of fewer than 10 people per km²?
2. Name three counties where the population density in the whole of each county is 10 or more people per km².
3. Name the physical region in north-west Co. Clare with a density of fewer than 10 people per km². Can you explain why the region has such a low density?

Link

The Dublin and Western regions, *Today's World 1*, Chapter 19.

The lightly populated lowlands of Co. Offaly, with boglands in the foreground.

The densely populated valley of the River Barrow, with Carlow in the left centre.

CASE STUDY

Population density in France

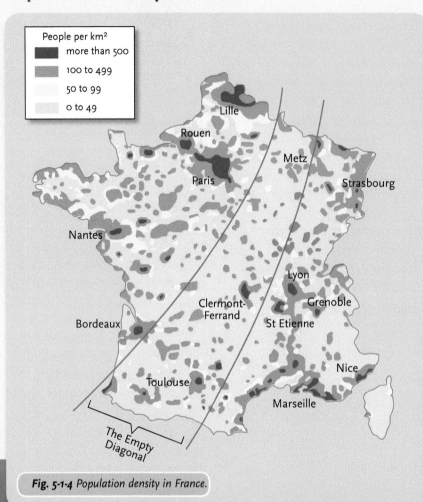

Fig. 5-1-4 *Population density in France.*

Legend — People per km²:
- more than 500
- 100 to 499
- 50 to 99
- 0 to 49

Map labels: Lille, Rouen, Paris, Metz, Strasbourg, Nantes, Clermont-Ferrand, Bordeaux, Lyon, Grenoble, St Etienne, Toulouse, Nice, Marseille, The Empty Diagonal

Regions with high densities

1. Greater Paris and the Seine Valley

The Seine Valley has attracted high densities. The greater Paris area has around 11 million people. Paris is a world city and supports industries of global importance, such as fashion and hi-tech industries. Paris is a great tourist city and has many service industries. As the capital of France, the city has a huge public service sector.

Further downstream, Rouen is an important city and port. Rouen supports port-related industries, providing thousands of jobs. The port of Le Havre at the mouth of the Seine has major oil refining and chemicals industries.

A view of part of the densely populated city of Paris.

8

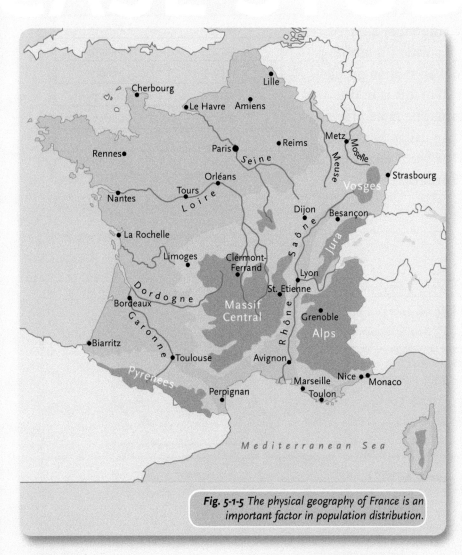

Fig. 5-1-5 *The physical geography of France is an important factor in population distribution.*

is the oldest and most famous hi-tech park in the region.

Regions with low densities

The **Empty Diagonal** stretches diagonally across France. This is a largely rural and agricultural area that passes through the Massif Central. The factors that lead to low densities in the Empty Diagonal include the following.

■ The region has few large cities that could attract large-scale manufacturing. Inward investment has been much lower than along the Mediterranean coast.

■ Mechanisation of agriculture in the last several generations has reduced jobs in agriculture.

■ The region has traditionally had a history of out-migration to Paris and the Rhone valley. The flight from the land to the cities of France has particularly affected the Empty Diagonal.

2. Nord

This region was an important region of coal mining and heavy industry until the middle of the 20th century. It supported tens of thousands of jobs in coal mining, steel manufacturing and heavy engineering. While this region has suffered from industrial decline, the government has helped to revitalise it. Today, cities in Nord, e.g. Lille, have modern industries such as car assembly and computer manufacture. Lille is also a TGV junction. This brings businesspeople and tourists to the region from London, Paris and Brussels.

3. The Mediterranean coast

This region has high densities from the Spanish to the Italian border. The region has one of the greatest tourist industries on the whole Mediterranean. The French Riviera has older resorts such as Nice and Cannes, each with beaches and large marinas. West of the mouth of the Rhone, Languedoc has irrigated farms and modern resorts. In the past 50 years, the population of this region has grown as the tourist industry has developed.

Marseille is one of Europe's largest ports, with oil refineries, chemical industries and gas storage facilities. The region has hi-tech parks, part of the French government's policy of regional industrialisation. Sophia Antipolis

Rural France has low population densities because of mechanisation and migration to the cities.

POPULATION GROWTH

The world's population reached 7 billion in the autumn of 2011. At this time, the population is growing at a rate of about 80 million people a year. Almost all of this is in **the developing world**. The rapid growth in the world's population in the last two centuries has been called the population explosion.

Year	Population
1804	1 billion
1927	2 billion
1959	3 billion
1974	4 billion
1987	5 billion
1999	6 billion
2011	7 billion

Table 5-1-3 *World population growth, 1804–2011.*

Geofact

There are people still alive today who have seen the world's population triple during their lifetime.

Geofact

It took the human population all of human history up to 1804 to reach 1 billion people. Today, the world gains 1 billion people in 12 to 14 years.

Activity

Calculate the annual percentage increase in the following example:
Population of a country: 1 million.
Birth rate per thousand in one year: 15.
Death rate per thousand in one year: 10.
Natural increase per thousand in one year: 5 = ...%

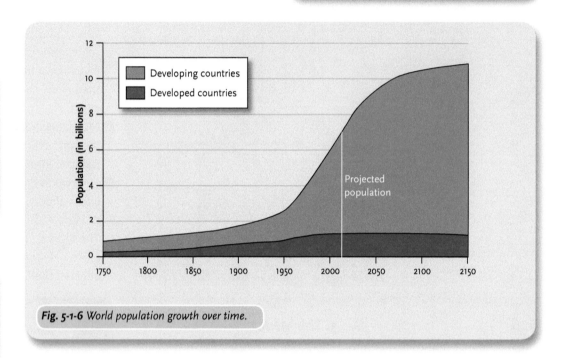

Fig. 5-1-6 *World population growth over time.*

POPULATION CHANGE

Population change occurs in a country because of three factors: birth rates, death rates and migration.

We measure birth and death rates per thousand of population. A **natural increase** occurs when the birth rate is higher than the death rate, as the following calculation shows:

> Birth rate per thousand in one year: 30
> Death rate per thousand in one year: 10
> Natural increase per thousand in one year: 20 = 2% increase

A **natural decrease** occurs when birth rates are lower than death rates. The following calculation shows this:

> Birth rate per thousand in one year: 10
> Death rate per thousand in one year: 12
> Natural decrease per thousand in one year: 2 = 0.2% decrease

Fertility rates among mothers around the world

Fertility rates refer to **the number of children per mother** in a country. These differ significantly around the world. In poor countries, parents have more children because:

- some of their children may die very young
- parents need to be looked after in their old age
- women have low status and are poorly educated
- children are an economic asset.

Geofact
A birth rate of 2.1 children per mother is necessary to maintain a country's population at replacement levels.

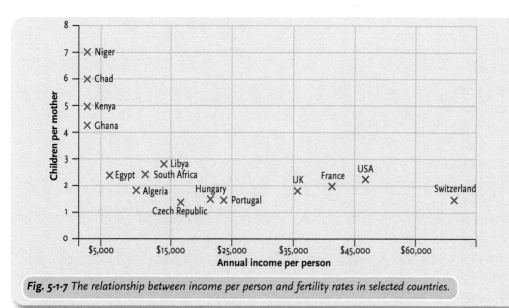

Fig. 5-1-7 *The relationship between income per person and fertility rates in selected countries.*

Geofact
2.1 children means that 10 mothers have 21 children between them.

In wealthy countries, parents have far fewer children because:

- child mortality is very low
- parents have pensions and are less dependent on their children in their old age
- women are well educated and practise family planning
- children are an economic liability.

Questions
1. Name one country in Africa where the fertility rate per mother is more than three children.
2. Name the country with the highest fertility rate per mother in Fig. 5-1-8.
3. Name one country in the EU with a birth rate that is lower than replacement levels.
4. What is the fertility rate per mother in Brazil?

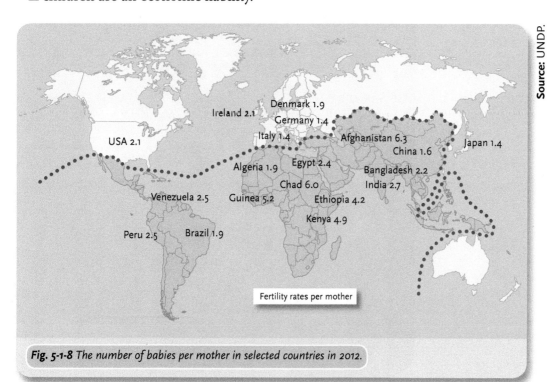

Source: UNDP.

Fig. 5-1-8 *The number of babies per mother in selected countries in 2012.*

Geofact
The global fertility rate is now 2.5 babies per mother.

ELECTIVE 5 – THE HUMAN ENVIRONMENT

Government intervention in fertility rates and population control

In addition to economic development, the education of women and the change in the status of women, **government policies** also influence fertility rates. China's one-child policy is a case in point.

CASE STUDY

China

Governments can influence a decline in the fertility rate. China, the world's most populous country, began its one-child policy in 1979. The policy is strictly enforced, especially in urban areas. However, it has led to a gender bias in favour of sons. Sons are highly prized in China. A high level of female abortions has led to greater numbers of baby boys than girls. More than 90% of children in orphanages are abandoned girls. In several provinces, the ratio of boys to girls is 117 : 100.

The one-child policy has pushed China through the demographic transition from stage 2 to stage 4 very quickly (see page 15). China's fertility rate is now below replacement levels. Population growth has slowed so much that China's population will be overtaken by India's in the coming decades. The population of China is now nearly 1.3 billion, which is almost one-fifth of the global population.

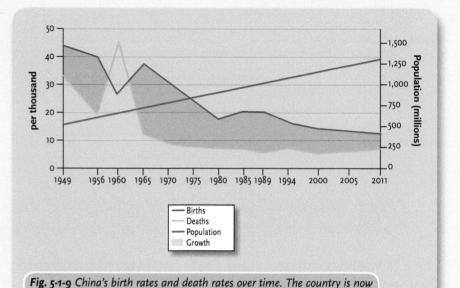

— Births
— Deaths
— Population
░ Growth

Fig. 5-1-9 *China's birth rates and death rates over time. The country is now at stage 4 of its demographic transition because of its one-child policy.*

Questions

Look at Fig. 5-1-9 and answer the following questions.
1. What was the birth rate per thousand in China in (a) 1949 (b) 2011?
2. What evidence in Fig. 5-1-9 suggests that population growth in China has declined significantly in recent years?

A one-child family in China.

CS

Birth rates in Ireland: Changes over time

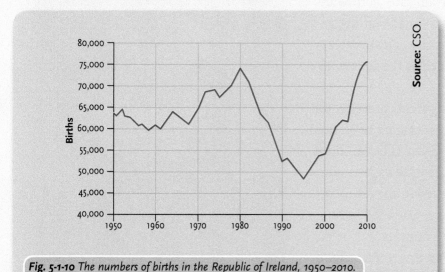

Fig. 5-1-10 *The numbers of births in the Republic of Ireland, 1950–2010.*

Source: CSO.

Birth rates per thousand in Ireland have generally been among the highest in Western Europe for many decades. How do we explain the variations in the Irish birth rate over the last 60 years?

The 1950s and 1960s
Even though the population of the Republic was only 2.8 million in 1960, the number of births was generally more than 60,000 in the 1950s and 1960s. The factors that account for this include the following.
■ The influence of the Catholic Church, which forbids artificial means of contraception. This led to a high **fertility rate of four children** among mothers.
■ The large percentage of the population living on the

Definition
BABY BOOMERS: The increased number of children born in the years after World War II (1939–45) in Europe and the US.

land. Children were **an economic asset** as they could help on the farm.

The increase in births in the 1970s
Births increased in the 1970s, reaching a high point in 1980, with 74,000 births. Reasons include the following.
■ The baby boomers born after World War II were now young adults and began to have families of their own.

■ The 1970s were years of economic growth. For the first time since the Great Famine, inward migration was greater than outward migration. In many cases, returning migrants were young couples in their childbearing years.

The decline in births in the 1980s and beyond
Births declined from 1981 onwards to a low of 48,000 in 1995. This was a decade of economic recession and high outward migration. Ireland lost more than 200,000 young adults who were entering their parenting years. Other factors include the declining influence of the Catholic Church, with increased numbers of couples practising family planning. In addition, many mothers had begun to postpone starting families until their thirties.

1995 onwards
Why did the birth rate increase in recent years?
■ There are 1 million women of childbearing age in the Republic today, more than at any time in the history of the state.
■ Inward migrants also helped to increase the birth rate, with 27% of babies born to foreign-born mothers in 2009.

Geofact
The number of births in the Republic of Ireland in 2011 was 74,650.

Geofact
The fertility rate of Irish mothers declined to 1.9 at the beginning of this century. By 2011, it had climbed to almost 2.1, which is replacement level.

Geofact
Maternal mortality – the deaths of mothers in childbirth – is among the very lowest in the world in Ireland, at 4 per 100,000. In Sub-Saharan Africa, the figure is 640 per 100,000.

Death rates across the world

One of the great achievements of recent decades has been the decline in the death rate worldwide. Governments have made efforts to reduce the death rate. Death rates have been reduced in the following ways.

- **Clean drinking water** prevents the spread of illnesses such as typhoid and cholera, which killed millions in the past. Urban sewage systems, taken for granted in the developed world, are being extended in the cities of poor countries.

- **Better nutrition** improves human health. A balanced diet gives people better resistance to infection. People are more aware of the benefits of good nutrition for their children than in the past.

- As economies develop, **health services and mass vaccination** have become the norm. Smallpox, once a major killer, was eliminated in 1976. This was achieved because the disease was targeted by health departments and agencies across the world.

*A girl in Tanzania filling a container with filtered water. Clean water is vital to life. It is literally **aqua vitae** – the water of life.*

Country	Years
Italy	82
Belgium	80
Vietnam	74
Haiti	61
Guinea	58
Kenya	54
Niger	51

Table 5-1-4 *Life expectancy in selected countries.*

Activity

Using graph paper, draw a suitable graph of the information in Table 5-1-4.

Definition

HIV: Human immunodeficiency virus.

Definition

AIDS: Acquired Immunity Deficiency Syndrome.

It is clear that the wealthier a country is, the higher the life expectancy. People in poor countries have a poorer diet, are less likely to have clean drinking water and frequently suffer from killer diseases such as malaria, TB and parasitic infections. Therefore, many die at a much younger age than people in wealthy countries.

The HIV virus and AIDS began to claim millions of lives in the 1980s, especially in Sub-Saharan Africa, where it is mainly a sexually transmitted disease. Today, however, special drugs and awareness building have begun to turn the tide against this condition in many countries, such as Uganda.

THE DEMOGRAPHIC TRANSITION MODEL

The sharp increase in the world's population has been studied by population researchers for many decades. They have noticed that as a country develops economically and socially, the population goes through a demographic transition.

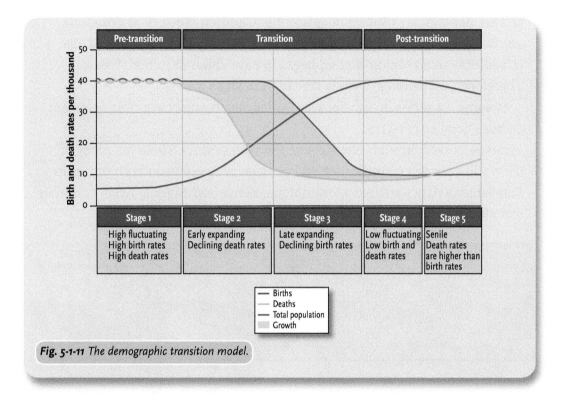

Fig. 5-1-11 *The demographic transition model.*

What is demographic transition?

This is a time of high population growth in a country, when there is a sharp decline in death rates and an increase in life expectancy. During the transition, birth rates remain higher than the death rate. The transition is achieved when birth rates decline to the same level as death rates.

Stage 1 – high fluctuating stage

In stage 1, birth rates and death rates are high. High birth rates are often cancelled out by high death rates. Therefore, there is no population growth. Europe's population was in the high fluctuating stage in medieval times. Death rates were high because of wars, plagues such as the Black Death and frequent famines. Many infants died because of infections. Birth rates were high because people had large families so that some would survive to become adults.

Rwanda found itself in stage 1 in the 1990s when a civil war led to a huge loss of life. Today, countries that experience famine, such as those in parts of Africa in recent decades, find themselves back at or close to stage 1 again.

Geofact
The demographic transition model is also known as the population transition model.

Link
We will examine the food crisis in East Africa in Chapter 2.

ELECTIVE 5 – THE HUMAN ENVIRONMENT

Stage 2 – early expanding stage

In this stage, death rates decline sharply. Fewer babies die because there are vaccines against childhood infections such as measles. Clean drinking water is available to greater numbers of the population as villages sink deep wells and stop using open ponds and rivers for drinking water.

However, birth rates remain high because most women are illiterate and are not familiar with family planning. **Children are seen as economic assets.** Parents have large families as an insurance policy for their old age. In addition, many young women begin to have children in their teens. Therefore, population growth is very high in stage 2.

In some countries in Sub-Saharan Africa, death rates have risen in recent decades because of AIDS.

Europe passed through this stage in the 19th century. However, many of the world's poorest countries are still in stage 2. These include countries in Sub-Saharan Africa such as Mozambique, Kenya and Nigeria. Asian countries include Afghanistan, Pakistan and Nepal.

Geofact

95% of the world's population increase is taking place in developing countries.

Children at school in Nairobi, Kenya. The education of large numbers of children in Africa's expanding population is very challenging.

Stage 3 – late expanding stage

Countries at this stage have a rapidly improving standard of living. People can afford better food and have good hygiene practices. In this stage, death rates continue to decline because of good health care, widespread vaccination programmes and good nutrition. **Mothers are also better educated** and many are practising family planning. Mothers realise that large families are not necessary because their babies are healthy and are likely to survive to become adults. More people are living in towns and cities, where accommodation is tight. In cities, children are no longer an economic asset. They are an **economic liability** because they cost money to educate. Therefore, parents have fewer children.

European countries passed through the late expanding stage in the earlier decades of the 20th century. However, large parts of the world are still at this stage, such as Latin America, India and some Islamic countries of the Middle East and North Africa.

Stage 4 – low fluctuating stage

In this stage, the population has passed through population transition. The developed world reached stage 4 in the second half of the 20th century. In this stage, the birth rates and death rates are very low. Birth rates are low because children are seen as an **economic liability** in developed economies. Their education is costly and parents realise that they can provide better for a small family. Most people live in towns and cities. Many mothers work outside the home.

Death rates are low because people have a high life expectancy of about 80 years. The higher the standard of living, the longer in general that people will live. Medicine is very advanced in developed countries. People live longer because of medical operations that free blocked arteries and because of medication that controls cholesterol and high blood pressure.

A French family trekking in the Alps. Family size in Europe is much smaller than in previous generations.

Stage 5 – old age or senile stage

Many countries in Europe, including Germany and Russia, are at this stage today. Japan is also at stage 5. At this stage, the death rates are higher than birth rates because with a very low birth rate, **the population ages**. Mothers are having fewer than two children each on average. That means that birth rates fall below replacement levels. Countries in stage 5 need young inward migrants to fill vacant jobs and to prevent the population from going into serious decline.

ELECTIVE 5 – THE HUMAN ENVIRONMENT

Question

At what stage of the model is each of the following countries?

Country	Birth rate per 1,000	Death rate per 1,000
Brazil	20	7
Italy	9	9.9
France	13	8.6
Nigeria	43	16.5

Table 5-1-5 Birth and death rates in selected countries.

Definition

DEPENDANTS: People aged 14 and under and 65 and over.

POPULATION STRUCTURE

Population structure is shown by using **population pyramids.** By studying population pyramids, we can see the following characteristics of a population:

■ the proportion of people of different age groups in a population
■ the proportion of males to females
■ the percentage or number of dependants in the population.

Three types of population pyramid

As countries advance economically over time, their populations go through demographic transition. As that occurs, the structure of their populations also changes. There are fewer children and more elderly people. That becomes clear in the changing shape of the population pyramid. Pyramids change from **progressive to stationary to regressive.**

A family in Kyrgyzstan, Central Asia. When you have studied the details on page 19, suggest which pyramid applies to Kyrgyzstan. Explain your answer.

CASE STUDY

Changing population pyramids in Japan over time

Japan's population pyramid in 1950 was **progressive**. The population was at stage 2 of the demographic transition cycle. Families were much larger than they are today in Japan and 35% of the population was aged 14 and under. The high death rate among young men during World War II is evident. Less than 5% of the population was aged 65 and over because life expectancy was much lower than today. Very few people reached pension age.

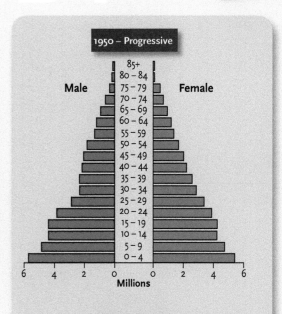

Japan had experienced more than 50 years of economic growth by 2007. The pyramid for 2007 was **stationary**, with a much narrower base because mothers had fewer children. Mothers were all well educated by 2007. Most practised family planning. By 2007, the percentage of the population aged 65 and over was far greater than those aged 14 and under.

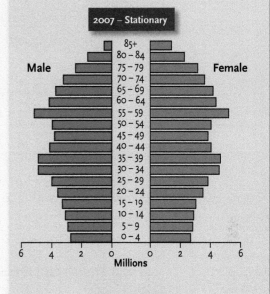

Question

At what stage was the population of Japan in 2007?

By 2050, Japan's pyramid will be **regressive**. That is because mothers will continue to have fewer than two children each. Many women will choose to have no children. The population will become older, with almost 40% of the population aged 65 and over. Life expectancy will continue to rise as health care improves and deaths from cancer and heart disease are reduced.

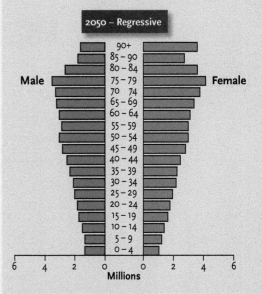

Question

Can you suggest two challenges that Japan's society and economy may face in 2050, when 40% of the population will be aged 65 and over?

Fig. 5-1-12 Population pyramids for Japan, 1950, 2007 and 2050 (projected).

ELECTIVE 5 – THE HUMAN ENVIRONMENT

Population pyramids in developing and developed regions today

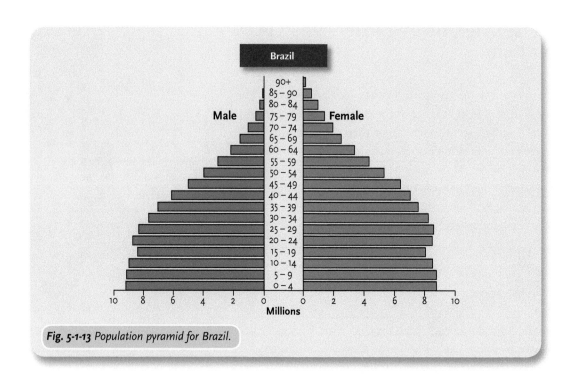

Fig. 5-1-13 *Population pyramid for Brazil.*

Questions

Examine Fig. 5-1-14 and answer the following questions.

1. What percentage of the population is aged 14 and under in France?
2. What percentage of the population of France is aged 65 and over?
3. Which of the three types of population pyramid is evident in the French pyramid?
4. Suggest and explain why the French pyramid is likely to become regressive in the future.
5. Describe and explain two ways in which the Indian population pyramid differs from the French pyramid.
6. At what stage of the demographic transition cycle is India? Explain your answer.

1. Brazil's population pyramid

The pyramid for Brazil shows that Brazil is at **stage 3** – the late expanding stage – of the demographic transition cycle today. That is because Brazil's economy is expanding rapidly. Mothers, who are better educated than the previous generation, are having fewer children than mothers had a number of years ago. It will take some time before the country's population becomes stationary.

2. The French and Indian population pyramids

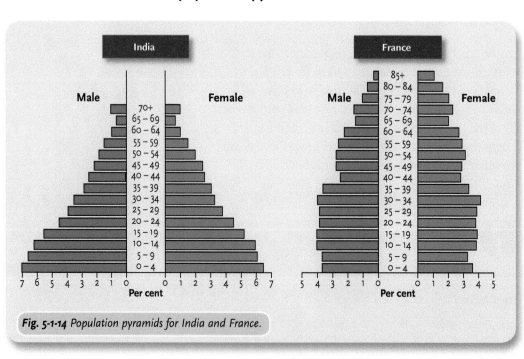

Fig. 5-1-14 *Population pyramids for India and France.*

Who uses population pyramids?

Government departments find the information useful. For instance, the Department of Education and Skills needs to know if the number of children aged under four is increasing. If it is, extra classrooms and teachers will be needed. The Department of Health needs to know if the population is ageing because if so, it will be necessary to provide services for expanding numbers of elderly people.

A group of mainly elderly people in Italy, where the percentage of elderly is high. Italy's population pyramid is becoming *regressive* because of the very low fertility rate in the country.

Link
Check Fig. 5-1-8 on page 11 for Italy's birth rate per mother.

The dependency ratio

Young dependants are aged 14 and under. Elderly dependants are aged 65 and over. The dependency ratio is calculated by expressing the young and elderly as a percentage of the working age population (those aged 15 to 64).

For example, to calculate the dependency ratio for the Republic of Ireland in 2011, we use the following formula:

$$\frac{\text{Children} + \text{elderly}}{\text{Working population}} \times 100$$

$$\frac{979{,}590 \text{ (children)} + 535{,}393 \text{ (elderly)}}{3{,}073{,}269} \times 100$$

$$= 49.3$$

The Republic of Ireland has 49.3 dependants for every 100 of the working population. That is shown as **a ratio of 49 : 100.**

CASE STUDY

The population structure of the Republic of Ireland

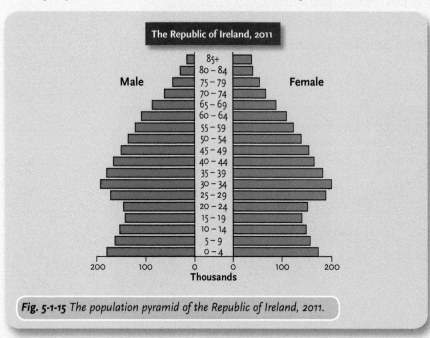

The Republic of Ireland, 2011

Male

Female

85+
80 – 84
75 – 79
70 – 74
65 – 69
60 – 64
55 – 59
50 – 54
45 – 49
40 – 44
35 – 39
30 – 34
25 – 29
20 – 24
15 – 19
10 – 14
5 – 9
0 – 4

200   100   0   0   100   200
Thousands

Fig. 5-1-15 *The population pyramid of the Republic of Ireland, 2011.*

The Irish population pyramid is **stationary**. The pyramid narrows sharply in the age groups from 15 to 29. However, there is one unusual feature in this pyramid.

The younger age groups (those aged 14 and under) show an increase over teenage groups, with **the sharpest increase in the 0–4 age group**.

Why has this occurred?
In the four years before the census of 2011, Irish women chose to have more babies than before. The recession that began in 2008 may have had something to do with this, in that people had more time to focus on family matters than on the frenzied pace of work during the Celtic Tiger years. In addition, many young adults migrated into Ireland during the boom. This increased the number of people of childbearing years; hence there is an increase in the number of young children.

This means that more teachers and classrooms will be required in the immediate future in those parts of the country where the child population is growing.

CASE STUDY

Irish census studies

A census is generally held in Ireland every five years. The census provides much information on population growth, population density and population change. The most recent census took place in 2011. We will now look at some results of the 2011 census.

The 2011 census
The 2011 census tells us that the population of the Republic of Ireland grew by 348,404 since 2006, an increase of 8.2% per annum. This was due to natural increase and inward migration. We will now focus on:
1. population change by county
2. the components of natural change in Ireland
3. population change, 1991–2011.

Population change by county: 2006–2011
Every county registered a population increase during this period. This can be explained by two reasons:
■ High fertility rates of slightly more than two babies per mother – the highest in Europe. Birth rates were higher than death rates, leading to a natural increase.

Source: CSO.

Question

What can we learn from an examination of Fig. 5-1-16?

■ Inward migration, especially in the years 2006 to 2008, when the economic boom was still occurring. Many inward migrants from Eastern Europe may have remained in Ireland even after the economic downturn.

1. The increase in Leinster

The population of Kildare, Meath, Louth, Longford, Cavan and Wexford grew by 10% to 15%, a very large increase in five years. The conclusion that we can draw is that the influence of Dublin has spread into these counties. We know that people moved there because they could not afford Dublin house prices during the boom years before 2008. Motorways such as the M1, M3, M4, M7 and M9 have made it possible for commuters to live in the Midlands and work in the Dublin region. By moving to these counties, thousands of commuters have tied themselves to long-term car dependency.

2. Co. Laois – the star performer

Co. Laois has grown by more than 15% in five years – the highest in the country (the actual figure for Co. Laois is 20%). Towns such as Portarlington and Portlaoise, both served by mainline rail, have really grown in recent years. The county has frequent trains to Dublin every day. Park-and-ride facilities at the train stations are provided for daily commuters to travel

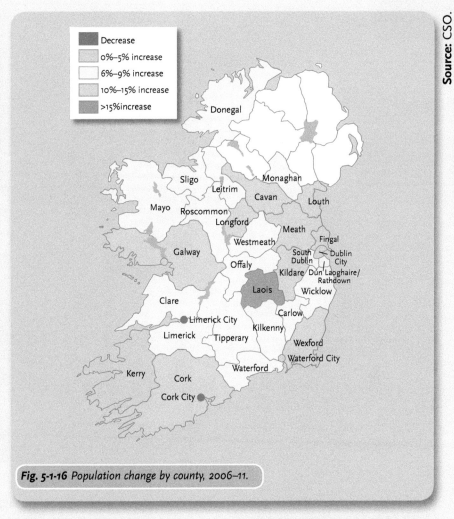

Legend:
- Decrease
- 0%–5% increase
- 6%–9% increase
- 10%–15% increase
- >15% increase

Fig. 5-1-16 *Population change by county, 2006–11.*

the 80 km a day to the capital to work. Portlaoise has a large Polish and Czech community, many of whom have put down roots in the community.

Geofact

Co. Cavan saw the next highest population growth after Co. Laois, at 13.9%, with many people commuting from Cavan to Dublin daily.

3. The Atlantic counties

All counties on the Atlantic seaboard saw an increase, ranging from less than 5% in Kerry to more than 10% in Co. Galway. Galway's growth can be partly explained

by the large student population at third level and by the large numbers of people in the medical devices sector.

4. Evidence of increased suburbanisation

The cities of Dublin, Waterford and Galway all grew by less than 5%. However, the areas around them all show higher percentage increases. This shows that many people are leaving the cities for the suburbs. Why is this? Reasons include the following.

■ The empty nest syndrome, with young adults leaving home in the city and establishing a home in the suburbs.

■ Cheaper homes in the suburbs and beyond.

CASE STUDY

Recent urban growth in Navan, where urban sprawl is evident.

All of this suggests continued urban sprawl as urban centres extend into the countryside.

The decline in the populations of the cities of Cork and Limerick is further evidence of the flight to the suburbs. While Cork's decline was marginal, Limerick city lost 5%. This is a major decline in five years and needs to be halted because a continuation of this trend could lead to a serious decline in services in the city. Many Limerick people have moved to Co. Clare, where the population has increased because of this.

The components of natural change

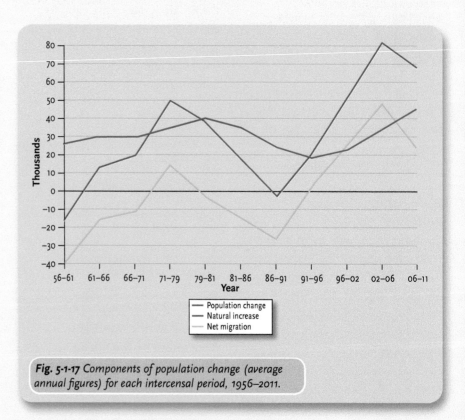

Fig. 5-1-17 Components of population change (average annual figures) for each intercensal period, 1956–2011.

CASE STUDY

There are three graphs in Fig. 5-1-17.

- **Natural increase:** This is the difference between births and deaths. The birth rate was always higher than the death rate over the 60 years shown. By 2011, the rate of natural increase was about 45,000. That means that births outnumbered deaths by 45,000.

- **Net migration:** Migration will be fully examined in Chapter 3. Here, we merely observe that net migration is one of the factors in population change. High outward migration existed in the 1950s and the 1980s, which affected population change. However, high inward migration occurred in the years 1991–2011.

- **Population change** occurs because of the combination of natural increase and net migration. The graph of population change shows that the population declined in the 1950s and in the period 1986–91 because outward migration was very high. However, strong natural increase and inward migration combined to increase the population in the 1970s. Population grew by 80,000 per annum in the period 2002–06 and by 70,000 per annum in the period 2006–11.

Census year	Population	Change	%
1991	3,525,719	−14,924	−0.4
1996	3,626,987	100,368	2.8
2002	3,917,203	291,116	8.0
2006	4,239,848	322,645	8.2
2011	4,588,252	348,404	8.2

Table 5-1-6 *Population change, 1991–2011.*

Population change: 1991–2011

Looking at Table 5-1-6, we can see that the population declined by 14,924 in 1991 from the previous census. However, the 1996 census showed an increase of 100,368, or 2.8%. The economic boom had begun at this time and there were many jobs available. The increase was 8% or more for the census of 2002, 2006 and 2011. By 2011, the population had grown by **more than 1 million people** in 20 years. This means that the population had grown by more than 30% in 20 years. We can conclude that inward migration was an important factor in the large increase in population.

Definition
NET MIGRATION is the difference between inward and outward migration.

Leaving Cert Exam Questions

1 **World population**

Study Fig. 5-1-18 showing world population density and answer the following questions.

(i) In what category of population density is Ireland?

(ii) Name any **one** country in the 0–9 category of population density.

(iii) Explain briefly what is meant by population density.

(iv) Explain briefly **one** negative effect of **high** population density.

(v) Explain briefly **one** negative effect of **low** population density. (30 marks)

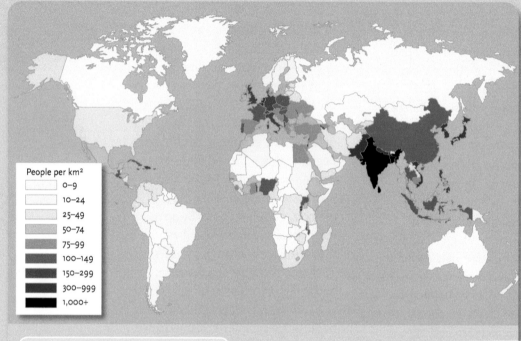

People per km²
0–9
10–24
25–49
50–74
75–99
100–149
150–299
300–999
1,000+

Fig. 5-1-18 *Population density per country.*

2 **Population change**

Examine the demographic model in Fig. 5-1-19, which shows population change over time in a developed country. Answer the following questions.

(i) Name **one** stage in the diagram where the birth rate and death rate are nearly equal.

(ii) At what stage in the diagram is the natural increase highest? (30 marks)

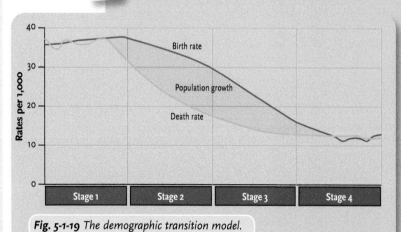

Fig. 5-1-19 *The demographic transition model.*

3 Population density

Examine the population density map of Ireland in Fig. 5-1-20 and answer the following questions.

(i) Name the county with the highest population density.

(ii) Name the **two** counties with the lowest population density.

(iii) What is the population density for Co. Kerry?

(iv) Name any **two** counties with a population density of 50–99 people per km². (30 marks)

4 Population structure

Examine the population pyramid in Fig. 5-1-21 for Cork city and answer the following questions.

(i) What percentage of females is in the 10–14 age group?

(ii) Which age group is the largest?

(iii) Which is greater: the percentage of males or females in the 80–84 age group?

(iv) Calculate the percentage of children, both males and females, in the 0–4 age group.

(v) Explain **one** way this population pyramid differs from the population pyramid of a city in the developing world. (30 marks)

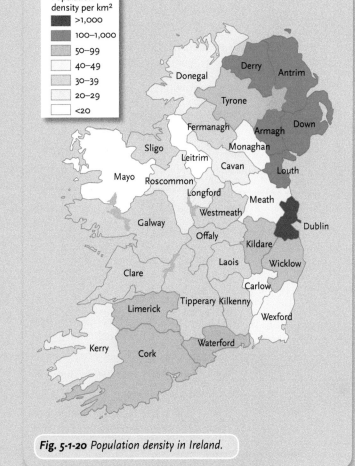

Population density per km²
- >1,000
- 100–1,000
- 50–99
- 40–49
- 30–39
- 20–29
- <20

Fig. 5-1-20 *Population density in Ireland.*

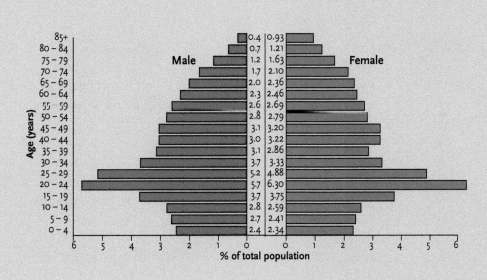

Fig. 5-1-21 *The population structure of Cork city.*

5   Population pyramids

Examine the population pyramids in Fig. 5-1-22 for Tanzania and Germany in 2000. Describe **two** differences between the population structure of Tanzania and Germany as shown by the pyramids. (30 marks)

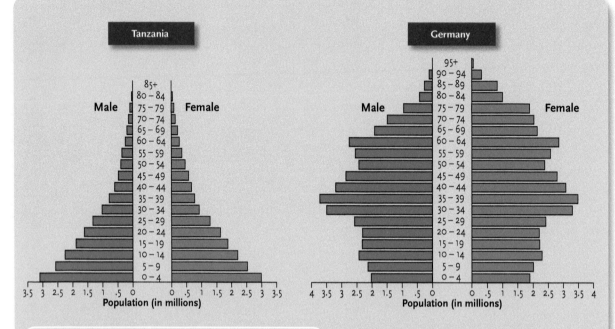

Fig. 5-1-22 *The population structure of Tanzania and Germany.*

6   Population structure

Examine the population pyramids in Fig. 5-1-23. Describe **two** differences between the structure in 2000 and the projected structure for 2050.
(30 marks)

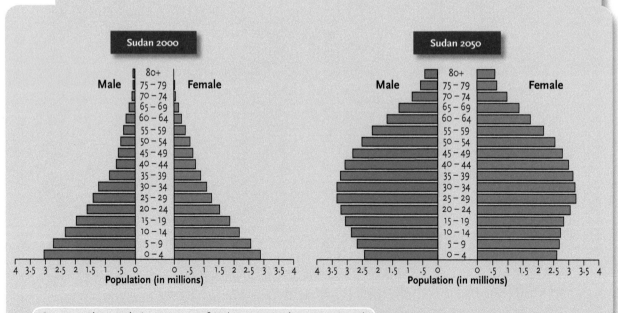

Fig. 5-1-23 *The population structure of Sudan, 2000 and 2050 (projected).*

7 Ageing population

Name and explain **two** difficulties that an ageing population can cause for a country.
(30 marks)

8 Population dynamics

(i)   Use graph paper to draw a graph to represent the data in Table 5-1-7.
(ii) Explain why the infant mortality rate is higher in developing countries such as Kenya. (30 marks)

Country	Infant mortality rate (deaths/1,000 live births)
Kenya	55
India	30
US	6
Ireland	5

Table 5-1-7 *Infant mortality rates, 2009.*

9 Population growth

Explain **two** reasons why the population in poorer countries grows faster than the population in wealthier developed countries. (40 marks)

10 Population density and distribution

Using examples you have studied, describe and explain the difference between the terms 'population density' and 'population distribution'. (30 marks)

11 World population growth
Examine Fig. 5-1-24 of world population growth. According to this graph:
(i)   What was the world population total in the year 2000?
(ii) Approximately what will it be in the year 2050?
(iii) Briefly describe the differing trends shown for the more developed and the less developed countries (a) up to the present day and (b) in the future.
(20 marks)

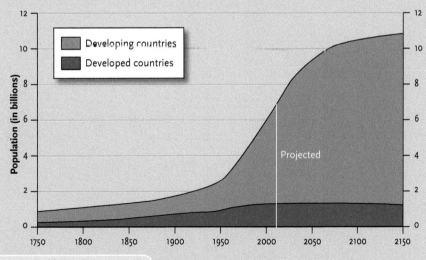

Fig. 5-1-24 *World population growth.*

12 **Life expectancy**

Examine the data in Table 5-1-8 showing female life expectancy at birth in a number of European countries.

(i) Using graph paper, draw a suitable graph to illustrate this data.

(ii) State **two** reasons why life expectancy in general is increasing in Europe. (20 marks)

Country	1990	2009
Bulgaria	75	77
Ireland	78	83
Germany	80	83

Table 5-1-8 *Female life expectancy at birth (years).*

13 **Population pyramid**

Examine the population pyramid in Fig. 5-1-25 and answer the following questions.

(i) What is the percentage of males in the 5–9 age group?

(ii) What is the percentage of females in the 0–4 age group?

(iii) What is the total percentage of the population in the 45–49 age group?

(iv) State whether the pyramid represents a developed or a developing region.

(v) State **two** ways that the structure of a population pyramid for a developing region differs from the structure of a population pyramid for a developed region. (20 marks)

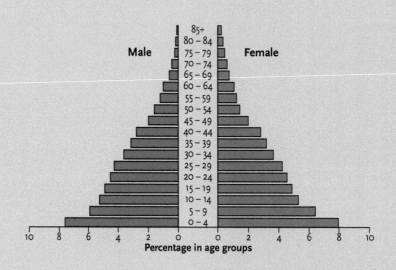

Fig. 5-1-25 *Population pyramid.*

14 Population structure

Examine the population pyramids of Japan in Fig. 5-1-26 and answer the following questions.

(i) What percentage of the population was in the 15–64 age group in 1950?

(ii) Which age group – 0–14, 15–64 or 65 and over – will have shown the greatest increase between 1950 and 2050?

(iii) What percentage of the population was classified as dependent in 2004?

(iv) Identify **one** socio-economic problem that might arise from the high percentage of population aged 65 and over in 2050. (20 marks)

15 Population structure

Examine the data in Table 5-1-9 below showing the percentage of the population aged 65 and over in a number of European countries.

(i) Using graph paper, draw a suitable graph to illustrate this data.

(ii) Name **two** problems faced by countries where the population of people aged 65 and over is increasing. (20 marks)

Country	1998	2008
Belgium	16	17
Ireland	11	11
United Kingdom	15	16

Table 5-1-9 *Percentage of population aged 65 years and over.*

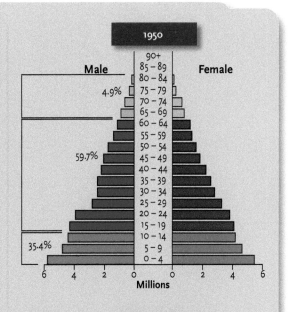

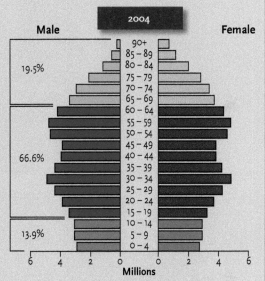

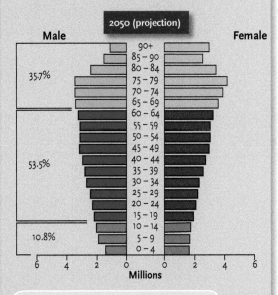

Fig. 5-1-26 *Population pyramids of Japan, 1950, 2004 and 2050 (projected).*

16 Birth rates

Using the map in Fig. 5-1-27 as a reference, answer the following questions.
(i)   What is the Netherlands' birth rate for 2007?
(ii) What is Switzerland's birth rate for 2007?
(iii) Identify **one** social factor that influences the birth rate.
(iv) Define the term 'mortality rate'. (20 marks)

Fig. 5-1-27 *Birth rates by country, 2007.*

Birth rate
per 1,000

9
10
11
12
>12
Data not available

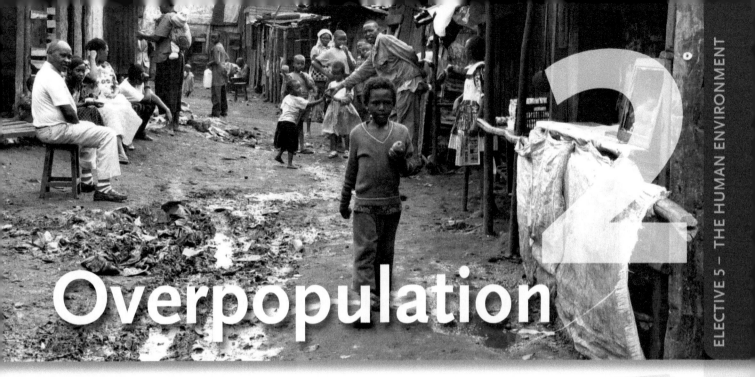

Overpopulation

INTRODUCTION

Today, many people are concerned that the **planet's carrying capacity** has been reached. Overpopulation exists in some regions of the world. Examples include the Sahel region of Africa, the Horn of Africa, Bangladesh, parts of India and north-east Brazil.

What is overpopulation?
Overpopulation occurs when the number of people in a region is too great to be supported by the available natural resources.

What is an optimum population?
An optimum population is the number of people who can have a high standard of living in a region using the resources and technology that are available to them at any time.

When does underpopulation occur?
Underpopulation occurs when there are too few people in a region to exploit the resources of that region. Examples are western Australia and the interior of Canada at the present time, where large mineral resources exist. Australia and Canada have held jobs fairs in Ireland and other countries to encourage engineers to emigrate to these countries to help in the exploitation of mineral resources.

Several factors must be considered in any discussion of overpopulation. These include:
- the resources of a region
- the income levels of the population
- social and cultural influences
- the impact of technology.

Learning objectives

After studying this chapter, you should be able to understand:

- the meaning of the term 'overpopulation'
- the causes and consequences of overpopulation
- that overpopulation exists in many parts of East Africa
- that population growth has an impact on development.

Definition
CARRYING CAPACITY is the number of people that an area can support, taking into account the quality of the natural environment and the level of technology of the population.

POPULATION DENSITY AND OVERPOPULATION

Overpopulation must not be confused with high population density. **Germany**, with a population of close to 82 million, has a population density of 234 people per km². However, as one of the most advanced economies in the world, with excellent resources, a strong work ethos, high income levels, modern technologies and strong exports, the population of Germany has high living standards. It is not at all overpopulated.

On the other hand, the Sahel countries have **very low income levels** and have a desert and semi-desert landscape. Climate change has reduced their carrying capacity even further in recent years. These countries have low life expectancy, high infant mortality and malnutrition. Therefore, the Sahel region, even with low population densities, is overpopulated because its resources cannot provide its people with a reasonable standard of living.

The Horn of Africa is also overpopulated. That region is examined in the following case study.

CASE STUDY

Case study in overpopulation: The Horn of Africa

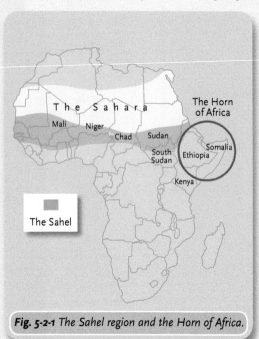

Fig. 5-2-1 The Sahel region and the Horn of Africa.

The Sahel region, a semi-arid region that lies south of the Sahara, and the Horn of Africa have suffered from frequent drought and crop failures in recent times. Burkina Faso, Niger, parts of Ethiopia, northern Kenya and Somalia experienced severe food shortages and overpopulation in the years 2010–12. We will now examine **overpopulation in the Horn of Africa.**

The depletion of the resources of the region

East Africa suffered from two consecutive failed rainy seasons in 2010–11. This drought was the worst in the region for 60 years.

As a result, the **water resources and food resources** of the region were severely depleted. According to local communities in Ethiopia, this is part of long-term climate change. They claim that drought occurred every six to eight years in the past but now occurs every one to two years. Livestock, a vital source of food, began to die. Trees and bushes also began to die and precious **soil resources** turned to dust and were blown away.

Geofact
The rainy season in the Horn of Africa is from March to June.

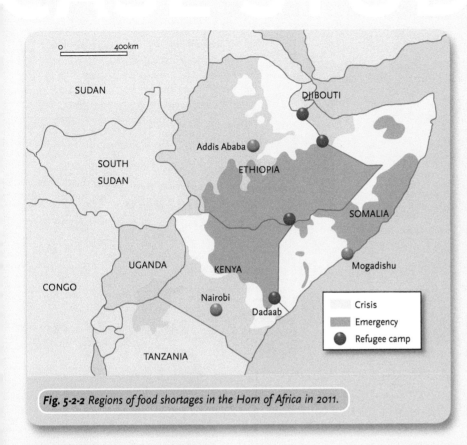

Fig. 5-2-2 *Regions of food shortages in the Horn of Africa in 2011.*

famine. Therefore, because **food and water resources were depleted** in the region, hunger and famine occurred.

The income levels of the population

Ethiopia, Somalia and Kenya are among the poorest countries in the world and people have very little income. While there is food in the shops in towns and villages, many people cannot afford to buy it. Therefore, their children go hungry.

These countries are poor partly because they are highly dependent on subsistence agriculture. Their exports are mainly commodities such as coffee, livestock, animal skins for the leather industry and bananas. During a drought, income that farmers derive from the sale of livestock collapses as animals die.

The crop failures in 2010 and 2011 led to a 300% rise in food prices in a short time. Prices shot up because of scarce **food resources**. The price of local maize, millet and sorghum was far beyond the reach of the poor. The poor account for the great majority of the population. Animals such as cattle and goats began to die because of a shortage of fodder.

The region had one of the highest rates of malnutrition in the world before the crisis of 2011, with at least one-third of the population suffering from malnutrition. The drought was the tipping point that plunged people over the edge into

A cattle market in Ethiopia. Healthy cattle are a vital source of food, including milk and meat, in East Africa. When drought occurs, animals die and this leads to a food crisis.

Country	Yearly income per person	Percentage of people living in relative poverty
Ethiopia	$390	39%
Kenya	$790	46%
Somalia	$150	81%

Table 5-2-1 *Income and poverty in countries in the Horn of Africa.*

CASE STUDY

Subsistence farmers who live in remote regions have no money put aside for periods of drought. As a result, a prolonged drought tips them into famine. Because these countries are among the poorest in the world, they have always suffered from **food insecurity**. That means they do not have reserves of food in granaries for periods of hunger. Many communities have been dependent on food aid for years. The region has been plagued by civil war and by corrupt and inefficient governments. Food security and children's health are forgotten in these situations.

Women breaking the ground with hoes in Kenya. Food output in East Africa per hectare is very low, partly because of poor technology, even where the soil is fertile.

Social and cultural influences

Population growth is very strong in each of the countries of Ethiopia, Kenya and Somalia. Each of them is at stage 2 of the demographic transition model.

Why are their populations growing so quickly? There are several factors, including the following.

- The poor status and educational levels of women – women are culturally tied to the traditional role of motherhood in these countries.
- The low percentage of couples who practise family planning.
- The absence of pensions for the elderly – children are seen as an economic asset by parents, as children will look after them when they grow old.

- High infant mortality rates – parents will have additional children since they know that some of them will die.

While Islam is the religion of a minority of the people of Ethiopia and Kenya, it is the religion of the overwhelming majority of the population of Somalia. Islamic communities have traditionally valued large families, although this is changing as women become educated and urbanised.

Because the populations of the countries of the Horn of Africa are increasing rapidly, the additional numbers of people put severe pressures on these countries when food and water resources dwindle in time of drought.

Geofact
An African saying: God causes drought but people cause famine.

The level of available technology

The countries of the Horn of Africa are among the poorest countries in the world. Their levels of technology are very low. The great majority of people in rural areas do not have electricity because electricity is confined to the cities. People do not have refrigerators and deep freezers to store food. They cannot afford electric or diesel pumps to pump water from deep wells. Only a very small number

Country	Population in millions, 1990	Population in millions, 2009	Annual population growth	Population 0–14 as a % of total	Birth rate per 1,000	Death rate per 1,000
Ethiopia	48.3	91	2.5%	44%	38	12
Kenya	23.4	41	2.6%	43%	38	11
Somalia	6.6	9.9	2.7%	46%	44	16

Table 5-2-2 *The populations and related factors of three countries in the Horn of Africa.*

of people in these countries have PCs and access to the internet – an item of technology that would give them access to news and events in the region.

Agricultural technology is generally primitive. Tractors are far beyond the means of almost all farmers. Farmers use oxen to pull ploughs. The **hand hoe** is also used to break the soil for crops. Farmers cannot afford to buy chemical inputs to boost their crops. Farm output is therefore very low.

Seed technology is poor. Farmers save seed every year from part of their crop. Modern high-output seeds that are used in Asia are generally not available in much of Africa. This also keeps food output low even at the best of times.

Irrigation technology such as dams, canals and plastic piping is in very limited use. Irrigation helps farmers to overcome the challenges of drought and to survive prolonged drought. Without irrigation, farmers are at the mercy of nature, which is very harsh in East Africa.

The effects of overpopulation in the Horn of Africa

1. Food shortages and famine

Food shortages have existed in the region for many years. Famine became a reality in the Horn of Africa in July 2011.

Hunger becomes a famine in the following circumstances:
- when 20% of households in a district face extreme food shortages
- when acute malnutrition rates affect more than 30% of the population
- when the death rates per day exceed 2 for every 10,000 people.

The reality that is masked by the coldness of these statistics is that for months before famine was declared official, cattle and goats were dying, grains and vegetables became very scarce and children were losing weight. People's immunity to infections was declining and parents were gripped by anxiety as they saw their children fade before their eyes.

2. The flight to refugee camps

The twin terrors of civil war and famine in Somalia forced tens of thousands of people to become famine refugees and to flee to the refugee camps across the border in Kenya and Ethiopia.

Dadaab in Kenya became the world's largest refugee camp in 2011, with the number of refugees approaching 500,000. The camp was built for 90,000 and became vastly overcrowded. Many walked

Link
Dadaab can be located in Fig. 5-2-2.

for weeks to reach the camps and lost family members to hunger along the way. The camp stretched for almost 50 km. The camp is in an arid and barren landscape where winds whip up the dusty soil to create blinding dust storms.

Geofact
In 2012, there were 985,000 refugees in the Horn of Africa and in Yemen.

Subsistence farmers who find themselves in this situation experience the loss of dignity in the camps as very degrading. **These proud, independent people want a hand up, not a hand out**. The world community responded by providing emergency food and medical aid to the camps. The role of TV news coverage was vital in raising awareness of the famine, as the currency problems in the eurozone and the Greek debt crisis were grabbing the headlines at the time.

Dadaab refugee camp in Kenya in 2011.

CASE STUDY

3. Migration

Overpopulation leads to outmigration. As resources dwindle, people migrate to places where they feel they will have a better life. People are pushed out of the region because of hunger but also because of violence in Somalia.

The collapse of the central government in Somalia in 1991 led to years of bloodshed between rival clans. The weak Somali government that now exists controls very little of the country and is hopelessly corrupt. The Islamic militant organisation Al-Shabaab prevented many aid organisations from operating in the area under its control. Al-Shabaab even claimed in July 2011 that while there were some food shortages, famine did not exist in Somalia and that the international media was exaggerating.

Many thousands of people from the Horn of Africa have crossed the Red Sea into Yemen, another Muslim country, in search of a better life. The sea passage across the Red Sea is one of the most dangerous on Earth because it is a busy shipping lane. Yemen is a very poor country and finds it difficult to cope with the influx of refugees from the Horn of Africa.

Most of the migrants are impoverished and they face many challenges, such as poverty, cultural differences and prejudice.

The situation in 2012

While seasonal rains have returned to the Horn of Africa, 13 million people are still at risk of hunger. The World Food Programme continues to provide food aid to 7.9 million people. The political disorder in the region continues. We can conclude therefore that the region remains highly vulnerable, and overpopulated.

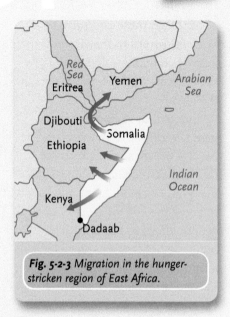

Fig. 5-2-3 *Migration in the hunger-stricken region of East Africa.*

Link
You will learn more about outmigration in Chapter 3, pages 45–70.

THE IMPACT OF POPULATION GROWTH ON DEVELOPMENT

Population growth takes place because of a high birth rate and/or inward migration. Population growth influences development in the following ways:
- A rapidly growing population provides workers for an expanding economy.
- The market for food, goods and services also causes farming, manufacturing and services to expand in order to meet the needs of a growing population.

Population growth and developing economies

Population growth presents **an opportunity and a challenge** for developing countries. A young population is a **country's greatest asset**. High population growth also provides a large labour force. Several East Asian countries used this asset to create economic growth as they focused on **labour-intensive industries**. These countries, known as newly industrialised countries (**NICs**), have developed rapidly since the 1960s. Asian NICs include South Korea, Taiwan and Singapore. These have been joined today by Vietnam, Thailand, Malaysia and the Philippines. East Asian goods such as TVs, sound equipment, mobile phones, toys and sports gear are sold in the EU and the US.

China's economy has expanded rapidly partly because it has a huge **pool of young workers**. Its annual economic growth exceeded 10% over many years because of rapid industrialisation and **labour-intensive manufacturing**. China's economy is now the second largest in the world and is likely to surpass that of the US before 2020.

The challenge of population growth for developing countries

Most developing countries are in stages 2 and 3 of the demographic transition model. Up to one-third of their population is aged under 15. These countries have a **high youth dependency ratio**, as shown in Fig. 5-2-5. Providing education and health services for these countries is challenging. This is especially the case in Sub-Saharan Africa, the world's poorest region, where political corruption and civil wars lead to these services being neglected.

Young workers in a garment factory in China.

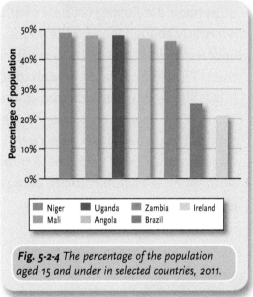

Fig. 5-2-4 *The percentage of the population aged 15 and under in selected countries, 2011.*

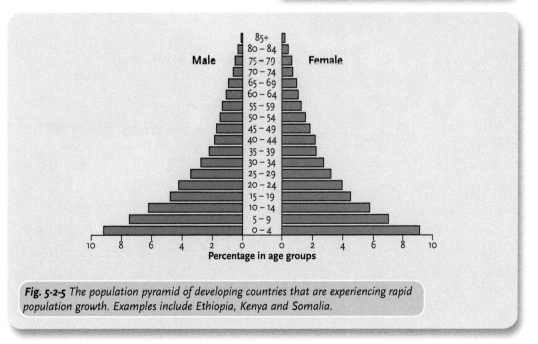

Fig. 5-2-5 *The population pyramid of developing countries that are experiencing rapid population growth. Examples include Ethiopia, Kenya and Somalia.*

A classroom in Tanzania, where large classes and poor facilities exist.

Activity
Check the country and
location of the cities
named in the paragraph
opposite.

In many developing countries with high population growth, there are
not nearly enough jobs for the young. Huge numbers are **unemployed and
underemployed**. Lack of opportunity in rural areas causes migration to the
cities. This leads to **rapid urbanisation** in developing countries. The result
is that shanty towns mushroom in these cities. Bangkok, Djakarta, Kolkata,
Mexico City, Bogota, Nairobi and many other cities have grown rapidly. It
took London 130 years to grow from 1 million to 8 million. **However, Mexico
City has grown from 1 million to more than 18 million in 50 years.** Providing
clean water, sewage, electricity, education and health in those circumstances
is difficult, to say the least.

Mathare, a shanty town in Nairobi, Kenya. Poor services are evident here.

The impact of population growth on developed countries

In the 19th century, European countries were in the expanding phase of the population transition model. This period of population growth occurred during the Industrial Revolution. The economies of Britain and Germany expanded rapidly because they had the labour supplies to work in the steel, railway and textile industries.

The population of the US has more than doubled since 1950. Inward migration to the US was very strong during those years. Migrants moved to the land of opportunity with a will to work hard and succeed. The US became the largest market and also the foremost economic power in the world. Population growth was vital to its development.

As already mentioned, the economies of Australia and Canada are short of workers in the mining and engineering sectors. Australia and Canada **need population growth** to help develop their mineral resources. They are encouraging inward migration, especially of people with engineering skills, from abroad. Irish workers are emigrating to those countries to help fill those jobs.

A queue outside the Working Abroad Expo in Dublin in March 2012.

Geofact
The population of Britain grew from 16 million to 41 million during the years 1801 to 1901.

Geofact
The population of the US grew from 152 million in 1950 to 315 million in 2013.

A jobs fair in Dublin in February 2012.

ELECTIVE 5 – THE HUMAN ENVIRONMENT

AGEING POPULATIONS IN THE DEVELOPED WORLD

Today, the populations of many countries such as Japan, Britain, Germany and Italy have an ageing population. These countries are in **stages 4 and 5** of the demographic transition model. In these countries, **death rates are higher than birth rates**. An increasing number of women in the developed world do not have children because family planning services give them a choice of having children or not.

The result is that with fewer children being born, the population ages. Today, more than 18% of the population is aged 65 and over in many EU countries. This has economic implications:

- The state has a high pension bill.
- Older people spend less on consumer goods than young people.
- Health care of the elderly is expensive.
- A shortage of workers in the economically active age group means that inward migration to the EU and Switzerland is necessary to fill jobs in many sectors.

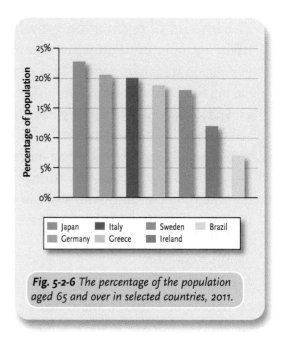

Fig. 5-2-6 The percentage of the population aged 65 and over in selected countries, 2011.

Geofact
Today, 20% of British women in their forties have no children.

Geofact
In Ireland, 12% of the population was aged 65 and over in 2011. We are still the young Europeans because of a strong birth rate.

Question
Several EU countries are planning to raise the retirement age over the next several years. Can you suggest two advantages of such a plan?

Senior citizens enjoying a game of chess in Zurich.

Leaving Cert Exam Questions

1 Overpopulation
Some parts of the world are overpopulated. Overpopulation occurs when there are too many people in a region relative to the resources available to provide an adequate standard of living.
(i) Name any **one** region of the world that is overpopulated.
(ii) Explain in detail **one** cause of overpopulation in the region you have named.
(iii) Describe in detail **one** problem caused by overpopulation.
(iv) Suggest **one** solution to the problems of overpopulation. (40 marks)

2 Overpopulation
(i) Explain what is meant by 'overpopulation'.
(ii) Explain **two** effects of overpopulation in a region or country you have studied. (30 marks)

3 Population
(i) Explain the term 'birth rate'.
(ii) Explain how any of the following factors influence birth rates:
  ■ Medical technology
  ■ Culture and society
  ■ Income levels (30 marks)

4 Overpopulation
Discuss the causes of overpopulation, referring to example(s) you have studied. (30 marks)

5 Overpopulation
Examine **one** cause and **one** effect of overpopulation with reference to an example(s) that you have studied. (30 marks)

6 Overpopulation
(i) Explain the term 'overpopulation'.
(ii) Examine **two** causes of overpopulation in one area you have studied. (30 marks)

7 Overpopulation
Overpopulation can be defined as the condition whereby the number of people in an area is too great to be supported by the available natural resources. Examine **one** cause and **one** effect of overpopulation, referring to examples you have studied. (30 marks)

8 Demographic change
Explain how improvements in technology impact on population growth, with reference to examples you have studied. (30 marks)

Population movements

INTRODUCTION

Migration is part of human history. Thousands of years ago, people migrated from the cradle of humankind in the East African Rift Valley to every corner of the globe. People have continued to migrate in search of food, riches, conquest and a better life. In modern times, people move for economic reasons and sometimes as environmental, political and religious refugees. At the present time, rural to urban migration is occurring in Asia, Africa and Latin America. More people now reside in cities than in rural regions. Population movements have an impact on donor and recipient (receiver) regions.

PUSH AND PULL FACTORS AND OBSTACLES TO MIGRATION

Push factors such as unemployment, poverty, hunger and violence push people into a decision to migrate. **Pull factors** such as relatives and friends abroad, a desire to see the world, better economic opportunities and better employment prospects also cause people to migrate.

However, migrants face **obstacles**. Travel is expensive. Many countries place restrictions such as **quotas** and **visas** on inward migration. Migration can be dangerous for migrants. Many asylum seekers have died on the dangerous and stormy route as they crossed the Straits of Gibraltar in small boats. In addition, migrants may face prejudice and discrimination when they reach their destination.

Learning objectives

After studying this chapter, you should be able to understand:

- that migration has several effects on both donor and host/recipient countries
- that Ireland has experienced changing patterns of migration
- that migration policies are difficult to put into place, both for economic migrants and for asylum seekers
- that cultural issues arise as a result of migration
- that rural to urban migration occurs in the developing and the developed world.

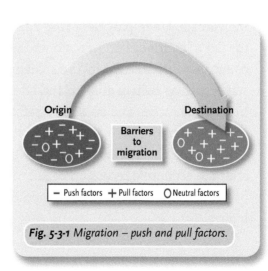

Fig. 5-3-1 Migration – push and pull factors.

(diagram labels: Origin, Barriers to migration, Destination; − Push factors + Pull factors ○ Neutral factors)

ELECTIVE 5 – THE HUMAN ENVIRONMENT

DONOR AND RECIPIENT COUNTRIES

Migration is a fact of life in the EU. In recent times, countries such as Germany, the Netherlands, France, Britain and the Republic of Ireland have been recipient/host countries for migrants, while Eastern European countries, Greece and Turkey are donor countries.

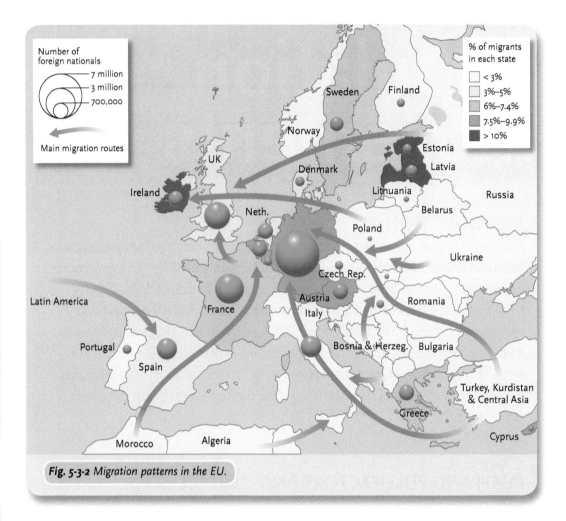

Fig. 5-3-2 *Migration patterns in the EU.*

Definitions

DONOR COUNTRY:
The country from which people migrate.

RECIPIENT COUNTRY:
The country that receives inward migrants (also called the host or receiver country).

Questions

Study Fig. 5-3-2 and answer the following questions.

1. Name three donor countries and three recipient (receiver) countries.
2. What is the approximate number of non-Irish people in Ireland?
3. Name one country from which people have migrated to Ireland.
4. Which country in Europe has the largest number of migrants?
5. What percentage of French people are migrants?

Donor countries: The advantages of outward migration

1. Reduction in the unemployment rate

Unemployment is a major challenge for an economy, for society and for individuals. Unemployment rose sharply in Eastern European countries after the fall of communism in 1990 and was still very high when Poland and other countries joined the EU in 2004. Many young adults migrated to older member states such as Britain and Ireland after that date. This reduced unemployment in those countries and acted as a safety valve that reduced the possibility of social tensions.

In Ireland, the unemployment rate shot up from 4% in 2007 to 14.3% in 2012 after the economic recession began to take effect in 2008. Outward migration began again. Without this, the unemployment rate would have been much higher.

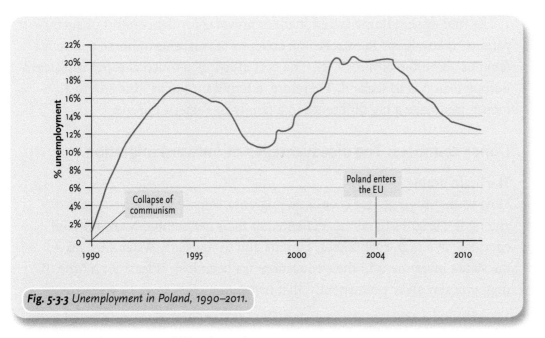

Fig. 5-3-3 Unemployment in Poland, 1990–2011.

2. Migrants learn new skills abroad

In the 1980s, the net migration of 200,000 people from the Republic of Ireland was a major loss of people. However, this loss proved temporary in many cases. Young Irish migrants worked in the US software industry and gained skills and expertise. They learned at first hand how people do business in the world's leading economy. When many of them returned during the years of the Celtic Tiger, they helped to place Ireland at the forefront of the software industry. A number of them set up their own companies and others took up work with leading multinationals in the software industry, such as Microsoft and Oracle in Dublin.

3. Remittances

Many migrants working abroad send money (called remittances) back home to their relatives. Older people in Ireland remember the **American letter** that contained welcome dollars from family members in the US. In recent years, foreign workers in Ireland have sent money home to their families in Poland, the Balkan states and the Philippines.

Elderly women in Poland. People in this age group depend on remittances.

Question
Can you suggest one reason for the decline in the Polish unemployment rate since 2004?

Geofact
Since 2004, Polish migrants have moved to Germany, France, the UK, the Netherlands and Spain as well as Ireland in search of work.

Geofact
Today, great numbers of Mexicans who live illegally in the US send remittances home to their families.

The money sent home as remittances provides for the comfort of ageing parents. It also helps to educate the children of migrants at home and to lift families above the poverty level. The cost of living is much cheaper in Eastern Europe than it is in Ireland. Therefore, a remittance of as little as €50 a month can make a big difference to a family in Eastern Europe.

Donor countries: The disadvantages of outward migration

The brain drain

Most young migrants are economic migrants. People who leave are often among the brightest and most talented of their generation. Many are well educated, at a high cost to their parents and to the state. When they leave, the state's investment in their education has been lost, at least for a time. If migrants stay away permanently, that investment will never be recovered.

Geofact
Irish migrants were granted 22,000 Australian visas in 2010.

Dublin Airport – the exit point for many Irish emigrants in recent years.

The Republic of Ireland is a case in point. Outward migration increased in 2009 due to the economic downturn. Many construction workers went abroad. Large numbers of junior doctors emigrated. Their countries of choice were Australia and New Zealand, because these countries present no obstacles to entry for young doctors. No exams are required to register, English is the spoken language and there is a plentiful supply of work. Even though they are a major loss to Ireland, many doctors return after a few years with a wide set of skills and experience that they received abroad. It is because of the shortage of doctors that the HSE has had to recruit additional foreign doctors to work in Ireland.

Recipient/host countries: The advantages of inward migration

1. Skills enrichment

Inward migrants bring skills with them from abroad. Most migrants are young adults who are trying to better themselves and work hard. The host country benefits from their ambition and drive. Many bring entrepreneurial skills with them.

Ireland has benefited from these factors. MNCs that are located in Dublin, such as Google, require large numbers of people who are skilled in foreign languages. Foreign workers are employed by these companies because of their languages – Irish graduates may not have the diverse language skills that some of the jobs require. Reference has already been made to the foreign medical staff, from as far away as the Philippines, who are filling vacancies in the Irish health services. Inward migrants spend money in Ireland on rent, food, entertainment and other needs. This benefits the Irish economy.

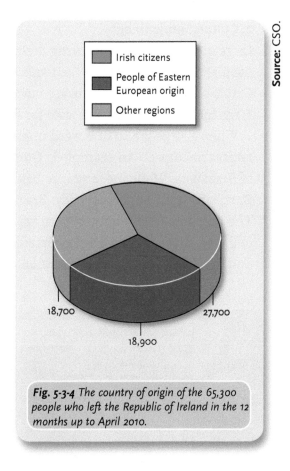

Source: CSO.

Irish citizens

People of Eastern European origin

Other regions

18,700

27,700

18,900

Fig. 5-3-4 *The country of origin of the 65,300 people who left the Republic of Ireland in the 12 months up to April 2010.*

Participants at the Web Summit in Dublin, 2012. Tech giants such as Google and AOL were represented. They have an international workforce in Ireland.

2. Cultural enrichment

Large groups of emigrants bring their culture with them. The local population is introduced to the foods, music and customs of inward migrants. Ethnic shops and restaurants are now found in every Irish town and city. Many local people acquire a taste for foreign ethnic dishes as a result.

When a large group of inward migrants settle in a town, they have a noticeable impact. An example is Gort, Co. Galway, which has a large group of Brazilians. While the language has been a problem for the migrants, young Brazilians learn English quickly. Brazilian foods are available in some shops. The migrants hold their own carnival each summer and the streets come alive to the sounds of samba music. Brazilians bring great excitement to the town during World Cup soccer tournaments.

Link
Gort in the Western region, *Today's World 1*, page 305.

Members of the Brazilian community celebrate their culture in Gort at their annual festival.

Geofact
766,770 people living in Ireland at the time of the 2011 census were born outside the state.

Host countries: The disadvantages of inward migration

1. The downward trend in wages

When inward migrants enter a country, the labour supply increases. The result is that many inward migrants may be prepared to work for less than local people, especially in unskilled jobs and in provincial towns where rented accommodation is cheaper than in the cities. This drives down the cost of labour and in turn can cause a reduction in the wages of the host population. Such a situation is good for the person who wants her home painted, for example, but it makes life difficult for local painters who have a mortgage to meet every month.

Link
Inward migration in the Paris basin, *Today's World 1*, pages 325–6.

2. The challenge of the language barrier

This is a major barrier to integration among inward migrants. The language barrier means that the migrants are sometimes exploited by employers.

Children are at a disadvantage at school, especially in secondary school, where all subjects have to be learned in the local language. Language teachers have to take small groups of migrant children to give them intensive language classes. This makes the provision of education more expensive for the state. The children of inward migrant parents who settle in the Gaeltacht face an even greater linguistic challenge.

3. The challenge of integration

When migrants from the same country settle in the same urban centre, they tend to congregate among their own people. This can make integration difficult because migrants speak their own language daily and have less contact with the host community. This trend can also lead to the emergence of **ghettos**. In some countries, distrust and prejudice against inward migrants can grow among the host community. This can lead to violence between the host and migrant communities. Tensions between the host and immigrant communities flare up periodically in the Netherlands, Belgium, Britain and other countries in the EU. As we have seen, a number of governments in Europe are moving to the right and calling for a reduction in inward migration. In fact, racism and **xenophobia exist to some degree in many European countries**.

Governments in host countries need to take the lead in measures that encourage integration. The Irish government appointed Conor Lenihan, TD, as Minister of State for Integration in 2007, a far-sighted step towards building harmony in Irish communities. However, this department became part of the Department of Justice in 2010.

'We asked for workers and we got people instead.' – *Max Frisch, Swiss novelist, referring to Swiss guest workers*. What do you think he meant by that?

Link
Migration patterns in the Mezzogiorno, *Today's World 1*, page 340.

Link
Inward migration – Paris Basin, *Today's World 1*, page 325.

Definitions
A **GHETTO** is an area in a city where the same cultural group lives.

XENOPHOBIA: Fear of foreigners.

A group of school children in Mullingar Educate Together NS. These children reflect the multiethnic nature of Irish society today.

CASE STUDY

The changing patterns of migration in Ireland

Migration has been a feature of Irish society since the Great Famine. Ireland experienced a pattern of high outward migration for more than 100 years after the Great Famine. In the last 50 years, while outward migration has occurred during economic recessions, new patterns of inward migration have also occurred. The Irish economy needed workers from abroad during the Celtic Tiger years.

Geofact
The southern Irish state has been known by different names since it was established in 1922:
■ 1922–37: **The Irish Free State**
■ 1937–49: **Éire**
■ 1949–the present: **The Republic of Ireland**

THE SOUTHERN IRISH STATE: PATTERNS OF MIGRATION

Outward migration

Outward migration, which had blighted the country since the Great Famine, continued in the decades after independence was achieved in 1922. The factors that caused outward migration from Ireland included the following.

■ **Push factors:** The Irish fertility rate was high, with an average of more than four children per mother. As large numbers of children grew up, there were no manufacturing jobs for them until the 1960s. The Irish economy continued to supply Britain with unprocessed agricultural products, mainly live cattle. No processing meant no industrial jobs.

■ Poverty and the lack of opportunities pushed people onto the emigrant boat.

■ **Pull factors:** Work opportunities existed in Britain and in the US. For example, during World War II, large numbers of outward migrants found work in Britain. Thousands of young Irish women trained as nurses in British hospitals. In addition, many Irish young people had relatives abroad who provided them with the support they needed to get on their feet in a foreign land.

A young Irish girl arriving in Britain to find employment in 1955.

The destinations of outward migrants

While many thousands of migrants made their way to the US, most went to Britain because it was much closer than the US and because Irish people could enter Britain without visas or other entry restrictions. A small number went to Australia, especially in the 1950s, when Australia needed workers and provided cheap ocean fares to Europeans.

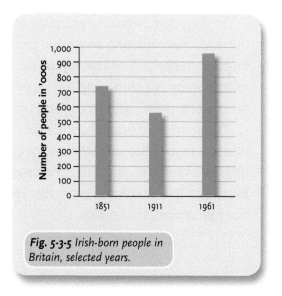

Fig. 5-3-5 *Irish-born people in Britain, selected years.*

The results of outward migration from the Republic of Ireland

A great wave of outward migration over the four decades after 1922 peaked in the 1950s. In the 1950s, net outward migration totalled **411,000 people**. The result was that the population continued to decline until the 1961 census, when it hit the floor at 2.8 million people – the lowest in the history of the state.

This had a serious effect on rural areas, especially in the west of Ireland. Migration was **age selective** – parishes lost their **young adults** and clubs were unable to field GAA teams. The life went out of communities and the percentage of elderly dependants increased. Boarded-up buildings and abandoned farmhouses were to be seen in every rural townland.

Inward migration to the Republic of Ireland

Fortunately, this devastating pattern of outmigration changed. The Lemass years of 1959–66 saw a major shift in government policy. Seán Lemass – guided by **Ken Whitaker**, his economic adviser – encouraged a policy of inviting multinational companies to become established in the Republic. These came in large numbers through the efforts of the IDA and the lure of tax incentives. **Net outward migration declined sharply** in the 1960s.

Jack Lynch signing the accession treaty when Ireland joined the EU.

© European Union, 2012

The Republic became a member of the EEC (now the EU) in 1973 and this encouraged strong economic growth. For the first time, the pattern of migration changed. **In the 1970s, net inward migration exceeded outward migration by 104,000 people.** The population increase of the 1970s was due to both relatively high fertility and inward migration.

The severe economic recession of the 1980s that was triggered by the increase in oil prices saw the return of outward migration. This time, outward migrants were well educated and caused a brain drain from Ireland. The Republic's loss was America's gain. However, a return to inward migration was just around the corner.

Definition
BRAIN DRAIN: The outward migration of bright, well-educated and highly skilled people from a country.

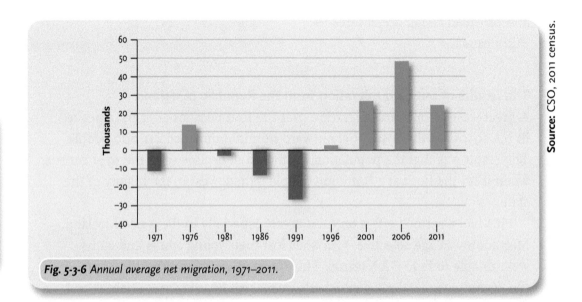

Fig. 5-3-6 Annual average net migration, 1971–2011.

Source: CSO, 2011 census.

Geofact
At the height of the boom around the beginning of the new century, 1,000 jobs a week were being created and thousands of jobs remained unfilled.

Inward migration becomes a stampede – the Celtic Tiger era
The Celtic Tiger era ushered in a period of amazing economic growth, when the Irish economy became the envy of the world. Even though the fertility rate was just below replacement level, the population grew rapidly during the years 1996 to 2011. This increase was therefore due to high inward migration. In fact, without inward migration, the Irish economy would have run out of workers.

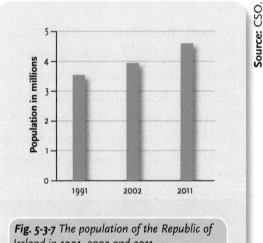

Fig. 5-3-7 The population of the Republic of Ireland in 1991, 2002 and 2011.

Source: CSO.

Question
Describe the information contained in Fig. 5-3-6.

The consequences for Ireland of inward migration
- Inward migration brought an immediate increase in population. By 2011, the population had grown by **more than 1 million people in 20 years.** This was unprecedented in recent Irish history.

■ This increase created more jobs, especially in the construction of homes, but also in school extensions, shops and services.

■ Inward migrants brought with them skills that they had acquired in work experience abroad. These were very valuable to the Irish economy. Many inward migrants with entrepreneurial skills set up companies and provided employment.

EU expansion led to unprecedented inward migration. Net inward migration peaked in 2007 at 71,800, mostly of young, energetic and well-educated people. While migrants came from many Eastern European countries, Polish people represented the largest group. As EU citizens, they were permitted to work in Ireland.

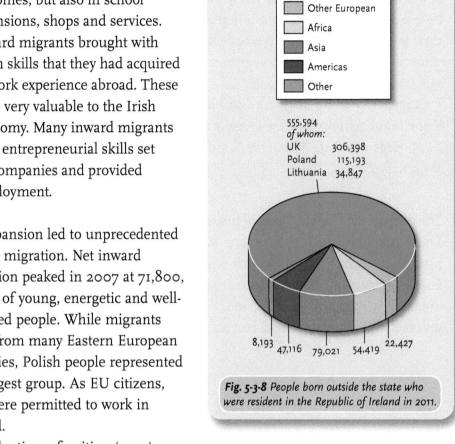

555,594
of whom:
UK   306,398
Poland   115,193
Lithuania   34,847

8,193   47,116   79,021   54,419   22,427

Fig. 5-3-8 *People born outside the state who were resident in the Republic of Ireland in 2011.*

At the time of writing (2012), outward migration is occurring because of the recession. However, as the 2011 census shows, it has been much less than feared at first.

Asylum seekers

Asylum seekers are allowed to enter Ireland to seek refugee status. While their application is being processed, they are entitled to accommodation, health care, a weekly allowance and education for their children. They may not engage in work while their application is being processed.

If their application for asylum is refused, they may be deported. However, they can appeal the refusal through the courts.

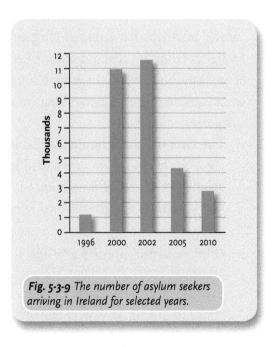

Fig. 5-3-9 *The number of asylum seekers arriving in Ireland for selected years.*

Refugee applications in Ireland

In 2010, Ireland was the EU member state least likely to grant refugee status following an application. **Almost 99% of applications were rejected** in 2010 compared to an average EU acceptance rate of one in four.

After the Good Friday Agreement of 1998, any child born in Ireland automatically became a citizen of the Irish state. Following this, the number of asylum seekers coming to Ireland rose sharply. However, in 2004 the Irish people voted in a referendum by a majority of 79% to withdraw the **automatic right to citizenship** to children born in Ireland of parents who were not EU citizens. This caused an immediate reduction in the number of asylum seekers coming to Ireland.

Citizenship would be granted to a baby born in Ireland after 2005 only if one of the parents had lived legally in the country for three years. After 2005, large numbers of parents/family members were deported because their asylum application failed.

The decision of the EU Court of Justice in relation to family members

The deportation of family members was challenged in the EU Court of Justice. The Court ruled in March 2011 that this policy was in breach of European law. This decision gave Irish children the right to have their parents live with them and work in Ireland. Families will no longer be separated unless there is an exceptional reason. As of 2012, this is how things stand.

MIGRATION POLICY IN THE REPUBLIC OF IRELAND

The Republic of Ireland is part of the global economy and needs highly skilled workers from abroad, especially in IT. Multinationals need to hire specialist workers from abroad for their Irish operations. Work permits – the equivalent of a working visa in the US – are available to foreign workers.

Work permits for inward migrants

Migrants from the EU and **other EEA countries** do not need work permits of any kind to work in the Republic of Ireland. However, inward migrants from outside these countries require work permits, of which there are four categories.

1. **The Green Card Scheme:** Available to workers with high skills in certain areas such as IT. The green card is available to workers who will earn salaries in excess of €60,000.
2. **Work permits** are given to workers earning between €30,000 and €60,000.
3. **Intra-company transfer permits** are provided to senior staff of MNCs who are transferred to Ireland.
4. **Spousal/dependant work permits** are available to husbands, wives and children of migrants who already hold work permits.

The rights of foreign workers in the Republic

■ Green cards and permits are now granted to the employee rather than to the employer. This allows the worker to move to another employer.

Question
Explain the meaning of the term 'hospitality industry'.

Geofact
In 2012, the IT sector of the Irish economy had 20,000 unfilled positions because of the shortage of workers with those skills in Ireland.

Geofact
The EU as well as Norway, Iceland, Liechtenstein and Switzerland make up the EEA – the European Economic Area.

- A work permit holder may apply to bring his/her family to Ireland and can apply for permanent residency within two years.
- Foreign residents may apply for citizenship within five years.
- Employers may not deduct recruitment costs from the wages of workers and may not hold their documents. These belong to the worker.

AN EU POLICY ON INWARD MIGRATION

Why is inward migration necessary for the EU?

- The EU's population is ageing due to its low birth rate. Already, many EU companies are having problems filling highly skilled job vacancies in research and IT. By 2020, the EU will need around 20 million legal migrants of working age.
- All the evidence suggests that the EU is losing out to the US, Canada and Australia in recruiting highly skilled workers from abroad. In order to remain competitive, the EU must make entry to the EU easier for specialist workers such as computer engineers and scientists.
- Multinational companies frequently need to transfer workers from outside the EU to their EU operations; and they want to do this easily and quickly.
- Until recently, EU countries have recruited workers separately in non-EU countries. Different countries have different entry requirements that are very difficult for would-be migrants to understand.

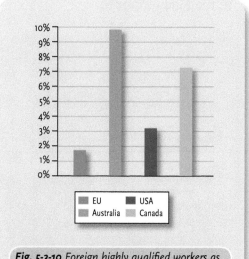

Fig. 5-3-10 *Foreign highly qualified workers as a percentage of the total working population in selected regions/countries. The EU needs to make entry into the EU more attractive for highly skilled people.*

Why is the US economy at the cutting edge of research and innovation? Partly because companies and universities in the US actively recruit bright young people in Taiwan, India and other developing states.

The EU Blue Card

The EU blue card is like the US green card. The card gives work and residence permits to non-EU workers. Under certain conditions, they will be allowed to move to another member state after two years of legal residence in the first state. To qualify for a card, an inward migrant must be offered a salary 1.5 times the average salary in the EU host country. The EU hopes that the blue card will give companies access to 'the right people with the right skills at the right moment'. The blue card came into operation in 2011.

AN EU POLICY ON ASYLUM SEEKERS?

Asylum seekers face several challenges when they enter the EU.

The Dublin System

Under the Dublin System (so-called after an EU meeting in Dublin in 2003), the EU country that the refugees first enter has to deal with their asylum application. This aims to prevent so-called 'asylum shopping'. An application by an asylum seeker can be examined by only one member state and this often means sending migrants within the EU back to their point of entry. Asylum seekers are fingerprinted at their point of entry and this information is collected in a computer database.

The number of asylum seekers and illegal immigrants entering Germany and other northern EU states has declined considerably since the Dublin System was introduced in 2003, as migrants are sent back to their EU point of entry. This puts greater pressure on Spain, Greece and Italy – entry points in the Mediterranean.

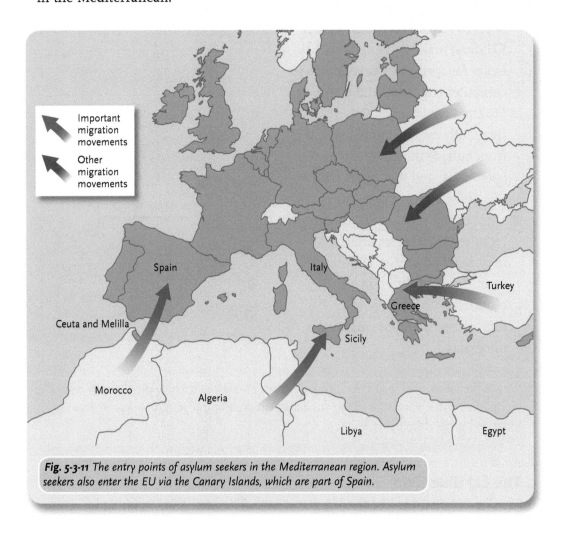

Fig. 5-3-11 *The entry points of asylum seekers in the Mediterranean region. Asylum seekers also enter the EU via the Canary Islands, which are part of Spain.*

Fortress Europe: FRONTEX

In 2004 the EU founded the border control agency FRONTEX. FRONTEX provides assistance to those member states that need help securing their borders. FRONTEX is active on the Greek-Turkish border, where between 200 and 300 illegal immigrants cross through Turkey every day. Greece is struggling to cope with controlling its Mediterranean border, which has become the gateway to Europe for many Asian migrants. FRONTEX assists the Italian authorities with the influx of refugees who come through Tunisia.

African refugees in Tenerife, one of the Canary Islands.

Right-wing groups within the EU

Anti-immigration sentiment has risen in several European countries in recent years, **especially with high youth unemployment in Europe** (see Fig. 5-3-13 on page 61). For instance, in Italy, Umberto Bossi's Northern League has wielded huge influence over domestic policy. Laws now allow authorities to fine and imprison illegal immigrants and to punish people who provide them with shelter. Even a country as tolerant as Denmark has made it more and more difficult for asylum seekers because of the influence of right-wing pressure. In these circumstances, the likelihood of a common EU asylum policy is remote.

Spain owns Ceuta and Melilla on the Moroccan coast, where Fortress Europe is very visible. These territories are heavily fenced and guarded to keep out asylum seekers. Many migrants receive serious injuries trying to scale these barriers in order to enter Spanish territory. Those who are caught by Spanish border guards are sent back to Morocco, where they face severe hardship and uncertainty.

ELECTIVE 5 – THE HUMAN ENVIRONMENT

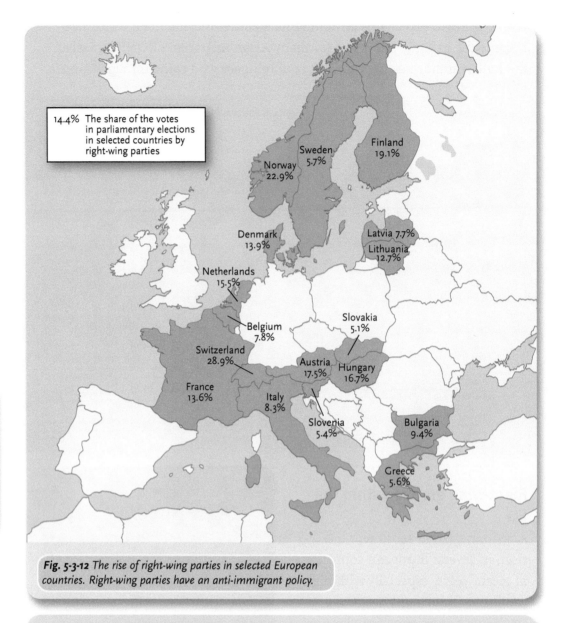

14.4% The share of the votes in parliamentary elections in selected countries by right-wing parties

Norway 22.9%
Sweden 5.7%
Finland 19.1%
Denmark 13.9%
Latvia 7.7%
Lithuania 12.7%
Netherlands 15.5%
Belgium 7.8%
Slovakia 5.1%
Switzerland 28.9%
Austria 17.5%
Hungary 16.7%
France 13.6%
Italy 8.3%
Slovenia 5.4%
Bulgaria 9.4%
Greece 5.6%

Fig. 5-3-12 *The rise of right-wing parties in selected European countries. Right-wing parties have an anti-immigrant policy.*

Geofact

In 2009, 260,000 people applied for asylum in the EU, of whom about 25% were successful.

In the US the message used to be: 'Give me your tired, your poor, your huddled masses yearning to breathe free.' In the EU the message seems to be: 'Give me your qualified and your educated only.' What do you think of that?

ETHNIC, RACIAL AND RELIGIOUS ISSUES THAT ARISE FROM MIGRATION

When migrants come to Europe from abroad, they bring their culture with them. Aspects of their culture are often very different to those of the host country in Europe. As a result, ethnic, racial and religious issues can arise between the host country and migrants.

Ghettos

Many migrants tend to live in one area of a city. This can lead to the establishment of a ghetto, where there are few links with the host community. Cities such as Antwerp, Marseille, Paris, Birmingham and Bradford are home to large migrant communities. When an immigrant community lives in a ghetto, its members are effectively cut off from the wider community. Some

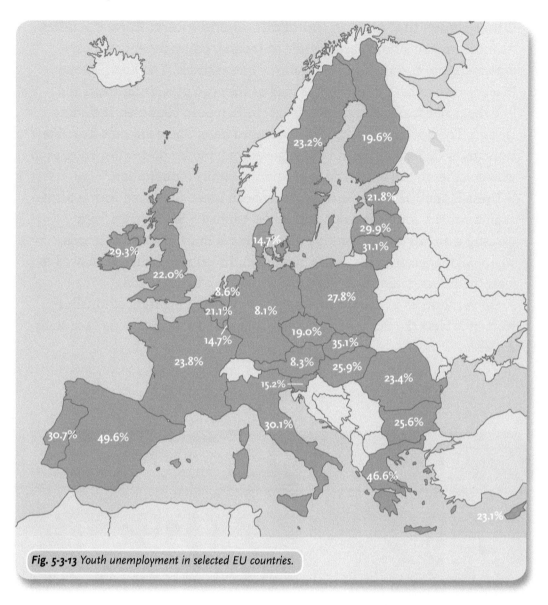

Fig. 5-3-13 *Youth unemployment in selected EU countries.*

Definition
RACISM: Abusive
behaviour towards
members of another
race or minority ethnic
group.

members of the ghetto may spend their whole lives in the ghetto and not learn the language of the host country.

Migrant communities are often neglected by the host country and remain impoverished. Recent years have seen riots by young people in Paris and among some migrant communities in Britain in protest at that neglect.

Racism

Sometimes people who come from a different racial or ethnic group become targets of jokes, taunts and discrimination. They are often stereotyped by the larger community. All of this adds up to racism. Some well-known football players in Britain have been the target of racism in recent times. Ireland has not been immune from racism.

An anti-racist rally by immigrants in France.

Other issues that arise in multicultural and intercultural societies

As more migrants from abroad settle in Ireland, issues never previously experienced in Ireland arise. **Polygamy** is one example. The Koran allows Muslim men to have four wives as long as they can provide for them and love them all equally. Polygamy is illegal in European countries, including Ireland. The law has already been challenged here. There are calls from the Immigrant Council of Ireland to the government to lay down clear rules as to who qualifies to live in Ireland in relation to family reunification.

Dress is another matter that has become an issue. Sikh men wear a turban at all times. In 2007, the garda authorities banned a Sikh recruit from wearing a turban during working hours. This is in contrast with Canada, where Sikh policemen may wear the turban. In Britain, Sikhs are allowed to wear the turban rather than the hard hat, even on building sites.

Some countries in Europe have begun to question the right of Muslim women to wear the facial veil, or niqab, in public, as the following case study shows.

Definitions

MULTICULTURAL SOCIETIES: The co-existence of people of different cultures and races in one country where people of different cultures may have relatively little contact with one another.

INTERCULTURAL SOCIETIES: People of different cultures live in the same territory and society. These groups interact with each other and have a sense of tolerance and mutual respect for each other.

Sikh men wear a turban throughout their lives.

CASE STUDY

The banning of the niqab in France

Muslim women wearing the niqab.

Geofact

The French government's message: The Republic lives with its face uncovered.

Geofact

As a secular state, the French census does not ask people what religion, if any, they belong to.

In 2010, a controversial French law was passed banning Muslim women from wearing the facial veil, known as **the niqab**, in public. The ban went into force in April 2011. France became the first country in Europe to do so.

France is a secular society and is guided by the principles of **liberty**, **equality** and **fraternity**. Supporters of the ban claim that the facial veil is a threat to women's rights, a symbol of oppression and enslavement, and that women wearing facial veils have to be liberated. In addition, the bill had overwhelming public support in opinion polls.

Those who oppose the ban claimed that the new law singles out a vulnerable group – Islamic women. They claim that the ban simply reflects a fear of those who are different – people who come from abroad and who have another set of values. They claim that walking on city streets represents freedom and that women should be allowed to wear the veil on every street in France.

It is not known how many Muslims are in France, but the figure is believed to be in the region of 5 million. Only a tiny minority of women – about 2,000 – wear the facial veil in public. Anyone wearing the facial veil in public now faces a fine of €150. More importantly, a person such as a husband or brother who forces the woman to wear the facial veil may be fined up to €30,000 and face a year in jail. Police do not ask the women to remove the facial veil in public. Instead, they are escorted to a police station and asked to remove it there for identification.

Many people see the law as a step towards ending multiculturalism. They believe that multiculturalism can lead to segregated communities, which is not at all desirable. The emphasis today is on the integration of minority communities in the society to which they migrate. European societies are becoming more assertive about the values they hold and the ones they want others to respect. That is what the French ban on the niqab is about. It is putting down a marker that living in France demands that people sign up to certain French values. Similar bans are being debated in both Spain and Belgium.

Link
See the population density map of Ireland on page 6.

RURAL TO URBAN MIGRATION IN THE DEVELOPED WORLD

The great majority of people in Western Europe are living in urban centres. Migration to cities from rural regions gathered pace at the end of the 18th century as the Industrial Revolution occurred. However, in some countries, such as Ireland, industrialisation only occurred in recent times. We will now examine rural to urban migration in Ireland.

CASE STUDY

Rural to urban migration in the Republic of Ireland

People have moved from rural areas to urban centres because of **push and pull factors**.

- The continued mechanisation of farming, including milking machines, tractors and silage harvesters, has reduced the number of workers on farms. There has also been a reduction in the actual number of farms, especially non-viable farms in the western peninsulas.

- Rural families in general place a strong emphasis on education. When young people go to third-level colleges, they get a taste for the attractions of urban life, such as nightlife and sport. Many remain in cities where jobs have been available during years of economic expansion.

- Manufacturing and industries are mainly located in urban areas. As the cost of petrol and diesel increases, young people are increasingly settling in urban areas rather than face the cost of a long commute.

A threshing machine in Bunratty Folk Park. Many farm workers were needed in the threshing operation in the past.

Combines have replaced workers for many decades.

Source: CSO.

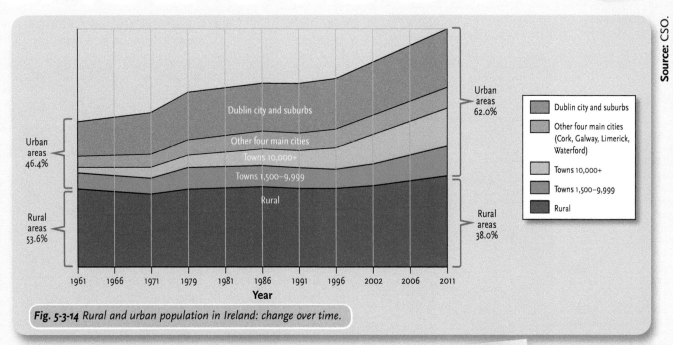

Fig. 5-3-14 *Rural and urban population in Ireland: change over time.*

The impact of rural to urban migration on urban areas

1. Population decline
Outward migration tends to be age selective, as young adults leave. Therefore, the number of marriages declines in these rural areas. This leads to a decline in the number of children in rural communities. Over time, the remaining population grows older and has a high percentage of elderly people. This leads to a high dependency ratio. The counties with the **highest dependency ratio** in Ireland are Leitrim, Donegal, Mayo and Roscommon, in that order. All are western counties. The exodus of the most active age group leads to a decline in parish activities, particularly sports.

2. Decline in services
Rural populations have declined in remote areas of the western seaboard. In turn, services such as schools, post offices and garda stations have closed. Small two-teacher schools have been amalgamated and children are brought to school by bus. The abolition of these services is strongly resisted by communities, but in a time of recession and scarce government resources, the pressure to withdraw these services is strong. Some village shops have closed.

3. Male/female imbalance
In remote rural areas in the past, migration led to an imbalance in the male/female ratio. In rural farming families, a son was

Geofact
The dependency ratio in Co. Leitrim in 2011 was 57.3%. Can you explain that?

Link
Dependency ratio, page 21.

Source: CSO.

Counties with the oldest populations		Counties with the youngest populations	
County	Average age	County	Average age
Mayo	38.6	South Dublin	34.1
Kerry	38.5	Meath	33.8
Leitrim	38.4	Kildare	33.5
Roscommon	38.4	Fingal	32.9

Table 5-3-1 *Average age of population in selected counties, 2011. The counties with the oldest populations are in the west, where migration has occurred over time. The youngest populations are in the greater Dublin area, where inward migration from within the Republic and from abroad is strong.*

CASE STUDY

Urban sprawl in Lucan, in West Dublin.

chosen by his parents to remain on the farm. However, girls were educated to a higher standard so that they could make a living. Girls became nurses, teachers and bank officials. The son remained on the farm, often a small one, with ageing parents. Young women, accustomed to city life and to financial independence, were not attracted to a rural lifestyle on a small farm. This has been the reason for the large number of lonely and isolated bachelor farmers in remote areas of the west.

The impact of rural to urban migration on urban centres

Urban centres have grown rapidly in recent years. This has occurred because of higher birth rates than in the rest of the EU, the influx of migrants from abroad and because of rural to urban migration. Rapid urban growth can have some negative consequences, outlined below.

1. Urban sprawl

To house the rapidly growing population, housing estates were built on the urban–rural fringe. Farmland was paved over as the built-up area invaded the countryside. Sprawl is evident not only in cities, but in towns across the countryside. Irish people seem to wish to live in homes that have front and back gardens. This leads to low-density housing.

In many cases, estates were built some distance from services such as schools and shops. Galway's population has trebled in size since 1946, partly because of inward migration.

Dublin has expanded outwards and has swallowed up communities such as Stillorgan, which are now part of the city. Dublin is now surrounded by several new towns, such as Adamstown, to cope with the increasing population. Urban sprawl has had a serious effect on the wildlife in the countryside.

Link
Urban sprawl, page 135.

2. Traffic congestion

The rapid growth of urban centres meant that urban streets quickly became congested. In towns that are not bypassed by motorways, this is a particular problem. Many small towns have narrow streets and find it difficult to cope with increased traffic. Country towns rarely have an internal bus service and are totally dependent on cars. Traffic congestion leads to air pollution.

Link
Traffic congestion, page 129.

RURAL TO URBAN MIGRATION IN THE DEVELOPING WORLD

The population of the developing world is growing rapidly. In many countries, especially in Asia and in parts of Latin America, there is much pressure on land. Across large regions, people are **pushed** from the land because of physical and economic pressures. They move to the cities because of the **pull** of opportunities.

CASE STUDY

Rural to urban migration in Brazil

The push factors

Many parts of rural Brazil are very poor. This is particularly the case in the north-east, an area known as the **sertão**. In the sertão, life expectancy, infant mortality and literacy are the lowest in Brazil. The people of the sertão have the same quality of life and standard of living as that of many Sub-Saharan countries. Great numbers of rural poor flock to the cities on the coast in search of a better life for the following reasons.

■ The **sertão** has a semi-arid climate. The dry season lasts from July to February and is often longer. Food crops are unpredictable and harvests are frequently poor; thus hunger is an ever-present reality for many families.

■ Population growth is among the highest in Brazil. However, there is a shortage of available land for the poor because so much land is in the hands of large landowners. Some of this land lies idle or underused. Large farms, known as **fazendas**, are devoted to crops such as cotton and cocoa. Increasing mechanisation is reducing the need for farm labourers and forcing down wages even further.

■ Services are poor. The police presence is haphazard. Schools and hospital services leave a lot to be desired. The quality of education is low, with poorly trained and badly paid teachers. Violence and crime are widespread.

The pull factors

■ For poor people in the sertão, the city offers people hope – of better services, better housing, clean drinking water, a better quality of life, the chance of a job and a better life for their children.

Question

Name three push factors and three pull factors that lead to rural–urban migration in Brazil.

Geofact

85.2% of Brazil's population live in cities.

Fig. 5-3-15 *The sertão of north-east Brazil. People from the north-east migrate to the cities in the south and on the east coast.*

The results of rural to urban migration

Because of migration, the overwhelming majority of the population of Brazil now live in cities. Cities such as São Paulo and Rio de Janeiro have grown rapidly because of this. **In fact, 65% of urban growth in Rio de Janeiro is due to inward migration.** The rest is due to natural increase. This rapid urbanisation results in a severe shortage of housing in cities and thus leads to the growth of shanty towns. Greater Rio now has more than 11 million people.

CASE STUDY

Shanty towns – favelas

Many favelas are built on the edge of cities, often on steep slopes. In addition, many factories are located on the edge of cities and jobs may be available near the favelas.

In the favelas, people construct homes from scraps of wood, galvanised metal sheets and plastic. Many people have to share one street water tap. In the early years of a favela, there is no sewage system and disease is common. People feel unsafe and criminal gangs roam the streets. Drugs are everywhere and many idle teenagers become involved in the drug trade as runners.

People's hopes are often dashed. A regular job eludes so many that mothers and their daughters are sometimes forced by poverty into prostitution.

Improvements in favela life

Politicians' neglect of favelas caused favela dwellers in **Rio de Janeiro** who were disillusioned with politicians to put up a monkey as a candidate for the position of mayor in 1988. The monkey, with the slogan *vote for a monkey, get a monkey*, got 400,000 votes and came in third.

This helped to focus the minds of the city authorities in Rio on the difficult lives of the residents of the favelas. Many improvements

have occurred in recent years. An example is the favela of **Rocinha** in Rio, home to 160,000 people. Here, local committees have established self-help projects. The city council provides bricks and mortar and local people build houses, lay water pipes and put down a sewage system, giving their labour free. Rocinha now has two newspapers, a radio station and waste collection. The streets are patrolled by police. Community websites are widely used by citizens.

Geofact
Favelas produced such sporting legends as Pele, Ronaldo and Rivaldo.

Geofact
Samba grew in the favelas of Rio de Janeiro.

Part of Rio de Janeiro, with a large shanty town (favela) in the foreground. Name one hazard that the people living in the left centre face.

Leaving Cert Exam Questions

1 Migration

(i) Describe and explain **one positive** effect of people migrating.
(ii) Describe and explain **one negative** effect of people migrating. (30 marks)

2 Migration

(i) Explain **two** reasons why people migrate from rural areas to cities.
(ii) Explain **one** effect that this has on the rural areas they have left behind.
(iii) Explain **one** reason why large numbers of people are emigrating from Ireland in recent times. (40 marks)

3 Migrants

Explain any **two** reasons why migrants might leave their native (home) countries. (40 marks)

4 Migration

(i) Explain **two** reasons why young people might migrate from rural areas to cities.
(ii) Explain **two** problems caused by this migration in the rural areas they have left. (40 marks)

5 Migration

(i) Explain **two** reasons why young people might migrate from places in the west of Ireland to the Dublin region.
(ii) Explain **two** problems caused by this migration to the Dublin region. (40 marks)

6 Population decline in Mayo, 1986–96

Fig. 5-3-16 refers to population decline in Mayo between 1986 and 1996.
(i) What area had the greatest drop in population?
(ii) By what percentage did the population of Swinford fall?
(iii) Explain **two** reasons why the population of rural areas such as these is falling. (40 marks)

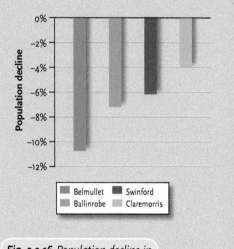

Fig. 5-3-16 Population decline in parts of Mayo, 1986–96.

7 Refugees

(i) Describe **two** problems faced by refugees when they seek asylum (a safe place) in a new country such as Ireland.
(ii) Explain **two** measures that governments could take to help refugees solve these problems. (40 marks)

8 Population change

With reference to Fig. 5-3-17, describe and explain **three** changes in Ireland's population between 1956 and 2011. (30 marks)

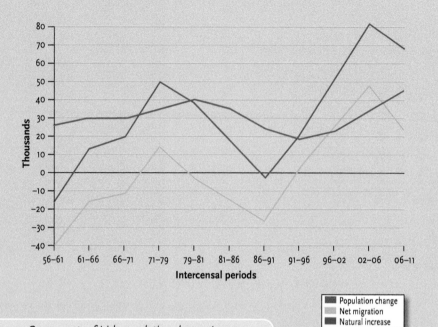

Fig. 5-3-17 Components of Irish population change (average annual figures) for each intercensal period, 1956–2011.

9 Population movement

Migration, both internal and international, continues to play an important role in shaping the population of states and regions. Examine **one** impact of population movement on the donor regions and **one** impact on the receiver regions. (30 marks)

10 Migration

Examine **one** positive and **one** negative potential consequence of human migration. (30 marks)

11 Migration

With reference to example(s) you have studied, examine **two** impacts of rural to urban migration. (30 marks)

12 Migration

Outline the effects of rural to urban migration in a developing region you have studied. (30 marks)

13 Migration

'Ethnic and religious issues can arise as a result of migration.' Examine this statement with reference to example(s) you have studied. (30 marks)

14 Migration and Ireland

Examine **two** major changes in the patterns of Irish migration within the last 100 years. (30 marks)

Settlement – site, situation and function

4

THE DEVELOPMENT OF SETTLEMENT IN THE PAST IN IRELAND

Type of settlement	Pre-Christian settlements	Christian settlements	Viking settlements	Norman settlements
Time	6000 BC	After the 6th century AD	After 795 AD	After 1169 AD
Examples	Lough Gur Céide Fields	Skellig Michael Cashel	Dublin Wicklow	Trim Athenry

Type of settlement	Plantation settlements	Landlord settlements	Canal and rail settlements	Recent settlements
Time	16th and 17th centuries	17th and 18th centuries	18th and 19th centuries	Modern times
Examples	Youghal	Birr Westport	Monasterevin Mullingar	Shannon town Tallaght

Table 5-4-1 Settlement in Ireland over time.

Learning objectives

After studying this chapter, you should be able to understand:

- how settlement in Ireland developed over time
- the importance of site, situation and function of settlements
- that the functions of settlements change over time
- that planning issues occur in rural areas.

EARLY SETTLEMENT

People have lived in Ireland for about 9,000 years. Over that time, people have lived in settlements in favourable sites. Sites that had a water supply, fertile farmland and security from attack were chosen. Archaeologists have given us an understanding of the past by excavating the sites of ancient settlements. We will now examine the evidence that remains of early settlements.

The Middle Stone Age

The first people came to Ireland during the Middle Stone Age around 7000 BC. The people were nomadic hunters and gatherers who collected food over a wide area. They picked seafood such as crabs and periwinkles from coastal areas and hunted small animals on land. They threw away the shells and animal bones in rubbish heaps, called **middens**. Archaeologists have learned about their foods from these middens.

The New Stone Age

The New Stone Age saw the development of farming. This era began in Ireland around 3500 BC. Animals were domesticated and cereals were grown for food. These developments caused people to settle in one place, where they tended their animals and grew crops. The light timber, skins and reeds that were used to build their homes have disappeared without a trace.

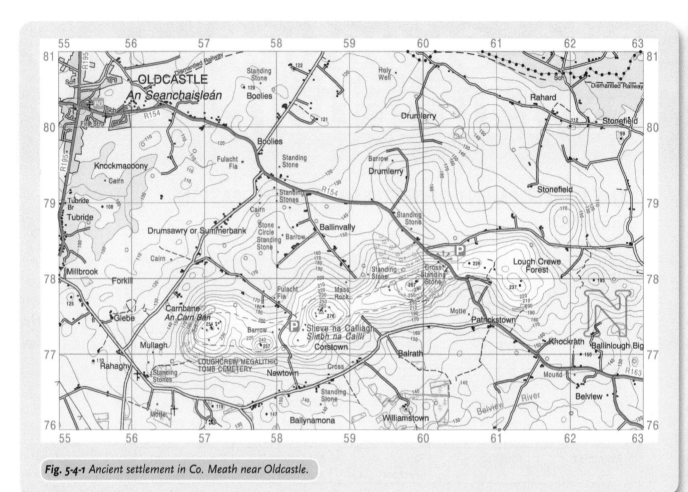

Fig. 5-4-1 *Ancient settlement in Co. Meath near Oldcastle.*

Question

Describe three ancient sites in the Loughcrew megalithic cemetery in Fig. 5-4-1.

Definition

The word **MEGALITHIC** refers to a structure made of large stones or rocks.

An ancient tomb in the Loughcrew megalithic tomb cemetery.

People from the New Stone Age, however, went to a great deal of trouble to bury their dead in elaborate fashion. The megalithic tombs such as **passage graves** and **court cairns** date from this era. **Portal dolmens** (graves with a large flat stone on top of standing stones) were also built in some areas, such as the Burren. The weight of the rocks that were used suggests that these people worked together as a community to lift heavy stones into place. These large graves suggest that people may also have believed in an afterlife.

An ancient stone circle in Drombeg, Co. Cork.

The Bronze Age

Bronze Age people who came to Ireland after this time tended to settle in areas where copper ore was found. *Fulachtaí fia* were used by earlier Bronze Age inhabitants too. A ***fulacht fia*** is a Bronze Age cooking pit. Bronze Age people dotted many parts of the landscape with **standing stones**.

Activity

Check out on the internet what a *fulacht fia* looked like.

Definitions

BARROW: An ancient burial place.

FULACHT FIA (singular); **FULACHTAÍ FIA** (plural): Ancient cooking sites.

Dún Aenghus in Inis Mór, Aran Islands – a promontory stone fort that is now much eroded by the sea. The defensive stones on the outside are known as a chevaux de frise to deter attackers.

Celtic settlement

The Celts came to Ireland around 600 BC. These were Iron Age people. They chose defensive sites. Since they were warlike and often involved in cattle raids, defence was important to them. The Celts lived in **ring forts, hill forts, promontory forts** and **crannógs**. **Crannógs** were artificial lake dwellings some distance from the shore.

Reconstructed crannóg dwellings in the Irish National Heritage Park, Co. Wexford.

The Celts spoke Irish and Irish place names from the Celtic era dot the landscape of Ireland today. *Lios* and *rath* were Celtic names for ring forts, while *dún* was a fortress made of stone. *Bally*, as in Ballyowen, is the English version of *baile*, meaning home.

The remains of the royal settlement at the Hill of Tara. The settlement dates back to the New Stone Age, when it was a burial site. It became the seat of Celtic royal power for hundreds of years. Its name in Gaeilge is Teamhair, meaning the place with the wide view.

Question

What was the main purpose of building crannógs some distance from the shore of a lake?

Question

Can you find any features of Celtic settlement and Celtic place names in Fig. 5·4·1?

Geofact

A *dún* was called a *caiseal* or a *caher* in some parts of Ireland.

Geofact

Doonbeg, Rathnew, Lissycasey, Cashel, Cahir and many more are names of Celtic origin.

HISTORIC SETTLEMENT

Christian settlement – from the 5th and 6th centuries

The word 'monastery' is found in many place names in Ireland. Examples include Monasterevin, *Mainistir na Buaille* (Boyle) and *Mainistir na Corann* (Midleton).

Ireland became Christian after 432 AD, when St Patrick came to Ireland. Irish men and women who wished to devote their lives to God joined monasteries and convents. During the 6th and 7th centuries, St Columba, St Brigid and St Ciarán developed monasteries that became great centres of prayer and learning. These centres grew into towns. Irish monasteries attracted students from abroad and Ireland became known as the **island of saints and scholars**. Many monasteries built round towers as bell towers and to protect their treasures from Viking raiders. Clonmacnoise and Kildare are examples of settlements that began as monastic sites.

Geofact

Cill (Kill in English) is the Irish word for a church or oratory. Examples include Kilmacud, Kildare and Killarney.

Glendalough, Co. Wicklow, showing a chapel and round tower.

Activity

Search on the internet for medieval monastic sites such as Clonmacnoise, Gougane Barra and Skellig Michael. Click on images to see photos of the ruins.

Viking settlements – the 9th century

Viking settlers began to settle in Ireland in the 9th century. They were seafarers, plunderers and traders who needed a quick escape route if necessary. They settled on the coast of Ireland for those reasons. They chose dry sites in sheltered bays. They were able to use their long boats to move inland and plunder monasteries on riverbanks.

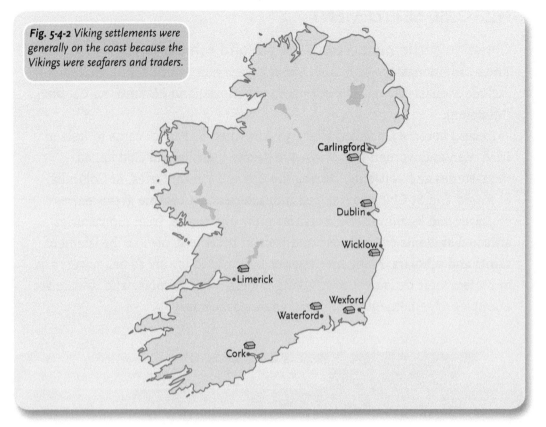

Fig. 5-4-2 *Viking settlements were generally on the coast because the Vikings were seafarers and traders.*

Many coastal towns and cities on the Irish coast owe their origin to the Vikings. Viking settlements such as Dublin, Waterford and Limerick grew as permanent settlements. Over time, Viking settlers remained and became part of Irish society.

Norman settlements – from the late 12th century

The Normans came to Ireland in 1169 from Britain. They valued land and moved inland to inhabit the fertile plains and river valleys in the south and east of Ireland in particular. They had an excellent eye for defensive sites, where they built their castles, first of wood and later of stone. Stonemasons, carpenters, wheelwrights, coopers and other craftsmen, traders and their families lived beside the castle. These settlements began to grow. Towns that owe their origin or growth to the Normans include **Kilkenny**, **Carrickfergus**, **Trim** and **Athenry**.

Athenry Castle dates from the 13th century.

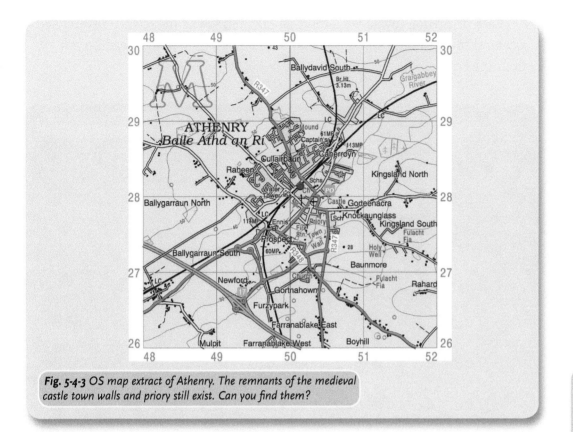

Fig. 5-4-3 *OS map extract of Athenry. The remnants of the medieval castle town walls and priory still exist. Can you find them?*

Unlike the Vikings, the Normans were Christian. Norman lords invited religious orders to establish abbeys beside their castles. This encouraged the further growth of Norman settlements.

Plantation settlements – 16th and 17th centuries

The English conquest of Ireland tightened in the 16th and 17th centuries. Plantations of English and Scottish settlers occurred in land that had been confiscated from rebellious Irish chiefs. Towns were built as part of these plantations as market centres and most of all to provide protection to the new settlers. Many plantation towns were built in Ulster, where the most successful plantation took place. Enniskillen, Donegal town and Derry are plantation towns. Several towns had walls for added protection.

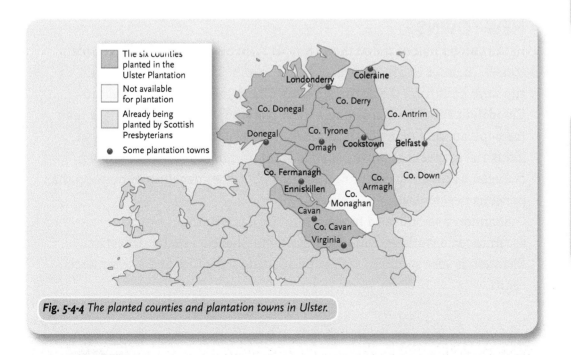

Fig. 5-4-4 *The planted counties and plantation towns in Ulster.*

Geofact

Planters in the Munster Plantation of the late 16th century built plantation towns such as Youghal.

Geofact

Virginia, a plantation town in Co. Cavan, was named after Queen Elizabeth, who never married.

Geofact

Unionists in Northern Ireland use the plantation name of Londonderry, while nationalists prefer to use the name Derry.

These plantation towns were the first planned towns in Ireland. Several had a central square in the shape of a diamond and straight streets leading out from the centre.

The walls of Derry. Plantation towns were heavily fortified.

Landlords' towns – the 18th century

By the 18th century, most of the land of Ireland was owned by people of English or Scottish origin. Many landowners owned very large estates. Some landlords built settlements beside their estates for their workers and to give status to themselves and their areas. **Kilrush**, **Birr** and **Westport** are examples. These towns were also planned with straight streets and a square.

NEW TOWNS

In the second half of the 20th century, Dublin began to suffer from urban sprawl. In order to control urban sprawl, planned towns west of Dublin city were built from the 1970s onwards. These towns – **Tallaght, Lucan-Clondalkin** and **Blanchardstown** – each has a population that is larger than the population of many Irish counties. They also have town centres and industrial estates that provide a significant number of jobs. **Adamstown**, west of Lucan, is the most recent new town, with higher densities of housing than previous new towns.

Shannon was built as a new town in Co. Clare in the 1960s to accommodate workers from the airport and Shannon industrial estate. Shannon is very spacious, with good sporting amenities and a commercial centre.

SETTLEMENTS: SITE AND SITUATION

Site

The site of a settlement refers to the land on which the settlement is built. For instance, settlers chose sites that were free from flooding, fairly level and close to a water supply. The site may have originally been chosen as a defensive site on the bend of a river.

Situation

The situation of a settlement refers to its location in relation to the landscape around it. A settlement may be situated in a river valley, at the mouth of a river, at a bridge point, in a sheltered bay on the coast or in a gap between mountains.

We will now examine the site and situation of Donegal town.

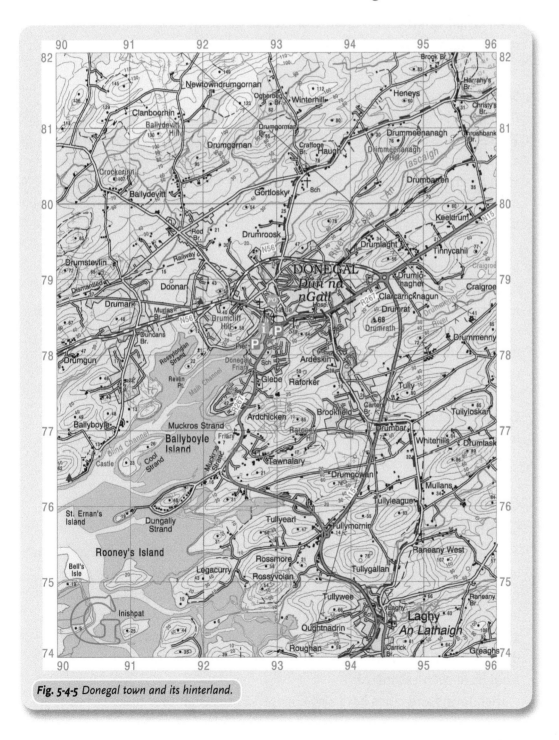

Fig. 5-4-5 *Donegal town and its hinterland.*

Site

Donegal developed at a **defensive** site. The centre of the town is built inside a meander of the River Eske. Thus, the river provided protection on two sides in earlier times. The word '*dún*' in the Irish name of the town means fort, suggesting that defence was a key point in establishing the settlement. The ring forts on Drumcliff Hill give further evidence of the importance of defence. There is a castle at G 928 785, suggesting that defence remained an important factor in the development of the town right up to the 16th and 17th centuries.

Donegal developed as a **crossing point** settlement and **nodal point**. The town is built on the River Eske and another unnamed river to the north-west. The town developed at the mouth of these rivers. As the estuary gets wider here, this is probably the lowest bridging point of the river. The river would also have been a source of water in times past. A number of roads meet here in a triangle at the centre of the town. Here the R267 meets an unnamed regional road linking with the N56.

Situation

Donegal is located at the **route centre** for many roads, major and minor. These include the national routes (N15 and N56), the regional route R267 and a network of third-class roads. Thus, Donegal could develop as a market town for the agricultural hinterland. The route taken by a section of the N56 bypasses the town to the north. This takes traffic around the town rather than through it – an indication of the level of business in the town.

Donegal has developed at the **mouth** of the River Eske. The land occupied by the town slopes gently from 30 m in height to sea level. However, to the south-west, Drumcliff Hill rises to 58 m and to the south-east an unnamed hill rises to 64 m. These hills shelter the town from the prevailing south-west winds. Its position at the mouth of the River Eske also links it to an inlet of the sea, with a deep channel. The pier at G 925 781 suggests that the town may be the focus of the fishing industry for the region. The town is also situated close to several strands on the inlet, e.g. Rossylongan Strand at G 916 780 and Muckross Strand. Strands situated nearby and the information centre in the town suggest that the town has a tourist function.

CHANGES IN THE FUNCTIONS OF URBAN CENTRES OVER TIME

The functions of urban centres change over time. An urban centre may begin as a port or as a mining settlement. However, as it grows it acquires other functions. Additional functions include residential, commercial and transport and other service functions. Former functions may cease when, for instance, a nearby mine the town depended on is worked out. Examples of this include the towns of Nord in northern France, where coal mines under the towns of Nord have been exhausted.

Irish towns and cities have also changed in function over time. We will now examine how this has occurred in **Galway city**.

Exam focus

Can you find 15 SRPs in the discussion on the site and situation of Donegal town?

Link

Remember Nord, *Today's World 1*, page 272, and Galway city, page 306.

Galway city: Change in function over time

Galway's origins

The Normans seized land at the mouth of the Corrib in medieval times. Richard de Burgo built a castle in the area. Over time, city walls were built to protect the settlement from raids. The Normans began to trade with France and the city became a port.

Galway's functions

1. Port function

Galway prospered as a **port city**. Fourteen families or tribes came to dominate the commercial life of the city. These tribes included families by the name of Lynch, Morris, Martin and Ffrench. The city's commercial life developed around the port. Ships exported hides, wool and smoked fish to France. Merchants imported textiles, wine, brandy and other goods from France.

Over time, the city became a **distribution centre** for imported goods. Galway also became a **route focus**, as materials from its hinterland were brought to Galway for export. Bridges were built over the Corrib. Port structures were expanded over time to cope with larger ships. Thousands of people emigrated from Galway during and after the Great Famine of the 1840s. The port declined in importance in the 20th century as ports in the east and south of Ireland became more important.

2. Educational function

Galway became a **university city** in the 19th century. The university was the only university in the west of Ireland and gave Galway an important educational status. The university, now known as NUIG, helped the city to grow. Additional accommodation, shops and other services for college staff and students expanded over time.

Galway is also the main centre for GMIT – the Galway Mayo Institute of Technology. Students come from many counties in Ireland and from abroad to attend Galway's third-level educational institutions. The **regional hospital is a teaching hospital** for medical students and nurses from the university. Galway is also an important centre for primary and second-level education.

3. Manufacturing function

Galway has become a major manufacturing centre in recent decades. The city has become the location for a number of multinational companies, especially American ones. Galway has become one of the most important centres for the manufacture of **medical devices** in the EU. Boston Scientific is the largest employer in the west of Ireland and a world leader in medical devices. The high quality of labour available locally is an important reason for Galway's success in attracting these companies. A high proportion of workers in these companies have third-level qualifications from Galway's third-level institutions. The large number of workers in manufacturing has helped to push the population of the city to more than 80,000. Galway is now the **third largest city** in the Republic.

4. Other functions

Galway has an important **transport function**. The M6 now connects Galway to the capital. Galway also has a rail terminal. The regional airport is important for business and tourism. Galway is the gateway to Connemara and has an important **tourist function**. The city has a unique character that is appealing to tourists.

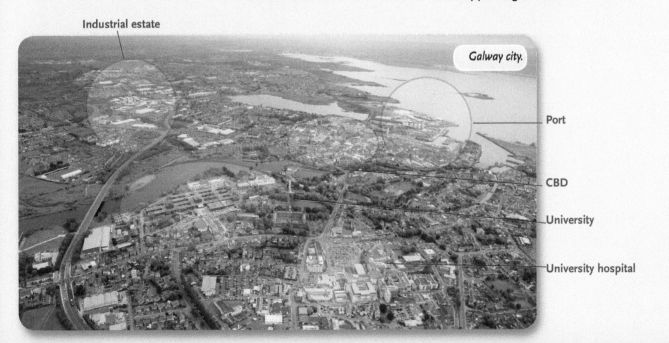

Industrial estate

Galway city.

Port

CBD

University

University hospital

URBAN HIERARCHY: CENTRAL PLACE THEORY

Walter Cristaller, a German geographer, devised **central place theory** to explain the size and distribution of settlements in a region or country. Cristaller studied the distribution of settlements in southern Germany in the 1930s and came to the conclusion that settlements are part of **a system of central places**. Settlements do not exist in isolation from each other. The function of a central place is to provide goods and services to the population of its hinterland. A central place is therefore a market centre.

Central place theory shows how settlements are located in relation to each other. Settlements located on a plain are spaced at a certain distance so that they do not compete for the same customers. Central places may be villages, towns or cities.

There are several elements in Cristaller's central place theory.

Urban hierarchy

The hierarchy of a country's urban system is arranged like a pyramid, with a small number of cities at the top and great numbers of villages and hamlets at the bottom.

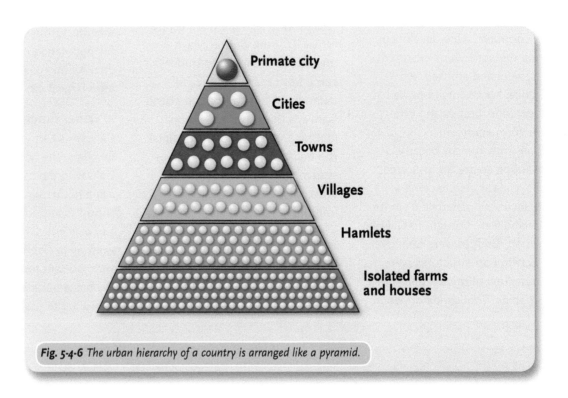

Fig. 5-4-6 *The urban hierarchy of a country is arranged like a pyramid.*

Hinterland

The hinterland is the area surrounding the central place. Customers who avail of goods and services of a central place live in the hinterland. Hinterlands that have circular shapes are not satisfactory. When central places are too close together, hinterlands overlap with each other. When towns are too far apart, some areas between the circles are not served.

Cristaller believed that the ideal hinterland for a central place was hexagonal, since no area of the hinterland is overlapped or excluded.

Range

The distance that people are prepared to travel for goods or services is known as the range. People are not prepared to travel far for goods that they require frequently, such as daily newspapers or fresh bread for breakfast. Frequent requirements such as fresh bread, scones and milk are low-order goods. A shop in a small hamlet or village will supply these.

On the other hand, customers will travel further for middle-order goods and services, such as shoes, clothing and visits to the vet, doctor and hairdresser. They will travel further still for a good selection of high-order goods, such as laptops or a new car and services provided by mortgage societies and law firms.

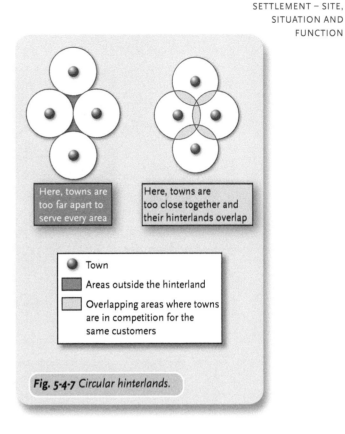

Here, towns are too far apart to serve every area

Here, towns are too close together and their hinterlands overlap

● Town

▮ Areas outside the hinterland

▢ Overlapping areas where towns are in competition for the same customers

Fig. 5·4·7 *Circular hinterlands.*

Threshold

The threshold is the minimum number of customers needed to maintain a service, i.e. the size of the market. A grocery shop in a village has a **low threshold** because customers from the area buy goods from the shop several times a week. People shop in a music shop or a pharmacy far less frequently than they do in the village grocery. Therefore, a pharmacy needs a **high threshold** – a larger pool of customers. This explains why pharmacies are found in towns rather than villages.

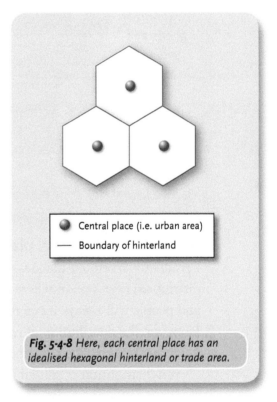

● Central place (i.e. urban area)

— Boundary of hinterland

Fig. 5·4·8 *Here, each central place has an idealised hexagonal hinterland or trade area.*

Conclusions

Cristaller's theory offers the following observations:

▮ Small urban settlements greatly outnumber large urban settlements.

▮ Small settlements such as villages have small hinterlands. Goods sold in village shops have a low range and low threshold.

▮ Large urban settlements such as Galway have large hinterlands.

▮ Large towns provide a greater variety of goods and services than small towns. The goods and services available in a large town have a high range and high threshold.

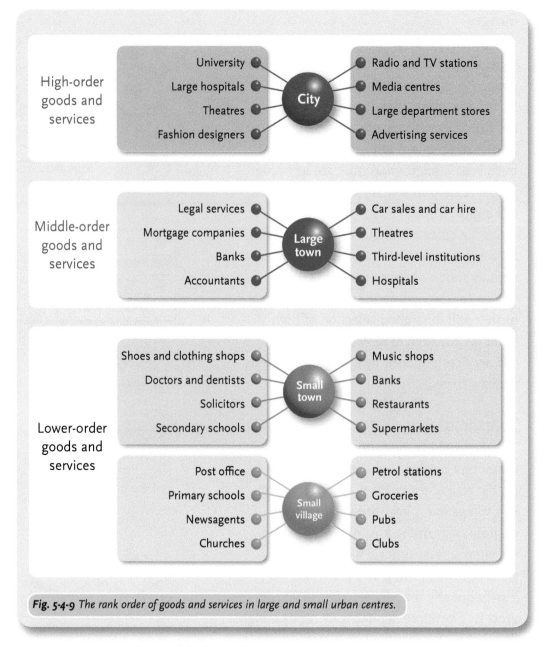

Fig. 5-4-9 *The rank order of goods and services in large and small urban centres.*

Weaknesses of central place theory

Cristaller worked out his ideas on the basis that the population is evenly distributed over a plain where transport links to market centres are the same and people will always travel to the nearest central place for their needs. However, the distribution of central places is changed by several factors:

■ Physical factors such as mountains, marshes and peatlands prevent the even distribution of settlements.

■ Urban settlements also develop because of local resources such as mines, tourist amenities and fishing harbours.

■ People do not always behave rationally when they are buying goods and services. They like novelty and change. Therefore, they may travel to a more distant central place just to give the car a good workout or to catch up with friends.

■ Modern transport facilities give the advantage to larger settlements. An example is the centres of excellence that are now part of HSE strategy. Some hospitals are being downgraded in favour of hospitals in larger centres.

Case study of a central place: Castlebar

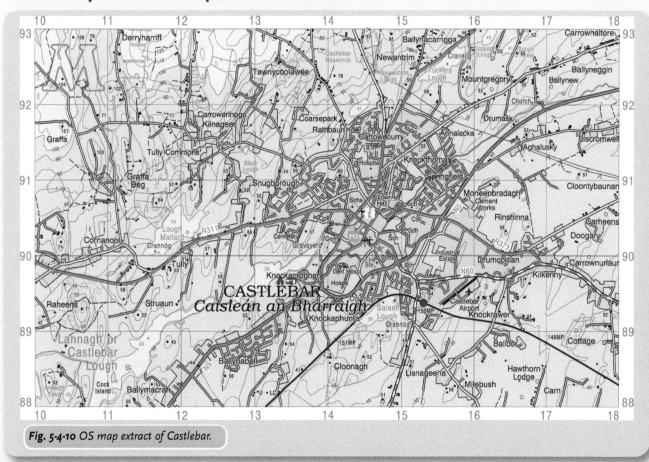

A route focus

Castlebar is a route focus, with national routeways such as the N5 and the N60 connecting it to its hinterland. Regional roads such as the R311 also focus on the town. A railway serves the town and there is a railway station at M 153 894. Several third-class roads link the town to its hinterland. Because it is a route focus, Castlebar is a **nodal centre**. People from the hinterland can easily come into the town by car, bus and rail to **avail of the goods and services** that Castlebar offers.

Higher- and middle-order services in Castlebar

Castlebar is a large town. The built-up area occupies more than **6 km²**. There are many people living in the hinterland of the town as well. The town has services including schools, a college, garda barracks, churches and an airport at M 158 895. There are hospitals

at M 143 896. At least one of the hospitals may be a **centre of excellence** because the town is served by national routeways. The airport may be used for recreational purposes. Castlebar has an industrial estate at M 155 900. Services and jobs are available to the people of the hinterland.

The range and threshold of services in Castlebar

Since Castlebar and its hinterland have a large population, the town can offer a wide variety of goods and services. These services vary from low-order services such as groceries to middle-order services such as doctors and dentists to higher-order services such as a college, a hospital and an airstrip. The middle-order and higher-order services have a wider range and customers from the hinterland can reach Castlebar easily because of the national and regional roads.

Because of the large population, high-order goods and services that have a **high threshold** can exist in Castlebar. Since there is a large pool of customers in the town and its hinterland, there is a sufficient number of customers to support high-order services. An example is the hospital services already mentioned.

Exam focus

Have you counted the 15 SRPs here? There are more than enough.

Link

The Western region, *Today's World 1*, pages 291–306.

RURAL SETTLEMENT PATTERNS

Clustered/nucleated pattern

This is a pattern where buildings are grouped around a particular point. Rural clusters of houses are a common sight in Ireland. In earlier times, small clusters of settlement developed around springs or dry points. Clusters of labourers' cottages were built for farm workers by landlords in the 18th century. Many of these stone buildings have been modernised and occupied.

Mills using water power were built beside a stream. Workers lived in a nearby cluster of homes. Small clusters of fishermen's homes are also found along the western seaboard.

Today, a cluster may offer a small range of services. A rural cluster may have a church, school, post office, pub, garda barracks, grocery store and a few homes. These services in turn attract more residents, leading to the growth of the settlement.

Dispersed pattern

A dispersed pattern is one where buildings are scattered throughout the countryside in a random fashion. It is often associated with agricultural activity and houses are frequently surrounded by farmland.

Irish farmers are mainly pastoral – they have animals such as cattle and sheep. Farmers live on their farms because they have to look after their animals on a daily basis. Cows have to be milked twice a day. Beef cattle have to be moved from pasture to pasture and observed for infections such as red murren. Therefore, farmers live in dispersed patterns of settlement on third-class roads and at the end of *bóthareens* (boreens).

Many of these farms are the result of the break-up of landlord estates more than 100 years ago. Landlords were obliged to sell their lands to their tenants. The farmers built houses and farm buildings on their farms. Therefore, settlement became dispersed. The density of this settlement pattern depends on farm size and soil quality.

Some dispersed houses represent the desire of people to live in the countryside while working in towns and cities. Other houses were built on sites farmers gave to their adult children.

Linear and ribbon pattern

In a linear settlement pattern, houses follow the line of a road or river or the foot of a mountain.

Some people prefer to live outside a town or village, as they may have been raised in the countryside. If one member of a young couple is from the locality and they need a house, they are likely to get planning permission in a rural area. The two-car family is normal today in many parts of the country. This allows people to live in the countryside if they wish. Farmers may wish to sell plots along the road front. These plots sold for a lot of money during the years of the economic boom before 2008. Services are usually available close to the public road.

Definition

A **DRY POINT** is a settlement site that avoids land that is marshy or likely to flood.

Geofact

Clachans were clusters of houses in rural Ireland where some farmers lived up to the 19th century.

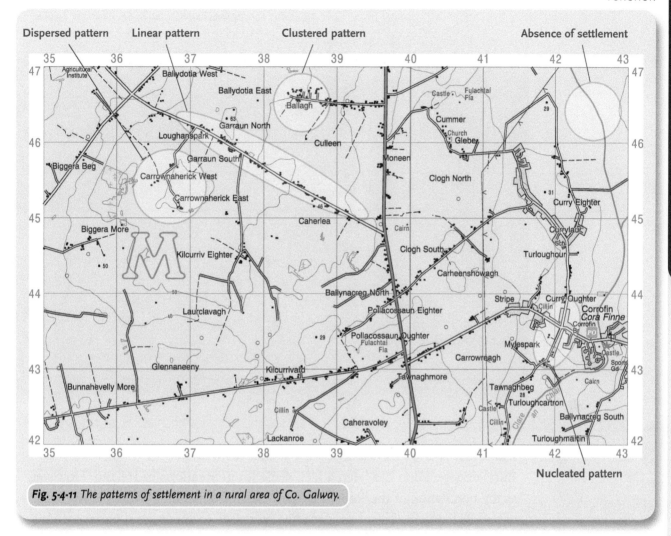

Dispersed pattern   Linear pattern   Clustered pattern   Absence of settlement

Nucleated pattern

Fig. 5-4-11 *The patterns of settlement in a rural area of Co. Galway.*

Linear development has aroused some opposition. Some people claim that drives that open onto the road are a hazard. Linear development has also given rise to the term '**bungalow blitz**'. Many linear developments in rural areas are not attached to sewage systems and have septic tanks. These became controversial in recent years because of a possible risk to groundwater.

Ribbon development occurs when housing and other buildings are built along main roads leading out of towns. It may lead to urban sprawl. Ribbon development is not an attractive pattern of development. It creates a built-up appearance, makes access to farmland behind it difficult and hinders the planned expansion of settlements.

Absence of settlement pattern

Settlement is absent from some areas. Reasons include:

- **Mountains and steep slopes**, for example in Connemara and west Mayo, where cold winds and thin or infertile soils make settlement impossible.
- **Bogs and marshes**, as in the bogs of the Irish Midlands.
- **Floodplains** that experience frequent flooding, for example along parts of the Shannon floodplain in the Midlands.
- **Areas that are short of water**, as, for example, in the Burren, where surface water disappears. The absence of soil over much of the Burren is also a factor.

Link
See pages 96–7 for a further study of rural settlement patterns on an OS map of part of rural Co. Galway.

A parcel of flooded land near Carrick-on-Shannon, Co. Leitrim.

Geofact
There were 289,451 vacant homes in the Republic of Ireland in 2011, most of them in rural areas. Of these, 59,000 were holiday homes (source: CSO, 2011 census).

Geofact
One-off homes brought about by counter-urbanisation are a spin-off from urban sprawl.

PLANNING STRATEGIES IN RURAL AREAS

Rural depopulation has been a fact of life for generations in Ireland. However, as the population of the Republic has increased since the 1970s, the number of people living in the countryside has increased in many rural parishes. This is especially the case in parishes that are close to towns and cities.

Rural population growth brings benefits to society. It helps to maintain rural communities. Young people and children bring energy and vitality to rural areas. Sport helps to maintain a community spirit and villages become vibrant market centres.

Counter-urbanisation

Counter-urbanisation occurs when people who work in the city or town decide to live in the countryside in a rural parish. This has led to many homes being built in recent years. There are several reasons for this.

■ Some farmers wish to increase their income by selling sites. Sites were sold for very high prices during the boom years that ended in 2008.

■ Homes in the city became very expensive during the boom years and young couples could build the house of their dreams in the countryside.

■ Many people who come from a rural background prefer country living.

■ People built holiday homes, especially in scenic areas in the west of Ireland. These homes remain vacant for most of the year.

■ Section 23 tax incentives were introduced by the government in the Rural Renewal Scheme in 1998. These incentives led to houses being built in the Upper Shannon Basin in counties such as Leitrim.

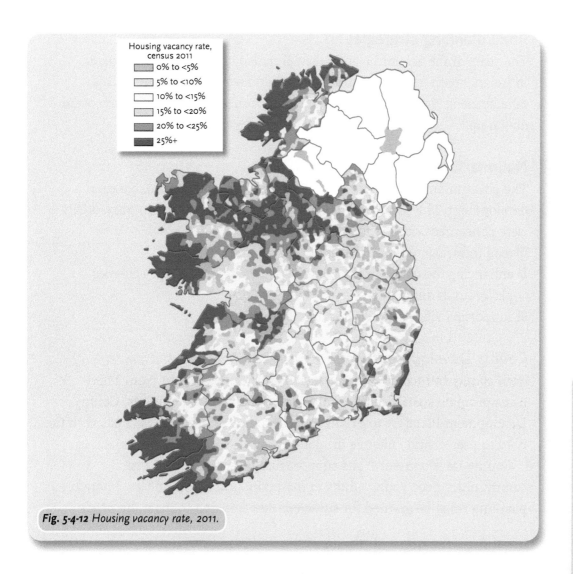

Fig. 5-4-12 *Housing vacancy rate, 2011.*

Questions

1. Name three counties with the highest percentage of vacant homes.
2. Can you explain why Counties Kildare and Meath have very few vacant homes?
3. What percentage of homes are vacant in Connemara?

Environmental and planning concerns: One-off homes

People who raise concerns about the environmental impact of the **huge number of one-off homes** that now exist in Ireland make the following points.

■ Services such as water, electricity and telephones to one-off dispersed homes are expensive. In addition, the countryside becomes criss-crossed with electricity and telephone cables.

■ The Republic now has 400,000 septic tanks. This has raised environmental concerns at EU level because of the risk to groundwater, especially in limestone areas. Rural dwellers now have to register their septic tanks, which are subject to inspection. This will help to keep contamination of the environment to a minimum.

■ One-off housing is unsustainable in the long term because rural dwellers are totally dependent on cars. In addition, the land bank of the country is a finite resource. One-off homes, each on 0.25 of a hectare, are a wasteful use of this resource.

■ One-off homes may present a traffic hazard along a busy road as cars enter and exit through entrances.

Question

Can you explain why septic tanks may pose a risk to the environment in limestone areas?

Rural planning strategies

The years of the economic boom saw frenzied development in housing in Ireland, both urban and rural. To give some degree of order to this development, National Development and County Development Plans were drawn up.

National Development Plans (NDPs)

The government has drawn up NDPs for orderly and sustainable rural development. The most recent one spanned the years 2007 to 2013. NDPs were concerned with the following:

- road infrastructure in rural areas
- enhancing the quality of village life with water and sewage schemes, playgrounds and parks
- supporting village enterprises and tourism.

County Development Plans

Each county council now produces a County Development Plan. These plans promote **sustainable planning and housing developments**. County Development Plans try to balance people's wish to live in rural areas with the need to protect and enhance the countryside.

County Development Plans support rural housing because rural communities need young adults to maintain local communities. Therefore, planning must be granted for sufficient new housing to meet the needs

The village of Newmarket in Co. Cork. This village, like many others, saw the development of new homes during the boom before 2008.

Examples of one-off houses in a rural area near Ballinspittle, Co. Cork.

of rural communities. However, in simple terms, it is easier to get planning permission in some rural areas of a county than in others. This is because some rural environments, such as areas of scenic beauty, can suffer as a result of development.

The economic downturn from 2008 onwards has seen a very sharp decline in house building.

Question

Name two advantages and two disadvantages of the settlement pattern that you see in this photograph.

CASE STUDY

Zoning in Co. Clare for rural housing

Vulnerable landscape
The Burren – a unique landscape – is a very sensitive and vulnerable area. In this area, an applicant must be a local rural person and have a need of housing. House design is also a sensitive matter.

Vulnerable landscape
Area under pressure from urban-generated housing
Structurally weak area
Open countryside

Source: Clare Co. Council Planning Office

Structurally weak areas
Structurally weak areas are heavily dependent on agriculture and have had a tradition of static or declining population. People may apply for planning permission if they are going to live in the house.

Open countryside
Areas zoned as open countryside are very rural in character and traditions. An applicant must be a local person and must have a need of housing.

Urban-generated housing
51% of the population of the county live in the area between Ennis and Limerick, which is a mere 18% of the total land of the county. An applicant for a rural house must be a local person and have a need of housing.

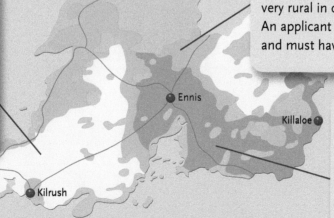

Fig. 5-4-13 Co. Clare is zoned into four types of rural areas. County Development Plans for other counties identify similar zones in their respective counties.

Leaving Cert Exam Questions

1 Urban functions

Describe how the functions of any urban area studied by you have changed over time. Clearly state the name of the urban area in your answer. (30 marks)

OL

2 Changing urban functions

Explain **two** functions of an urban area studied by you. Clearly state the name of the urban area in your answer. (30 marks)

OL

3 Dynamics of settlement

With reference to **one** Irish centre you have studied, examine how its functions changed over time. (30 marks)

HL

4 Central place theory

Examine Fig. 5-4-14, which refers to Cristaller's central place theory. Explain what you understand by this theory. (30 marks)

HL

5 Historical map

Examine the historical map of Carrick-on-Shannon in Fig. 5-4-15. Draw a sketch map of the historical map. On it, show and name each of the following:
- Two connecting roads/streets
- The Fair Green
- The school
- An administrative building (20 marks)

HL

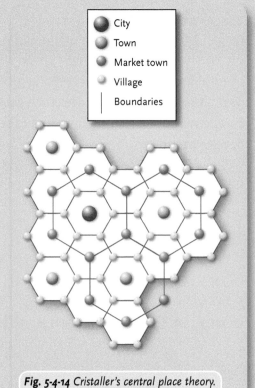

Fig. 5-4-14 Cristaller's central place theory.

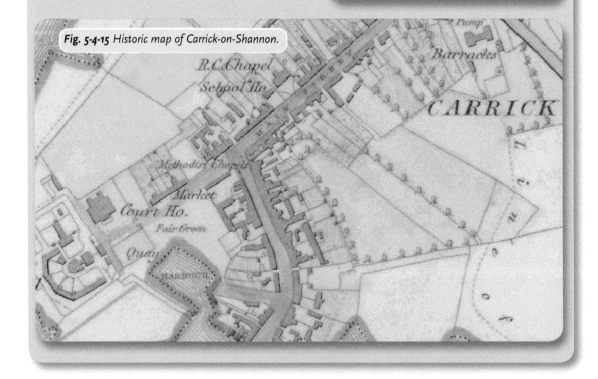

Fig. 5-4-15 Historic map of Carrick-on-Shannon.

Ordnance Survey maps and photographs

INTRODUCTION

In the Leaving Cert examination, students are asked to examine various aspects of social geography using OS maps and/or photographs. For instance, students can be asked about the following:

■ the patterns of rural settlement
■ the different types of historic settlement in an area
■ the functions of a town or city
■ the development of a town or city over time.

The questions below are Higher Level questions with Higher Level answers and are 30 marks each (15 SRPs).

THE HISTORY OF SETTLEMENT

```
• Holy Well (Early Christian)




• Cairn (Pre-Christian)

                                    Residential
                                    (Modern)
                                        •

        • Castle (Normans)
```

Fig. 5-5-1 *Sketch map (of the map extract on page 94) showing history of settlement.*

Question

Examine the OS map shown on page 94. Draw a sketch map to half-scale of the area shown on the map extract. On it, show and name evidence that the area has a long history of settlement.

Link

Sketch maps, *Today's World* 1, page 202.

ORDNANCE SURVEY MAPS AND HISTORIC SETTLEMENT

Question: Examine the OS map shown here. Using evidence from the OS map, describe and explain three different aspects of historic settlement.

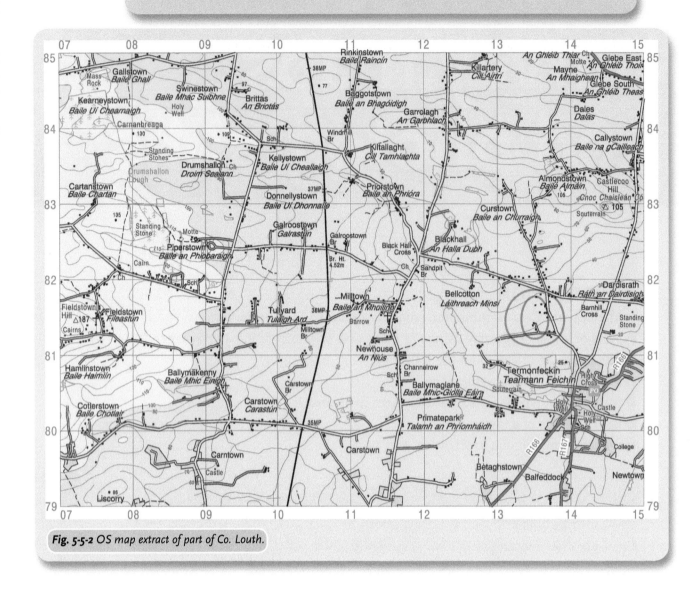

Fig. 5-5-2 OS map extract of part of Co. Louth.

Pre-Christian settlement

A ringfort is located at the top of Castlecoo Hill (O 145 830). This is a structure that is circular in shape. Its walls are made of either stone or clay. It served as a settlement but also had a defensive function against wild animals and hostile people.

Souterrains (O 144 829) were tunnels that were used for food storage in times of peace but also as a means of escape from a fort during times of strife. This souterrain may be linked to the nearby ringfort.

Standing stones are found near O 082 836. These could have had a number of functions, including marking the burial place of a chieftain or serving as a boundary mark, or they may even have been used in rituals.

Cairns (O 071 813) are ancient burial sites. They consist of a large mound of stones and are found on a site (on the 180m contour) that is higher than the surrounding landscape.

The barrow (O 113 815) marks an ancient burial site. Barrows are located in low-lying areas and consist of a large mound built of clay, which was used because stone was not available.

Early Christian settlement

There are two holy wells in Termonfeckin town. When Christianity came to Ireland, old pagan wells were adapted as Christian holy places. Many were named after local saints. It was believed that drinking from them would give wisdom, or in the case of people who were ill, cure them.

High crosses, such as that at O 143 806, were a follow-on from standing stones. They date from the 7th century onwards. Made of stone, they are carved with scenes from the Old and New Testament and were usually located at monastic sites. They served as picture bibles or marked the burial site of important figures.

The ruins of a number of churches are scattered throughout the extract, with one located at O 094 835. These were originally wooden structures that were later replaced with simple stone structures. Their location in the countryside is evidence that Ireland was then a rural society.

The Normans

The motte was the first type of fortification built by the Normans, who arrived after 1169. The remains of a motte are found at O 087 825. A motte was a circular mound of clay. Its function was defence. Mottes could be built quickly and were regarded as temporary until stone structures could be built. The motte overlooked an enclosed yard, called a bailey. The height of the motte made it difficult to attack.

The Normans built castles to control their territories. They built most of their castles on high ground for defence or near rivers for defence and water supply. Towns grew up around some of them, such as Termonfeckin (O 14 80). The castles were initially made of timber and later made of stone. These strong castles made it difficult for Irish clans to attack them.

This question may also be answered with the following headings:
■ Burial sites
■ Religious sites
■ Defensive sites
The information given above is valid for these headings but needs to be grouped differently.

ORDNANCE SURVEY MAPS AND PATTERNS OF RURAL SETTLEMENT

Question: Study the OS map shown here. Describe and explain three patterns of rural settlement evident in the map.

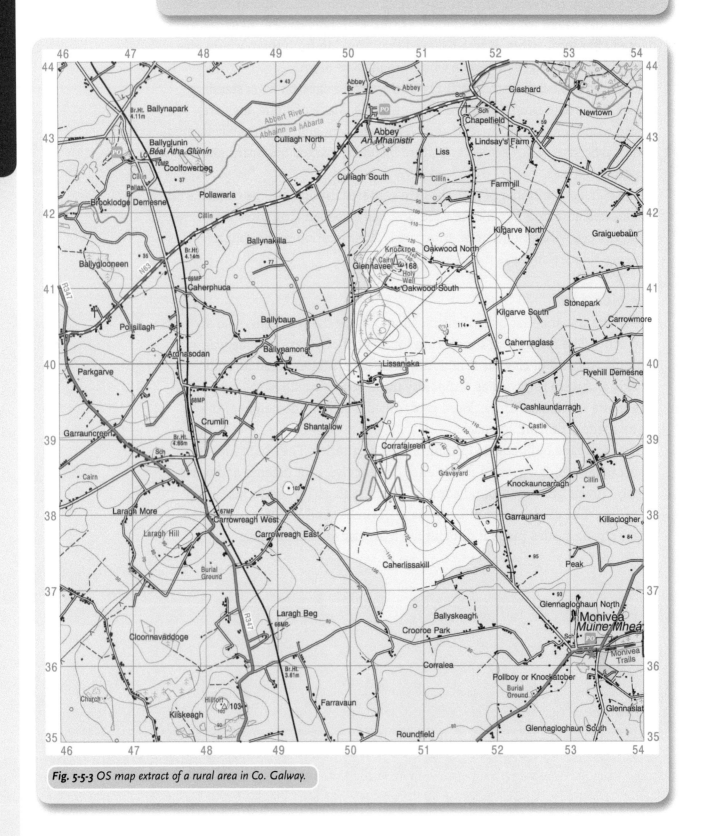

Fig. 5-5-3 OS map extract of a rural area in Co. Galway.

Linear settlement pattern

In a linear settlement, houses follow the line of a road, coast or river.

In this map linear settlement is found along the N63 at M 49 42 and also along third-class roads such as the one leading directly south from Chapelfield at M 517 433. Some of the homes here probably belong to farmers whose land is behind the houses, such as Lindsay's Farm.

Others are likely to be houses built by locals who purchased sites from farmers. Farmers may also have given sites to their adult children.

Services such as electricity, water and telephone cables are probably available along these roads, reducing development costs and making planning permission easier to obtain. Indeed, we see an electricity transmission line crossing the areas diagonally.

Many people like the quiet and quality of life in the countryside rather than living in an urban area. However, this is not an attractive pattern of settlement and may lead to bungalow blitz.

Clustered settlement

In this pattern, buildings are grouped around a particular point, such as a crossroads.

There are several rural clusters in this area, including Abbey at M 503 432 and Monivea at M 534 363.

Local inhabitants require services and these clusters provide some low-order services, such as primary schools and post offices.

Monivea also has a garda station and seems large enough to have a few shops. There are some unnamed clusters in the area, such as one near the *cillín* at M 534 387. The area around this cluster has no evidence of surface water, suggesting that the bedrock is limestone. Therefore, clusters of houses may have been built where a spring emerged. Indeed, the cluster at Knockatobar at M 527 358 suggests that. *Tobar* is the Irish for well or spring.

Dispersed settlement

Dispersed settlement consists of isolated houses scattered throughout the countryside.

This pattern is found on other roads or country lanes that are cul-de-sacs. An example is the area east of the railway line at Crumlin (M 485 393).

The inhabitants of these homes are farmers who live on their farms. This pattern developed when landlords sold their estates to former tenants at the end of the 19th and early 20th centuries.

Farmers in dispersed homes have livestock farms of cattle and/or sheep and need to live close to their animals. Herds have to be looked after daily and moved to fresh pastures.

Each house is surrounded by its own farmland, so the density of the houses depends on the size of the farm.

ORDNANCE SURVEY MAPS AND THE FUNCTIONS OF A TOWN

Question: Study the OS map shown here and examine the development of any three functions of Trim, both past and present, using evidence from the OS map to support your answer.

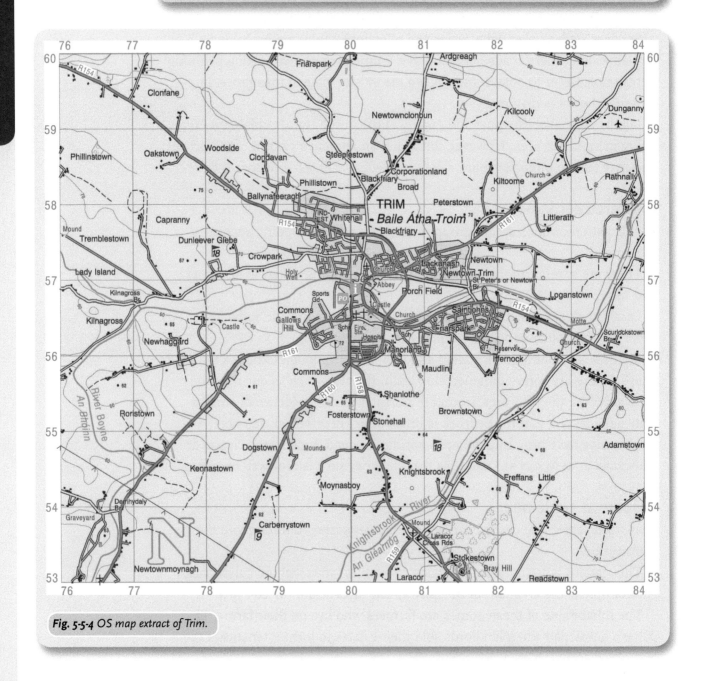

Fig. 5-5-4 OS map extract of Trim.

Question: Draw a sketch map (to half scale) of Fig. 5-5-4 above. Include:
- A named river
- The built-up area of Trim
- Two named regional roads
- A named historic site

Note: You must use graph paper.

Defensive

Trim may have grown around a castle. We see a castle ruins at N 803 567.
This may have been a Norman castle, built in the 12th century. The castle was
built on a defensive site on the south bank of the River Boyne, defending the
town from attack via the river.

The castle would have had knights, soldiers and saddlers, metal workers,
tailors, coopers and others supporting the Norman lord. This helped the
settlement to grow. People also lived outside the town walls but close to the
castle for protection.

The Normans established abbeys too. We see an abbey ruins at
N 803 569. The abbey helped the settlement to grow, as monks provided
religious services, education and basic health care.

A bridging point

The Irish name for Trim is *Béal Átha Troim*. *Áth* is the Irish word for a ford
or crossing point on a river. Later, Trim became a bridging point. The town
today has two bridges, with one at N 802 568. As a bridging point and the
home of a Norman lord, the town grew to be a route focus.

Today, several regional roads converge on the town. These include the
R154, the R161 and the R160. These routes connect Trim to the people of the
low-lying hinterland. This has helped Trim to grow as a central place and
market town serving the surrounding agricultural lowlands.

A services centre

The OS map provides evidence of several services.

A hospital is located at N 804 563. The hospital employs medical staff who
have added to the town's population and importance. The fire station, garda
station, two churches, a post office and a school are marked in the OS map in
Trim – all attracting people and trade to the town, thus helping it to grow.

The town also has a tourist industry. There is an information centre to
provide information on the castle, abbey and two church ruins. Tourists
visiting the town spend money in restaurants, hotels and filling stations. This
has encouraged people to open restaurants and provide employment.

The town is likely to have several shops that provide for many of the
shopping needs of the surrounding population, such as those in the planned,
and therefore new, housing development at Manorland (N 803 561).

ORDNANCE SURVEY MAPS AND THE DEVELOPMENT OF A TOWN

> **Question: Study the OS map shown here and, using map evidence to support your answer, explain three reasons why Killarney developed at this location.**

Tourist attractions

Killarney has a wide range of activities and attractions to bring tourists to the town. There is an information centre at V 965 904. This centre provides information and maps of the area.

Killarney has accommodation for tourists. There are four youth hostels in the town. The area has caravan parks, including one at V 972 890. These facilities bring tourists who spend money in restaurants and bars, thus maintaining employment and helping the town to grow.

The area has mountains, such as Purple Mountain south-west of Lough Leane. The region is ideal for trekking and cycling – the Ring of Kerry cycle route seems to begin and finish in the town. Motorists can use Killarney as a base from which they can drive to the many car parks east of Muckross Lake. Therefore, motorists bring money into the town and help to maintain jobs in filling stations and in shops.

Transport

Killarney has good transport services. A railway passes through the town, with a station in the centre of the town at V 970 907. The railway was probably built in the 19th century and has helped Killarney to grow since then. The railway brings tourist passengers to Killarney and was also used to transport bulky goods before the road system was developed.

The town is a route focus for roads. A national primary route (the N22) passes beside the town to the north-east. The N72, a national secondary route, approaches from the west, while another secondary route enters from the south. The immediate area of Killarney has many third-class roads. Therefore, the town is very accessible.

Motoring tourists and tour buses can reach Killarney easily. The dense network of roads has also helped Killarney to develop as a market town for the region.

Other services

Because the town is a route focus, it has become a nodal point. Therefore, it has become a services centre. A hospital is located at V 965 916. This hospital provides jobs for nurses and doctors, many of whom live in the town and do their shopping in the town every week. This maintains jobs in supermarkets and other shops.

Killarney has two churches, with one located at V 959 908, that provide religious services. People come to religious services at weekends and may spend money on newspapers and other needs in Killarney.

Killarney is a sizeable town and its CBD obviously has banks, shops and hotels that developed over time. The availability of these services makes Killarney an attractive place in which to live; hence the development of housing estates on the perimeter of the town. Building these homes provided jobs for builders and skilled tradesmen.

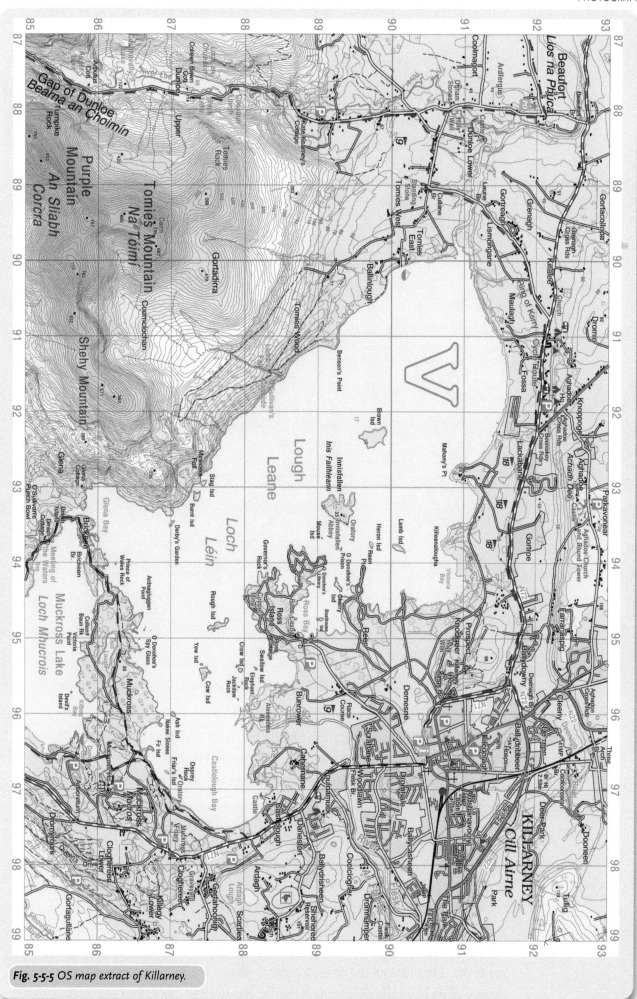

Fig. 5-5-5 OS map extract of Killarney.

ORDNANCE SURVEY MAP AND AERIAL PHOTOGRAPHS AND THE FUNCTIONS OF A TOWN

Question: Study the OS map and the aerial photograph of Mullingar. Examine any three functions of the town, using evidence from the OS map and the aerial photograph to support your answer.

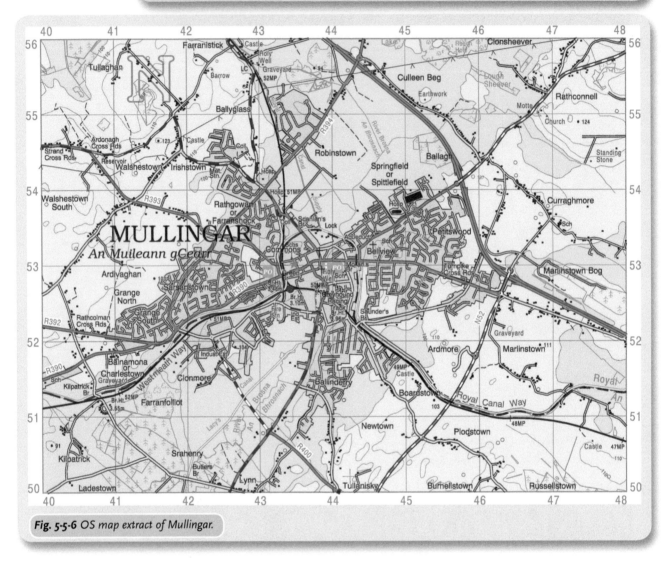

Fig. 5-5-6 *OS map extract of Mullingar.*

Transport function

The Royal Canal passes through Mullingar, with a lock at N 440 534. This indicates that it had a transport function for bulky goods as far back as the 19th century. The walk along the canal suggests that it is not used for this function today.

There is a railway station at N 434 527. Mullingar has a rail junction, with lines coming from three directions. The railway lines and station are clearly visible in the centre of the photo. The railway may be used to bring raw materials to the industrial estates. One industrial estate is located beside the railway at the right centre of the photo. The OS map indicates another nearby at N 424 518.

The town is a route focus. The N52, the R393 and the R390 converge on the town. This makes the town a central place or a market centre for the people of its hinterland. Through-traffic can bypass the town on the dual carriageway, which is not numbered.

Residential function

The photo provides evidence of the residential function of Mullingar in the left and right foreground and in the right background.

The right background has low-density modern residential estates, suggesting that the town expanded rapidly in recent years. These are mainly detached and semi-detached houses. The houses in the left foreground are terraced.

In the centre, large blocks of apartments have been built with higher densities than the residential estates. These seem to have been recently built and are close to the centre of town and the railway station, which is ideal for commuters.

We can also see evidence of residential areas in the OS map, especially in the north and eastern areas of the town, such as in Rathgowan (N 428 537). The OS map shows that the residential areas have expanded along each side of two regional roads in an easterly direction from the town centre.

Services function

The OS map shows the wide range of services available in Mullingar. The information centre at N 438 530 indicates tourist services, along with a canal walk and antiquities. The sports pitch in the left background and the wood in the left middle ground of the photo indicate the leisure functions of Mullingar.

Mullingar.

The town has three hospitals, e.g. N 432 540. Because the town is a route focus, one of the hospitals may be a centre of excellence of the HSE. Mullingar is also an educational centre, with several schools shown in the OS map, e.g. N 442 529.

The large new building with the flat roof in the centre foreground of the photo may be a shopping centre. There are shops along the street running from the foreground to background. These suggest that the town has a retail function.

ORDNANCE SURVEY MAPS AND AERIAL PHOTOGRAPHS AND THE DEVELOPMENT OF AN URBAN AREA

Question: Using the OS map and aerial photo of An Daingean/Dingle, explain three reasons for the development of the town at this site.

A sheltered harbour

The town is situated at V 44 00 and V 44 01 in a sheltered bay with a narrow exit called Dingle Harbour in the OS map. The photo indicates a large, fairly level and dry site on which the town is built. Quays are evident at Q 443 008 and also in the photograph in the left foreground. There are several fishing trawlers tied up on the quays in the left foreground of the photo. This suggests that Dingle is a large fishing port. The large building in the middle centre of the photo, with trucks parked outside, may be a fish processing plant. The fishing industry employs many workers who live in the town. Fishing has also helped the town to grow because the town supplies fish to the shops to sell to the community. Restaurants in the town can offer fresh fish on their menus to tourists.

The tourist industry

The OS map suggests this is an area of great scenic beauty, e.g. Connor Hill (Q 491 055), which has a viewing point, and the Dingle Way (Q 458 024). The area has several antiquities, such as the Gallain at Q 430 012. An Daingean is an ideal centre for tourists to explore the area and has an information centre. Tourists can easily reach the town because it is a route focus, with several roads, such as the N86 and the R559, converging on the town. Some of the buildings near the harbour at the left centre of the photo may be guesthouses for tourists. The port area has a marina at the left centre of the photo where leisure craft are tied up. Tourists bring business to the town and spend their money at petrol stations, restaurants and guesthouses, thus providing employment locally. There is a helipad at Q 447 004.

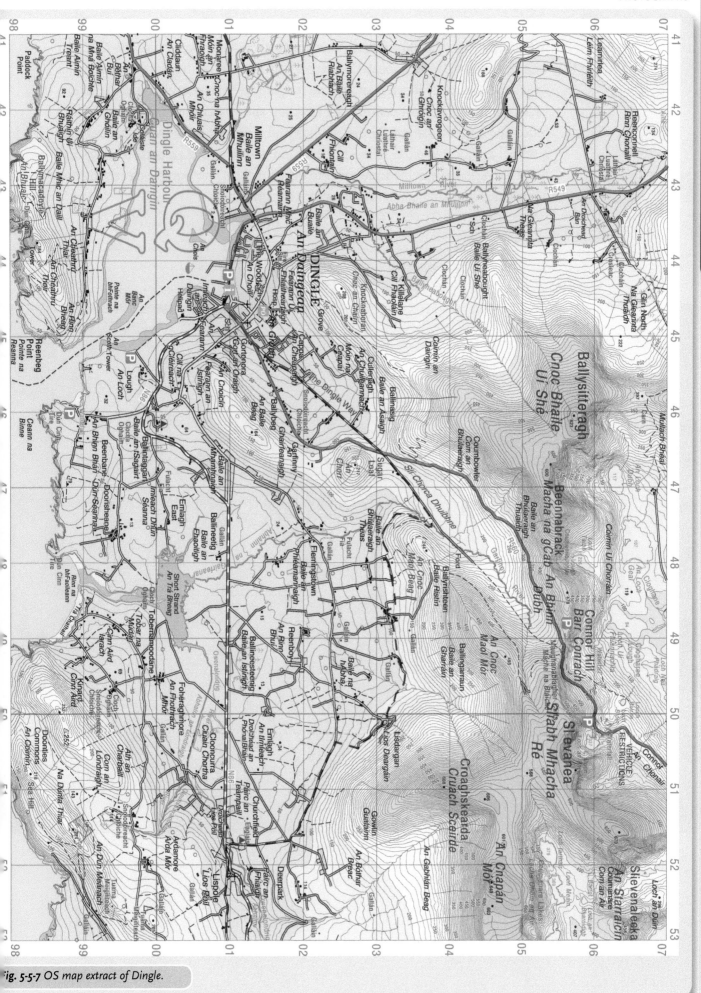

Fig. 5-5-7 OS map extract of Dingle.

Other services

An Daingean is a central place and a nodal point. It provides services for the community of its hinterland. The photo shows the location of the CBD where several shops are located. Shops are in the left centre, in the street in which the church is located and in the long street that extends from the left background to the right centre. The OS map shows that the town has a post office and a garda station. There is a hospital at Q 447 016. Two churches and a school are located close to the information centre at Q 444 010. Workers in these services have helped the town to develop. The photograph clearly shows a fairly new housing estate in the centre background.

An Daingean (Dingle).

Urban land use and planning

6

Urban settlements display an ever-changing land use pattern and pose planning problems.

ZONES WITHIN THE MODERN CITY

In cities today, separate districts are used for different purposes and activities. These include:

- commercial
- transport
- residential
- industrial
- recreational.

Learning objectives

After studying this chapter, you should be able to understand:

- that different land use zones develop in cities
- that urban land use theories explain land use zones in cities
- that changes in urban land use zones can lead to planning issues
- that land values vary within cities
- that the expansion of cities puts pressure on rural land use.

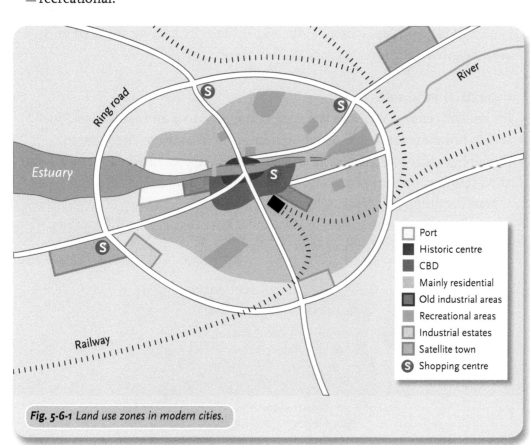

	Port
	Historic centre
	CBD
	Mainly residential
	Old industrial areas
	Recreational areas
	Industrial estates
	Satellite town
S	Shopping centre

Fig. 5-6-1 *Land use zones in modern cities.*

Local authorities devise long-term plans for the development of modern cities. This involves zoning land for specific economic or social activities. Zoning land means that a city will develop in accordance with a specific plan. Zoning is designed to prevent a free-for-all as a city develops. Zoning ensures that abattoirs are not built in residential areas, that industries with a lot of heavy goods traffic are located together and that residential areas are located close to recreational parks.

Commercial land use

Commercial districts in a city contain banks, building societies, department stores, cinemas, theatres, restaurants and offices. The CBD is the largest commercial district in cities. The CBD is found in the most accessible part of the city, where transport networks meet. Space is limited and rents are high in the CBD. Office buildings are multi-storey. Car park charges in the CBD are high.

Transport land use

Roads, car parks, bus depots, train stations and railway lines take up a lot of space in cities. European cities have grown outwards from a medieval core. Therefore, city centre streets are often narrow. Many modern cities are surrounded by ring roads.

Residential land use

This is usually the largest single land use in cities today. Housing densities vary within a city. High-density housing is found close to the centre because of the cost of land. Close to the city centre, many people live in multi-storey residential apartments, both social and private. Residential suburbs have more spacious homes, with front and back gardens. Large shopping centres for suburban residents are located at the edge of the city because these centres are accessible by car on ring roads.

Industrial land use

In the 19th century, factories were built close to canals and railway stations so that raw materials could be brought in easily. They were also close to residential areas because people walked to work. Today, heavy industries such as oil refining, cement plants and steelworks are found in port areas of cities.

Manufacturing is increasingly located close to the perimeter of cities, where large and relatively cheap sites are available. Ring roads allow truck transport to access these sites with components.

Question

Explain two advantages of zoning within urban areas.

Questions

Examine the photograph of Tralee on page 109 and answer the following questions.
1. Give two examples of zoning in Tralee, based on evidence in the photo.
2. Would you consider this town to have high- or low-density housing? Explain your answer.
3. Where do you think the CBD is in Tralee? What evidence supports your answer?

Activity

Draw a sketch map to half scale of Tralee (page 109). Include and name the following:
■ A sports ground
■ An industrial estate
■ A housing estate
■ A commercial centre

Transport

Manufacturing

Residential (houses)

Commercial (shopping centre)

Recreational

Residential (apartments)

Commercial (offices)

Recreational

Manufacturing

Commercial (retail shops)

Transport

Fig. 5-6-2 Tralee, Co. Kerry, showing examples of urban land use.

ELECTIVE 5 – THE HUMAN ENVIRONMENT

Recreational land use

Recreational areas are essential for the health of urban residents. Phoenix Park is one of the largest urban parks in Europe, where families can while away an afternoon. Central Park in New York and the Bois de Boulogne in Paris are also important recreational parks for city residents.

Limerick city on the River Shannon.

Questions

Examine the photograph of Limerick above and answer the following questions.

1. What evidence suggests that Limerick has a planned city centre?
2. Identify two areas of recreational land use.
3. Where do you think the CBD is? Explain your answer.

THEORIES OF URBAN LAND USE

Researchers have studied land use zones and social stratification in cities over many decades. Many theories have been developed to explain how different land use zones develop in cities. We will now examine three of those theories, all American. The problem with them is that they did not examine European cities. However, cities show some of the same characteristics all over the world.

E.W. Burgess's concentric zone theory, 1925

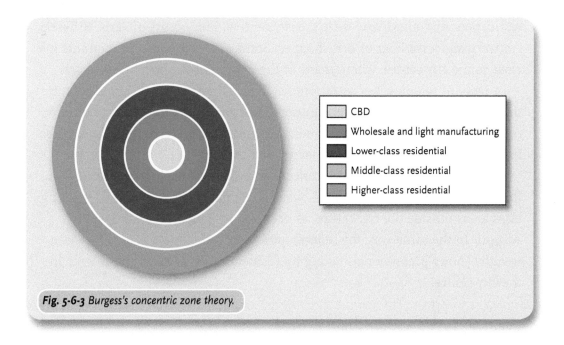

CBD
Wholesale and light manufacturing
Lower-class residential
Middle-class residential
Higher-class residential

Fig. 5-6-3 *Burgess's concentric zone theory.*

Geofact
Burgess really only attempted to explain Chicago.

Burgess's theory suggests that because urban land resources are scarce, there is competition between groups of people for land and space. This leads to people with the same income living in the same districts. Burgess's theory highlights the **relationship between income and distance** from the CBD.

Burgess's theory claims that cities are composed of **concentric zones** that become established as the city grows outwards from the centre.

Zone 1 is the CBD, the commercial heart of the city, with hotels, restaurants, offices and department stores. Because land is expensive and competition for space is strong, buildings are built upwards to make greater use of space.

Zone 2 is the transition zone between the CBD and residential zones. It is in a constant state of change as the CBD expands outwards. This zone has factories dating back to previous decades that are running out of space. High-density and old housing exist in this zone, with recently arrived migrants living in cramped quarters.

Zone 3 is lower-class residential. These are long-established communities of people who live close to zones 1 and 2, where many of them work. They have a short commuting time to their jobs. This zone has terraced homes. Blocks of flats may have replaced older terraced housing. Population densities are high.

Zone 4 is middle-class residential. Land is cheaper here than in zone 3 and has parks and recreational areas. Homes are spacious and have front and back gardens.

Zone 5 is high-class residential. It has spacious homes, with many properties enclosed in large plots. This zone includes towns and villages that are being surrounded by the growing city. Many residents in this zone commute to work in the CBD.

Is Burgess's theory relevant to cities today?

Some aspects of his theory still apply. For example, in cities in the developed world, poor migrants live close to the city centres. This occurs in Paris, Brussels, Antwerp and a number of British cities. Some of Dublin's recent migrants live close to the city centre, where many of them work in the hospitality sector.

In Dublin, middle-class communities live further away from the city centre than many working-class communities. The further one travels from the city centre, the more spacious the homes and gardens are. Ireland's urban centres have leafy suburbs on their perimeters.

However, very few cities have concentric circles of people of the same income. Local authorities have rehoused some inner-city residents in working-class areas outside the city centre, as occurred in Ballymun, near Dublin Airport. In the same way, the redevelopment of Dublin's docklands has seen wealthy young professionals taking up residence in expensive apartments in the city centre.

Homer Hoyt's sector theory, 1939

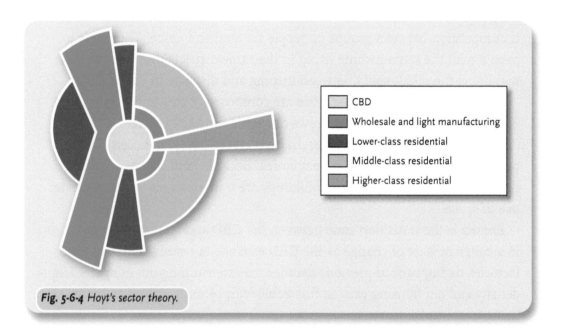

CBD

Wholesale and light manufacturing

Lower-class residential

Middle-class residential

Higher-class residential

Fig. 5-6-4 *Hoyt's sector theory.*

Even though Hoyt also used Chicago as a model, just as Burgess did, he broadened his research and studied other cities. He developed a theory that applied to many cities in America. For Hoyt, transport routes were important in the development of urban land use. He believed that cities grew outwards in wedge-shaped patterns, called sectors, along transport routes.

Zone 1 is the CBD.

Zone 2 is the wholesale and light manufacturing sector, which is located along routeways such as a river, a canal, or rail and road corridors. Zone 2 grows outwards along a wedge at each side of transport routes as more factories and wholesale premises are established.

Zone 3 is the lower-class residential sector. People choose to live in this zone because it is beside zone 2, where many of them work. They have a short and cheap commuting time. However, air and noise pollution are high here because of the factories and heavy traffic in zone 2. For that reason, this is the least desirable zone for people who can afford to live elsewhere.

Zone 4 is a middle-class neighbourhood, spacious, leafy and with a clean environment. Hoyt also accepted the idea of social stratification because it was so obvious in Chicago.

Zone 5 is the higher-class residential area. It is the most desirable part of the city to live in. It may be elevated and have good views of distant mountains, lakes and countryside. It has country clubs and golf courses.

Harris and Ullman's multiple nuclei theory, 1945

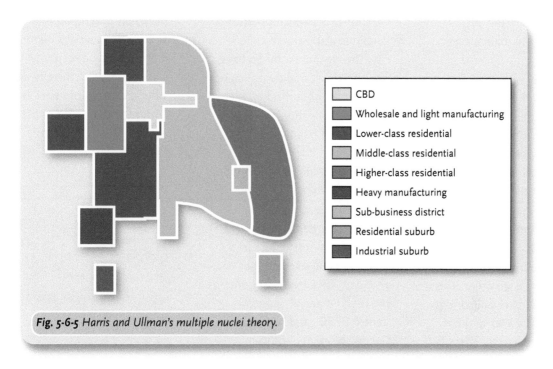

Fig. 5-6-5 *Harris and Ullman's multiple nuclei theory.*

Harris and Ullman believed that the two theories already examined do not explain the development of many cities. When this theory was developed in 1945, car ownership was much more important than in previous decades in the US. Cars allowed people to travel much more and allowed for the growth of specialised centres, such as heavy industrial districts, leisure areas and business districts. The result is that in many cities, **several nuclei or centres** develop in parts of the city where road access is good.

The main elements of this theory are as follows.

- A city grows from multiple centres, or **nuclei**, rather than from one CBD. As nuclei grow outwards, they merge to form one large urban area.
- **Economic activities of the same kind attract each other** because they can avail of the same services and customers. For instance, restaurants, cinemas and theatres are located in the CBD because they attract the large number of people who enter the CBD on a daily basis. Manufacturers locate in industrial suburbs because they can form links with nearby manufacturers.

■ **Some land uses repel each other**. Areas of heavy manufacturing will repel wealthy residents because of possible air pollution and odours. The poorest people will live beside areas of heavy manufacturing. The result is **social stratification**, with working-class, middle-class and upper-class residents living in different neighbourhoods.

CASE STUDY

Harris and Ullman's multiple nuclei theory applied to Dublin

This theory fits Dublin in several ways.
■ Dublin's CBD is in the city centre, where the main streets converge.
■ Dublin is a city with multiple nuclei. The city's expansion has absorbed villages with their own small business districts. Examples include Stillorgan and Dundrum, each with their own shopping centres and business districts. New towns such as Tallaght have their own CBDs outside the city.
■ In this theory, the same activities are attracted to each other. This is evident in Dublin. Ballsbridge has a large office area and has a cluster of embassies. There is a cluster of medical consultants in the Fitzwilliam Square area because the area is close to several hospitals.
■ Many manufacturers are attracted to the same areas. These are located in Dublin Port and in industrial estates

along the M50. In this way, manufacturers can buy and sell components to each other.
■ Dublin is a socially stratified city. The city and suburbs have working-class, middle-class and wealthy neighbourhoods. (See 'Social stratification' below and Fig. 5-6-6 on page 115.)

However, the multiple nuclei theory does not fit Dublin in every way.
■ The theory does not take account of urban renewal. The Dublin docklands is a case in point. Land use here has changed. This area now contains the Irish Financial Services Centre (IFSC), the National College of Ireland, offices, theatres and residential areas. The area has a mix of land uses.
■ The theory does not take account of city council housing decisions. An example is Ballymun, south of Dublin Airport. This was developed as a large working-class suburb of

tower blocks in the 1960s. The city authorities did not develop Ballymun around an existing nucleus or business district. Ballymun was a response to a housing crisis in the city, when inner-city residents were moved out to the perimeter of the city.

Geofact
The plural of nucleus is nuclei.

Link
Secondary economic activities in the Dublin region, *Today's World 1*, pages 280–3.

Link
Urban regeneration in Dublin, *Today's World 1*, page 290.

SOCIAL STRATIFICATION IN CITIES
Social stratification refers to the division of people into classes based on wealth and status. In cities all over the world, people of similar incomes and educational levels generally live in the same urban districts.

It is because of social stratification that some urban addresses are more sought after than others. House prices reflect this. Homes in middle-class and upper-class areas command high prices. Working-class areas have a higher proportion of social housing.

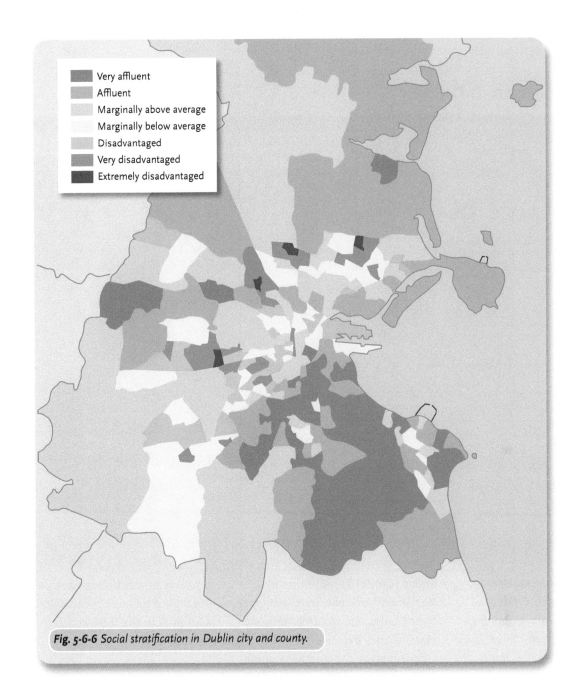

Very affluent
Affluent
Marginally above average
Marginally below average
Disadvantaged
Very disadvantaged
Extremely disadvantaged

Fig. 5-6-6 *Social stratification in Dublin city and county.*

An affluent suburban street in Dun Laoghaire.

Working-class apartments in Dublin's inner city.

CASE STUDY

Social stratification in Dublin

A view of the regenerated docklands on the Liffey's north bank, with the Samuel Beckett Bridge. The area has a mix of apartments and offices.

Social classification is evident in Dublin. Dublin can be divided into two sectors by a line running south-west from Howth. In general, the wealthiest people live south of this line in middle-class and upper-class areas. North of this line, residential districts are generally either working class or middle class. The inner city in Dublin is mainly working class. Ballymun is also a working-class area at the edge of the city.

However, the wealth generated in the Celtic Tiger years brought about some changes. In many working-class areas, people bought their homes and became middle class as they became better off. Working-class children have gone on to third-level education and joined the middle class. Education is therefore a great social leveller. These young people then buy homes in middle-class areas.

The docklands area of Dublin, once a working-class area, is now more mixed. The area is experiencing gentrification. Many expensive apartments in the regenerated docklands have been purchased by young professionals who work in the IFSC and in companies such as Google.

Question

Examine Fig. 5-6-6 on page 115. Write down five SRPs using information in the map.

Geofact

Google has more than 2,000 employees working in the city centre docklands south of the River Liffey.

Definition

GENTRIFICATION: The urban renewal of a run-down area and the influx of wealthy people who replace poorer residents.

Question

Explain how education is a social leveller.

CHANGING LAND USE ZONES IN URBAN AREAS

Older parts of cities show their age over time. Factories close their doors in the inner city and in port areas because of competition from modern factories in new industrial estates built along ring roads. Port areas suffer from economic decline because modern ships are larger and the port moves downstream to more modern and larger dockyards. As a result, unemployment occurs. People move out and many homes and factories become derelict. These areas include **brownfield sites** that have old rusting machinery lying around and which give a negative impression of an area.

Brownfield site in Dublin's docklands.

Definition

INNER CITY: A central and old area of the city where people live and where many problems exist, such as high unemployment, poverty and sub-standard housing.

The solution to inner-city decline is **urban renewal/regeneration**. Examples of urban regeneration include the following.
- Canary Wharf – a modern high-rise financial district in London's former docklands.
- The developing Titanic Quarter – a mix of residential, entertainment and hi-tech developments in the former Belfast shipyards.
- Dublin's Temple Bar area and the regeneration of Dublin's former docklands.

We will now examine **changes in land use** in Dublin's docklands over time.

Belfast's docklands before regeneration.

The futuristic architecture of Belfast's Titanic Quarter.

CASE STUDY

Land use changes in Dublin's docklands

Dublin's docklands, circa 1900.

Economic decline

The demand for manual labour declined sharply in the decades after 1950. This was mainly due to technological developments. These included:

- the growth of truck transport, such as roll-on roll-off ferries
- the introduction of heavy crane equipment, which replaced the need for manual labour in loading and unloading ships
- the decline in coal imports because of the switch to oil and gas
- the use of containers to transport goods.

Port-related land use in earlier times

Dublin became Ireland's premier port when Ireland was a colony of Britain. The port and city grew as a distribution centre for imports and as a focal point for exports. The port area had coal yards, warehouses and cattle yards. Flour milling, such as Boland's Mills, clothing workshops and iron foundries were located nearby. The port became the focus of canals and railway networks in the 19th century. The Royal and Grand Canals had large docks in the port area too. Land was given over to rail connections and warehouses, such as the Point Depot.

The area before regeneration.

Geofact

In the 19th century, Dublin's economy depended on its port work much more than on manufacturing.

Land use changes in Grand Canal Docks. The area now contains open space, the Grand Canal Theatre, offices and apartments.

The port moved downriver, away from the older docks to modern facilities at the mouth of the river. The older port area became derelict. Communities in the old port area around Sheriff Street suffered high unemployment. Only 35% of students reached Leaving Cert level. The port area was in crisis, socially and economically. Government intervention was needed.

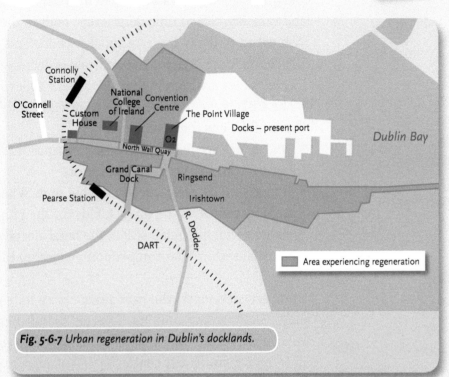

Fig. 5-6-7 *Urban regeneration in Dublin's docklands.*

Area experiencing regeneration

Question
Can you explain exactly how containerisation of goods reduced the workforce in ports?

Link
The IFSC in the Dublin region, *Today's World 1*, pages 284–5.

Recent land use change
Land use change began in Dublin's docklands in 1987 with the development of the IFSC. Where once there were abandoned warehouses and cattle yards, gleaming new high-rise office blocks now exist, supporting 450 companies engaged in banking, financial trading and financial services.

Definition
DDDA: Dublin Docklands Development Authority.

The success of the IFSC and the money made available by the growth of the Celtic Tiger led to further developments. The DDDA was established in 1997. Its role is the sustainable physical, social and economic renewal of the former docklands. It is responsible for 520 hectares north and south of the Liffey. The area is now impressive in many ways. It includes the National College of Ireland, the National Convention Centre, the O2, the Samuel Beckett Bridge, the Grand Canal Theatre and shopping areas. Hotels, restaurants and street furniture give the area a pleasant ambience. The Point Village near the O2 – a major office, hotel and apartment development – will grow over time.

Social developments are given major importance in the area. The aim is to repopulate the docklands with a projected population of 45,000 people. Many new apartment blocks are located in the docklands. This is another land use change. The population is growing. For instance, North Dock B showed a major increase in population in the 2011 census. Gentrification is also occurring as young professional people move into the area. Community training schemes have been put in place to upskill local people for employment.

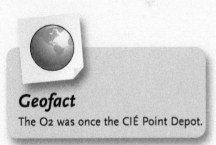

Geofact
The O2 was once the CIÉ Point Depot.

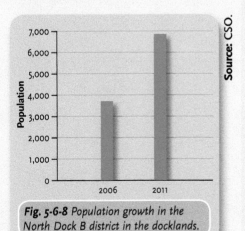

Source: CSO.

Fig. 5-6-8 *Population growth in the North Dock B district in the docklands.*

LAND VALUES IN CITIES

The property bubble that occurred in Ireland in the years before 2008 caused land values to rise to ridiculous levels, both in the centre and perimeter of Irish urban centres. Property bubbles aside, land values vary within cities. City centre space is expensive and values decrease towards the suburbs.

Land values are high in the CBD for the following reasons.

- The CBD is the focus of urban routes and is therefore the most accessible area of the city for customers.
- Land values are high in the centre because there is intense competition between competing economic sectors.
- Property values are related to the **bid rent**. When a city centre site or property comes on the market, bids for the property may come from the leisure sector, the retail sector, the hotel/hospitality sector and the banking/financial sector. That competition pushes up the price.

A property developer who pays a huge price for a city centre location will build a multi-storey building. The rent that comes in from the entire building will counteract the high cost of the land. That also explains why land use is most intense in the city centre.

The variation in land values and bid rents explains why different economic activities are concentrated in different parts of the city.

Definition

BID RENT: The rent that various economic sectors are prepared to bid for land or property at various distances from the city centre.

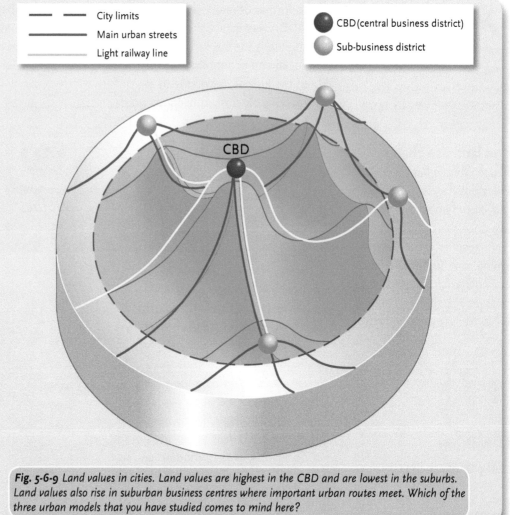

– – –	City limits	
———	Main urban streets	
———	Light railway line	

● CBD (central business district)

○ Sub-business district

Fig. 5-6-9 *Land values in cities. Land values are highest in the CBD and are lowest in the suburbs. Land values also rise in suburban business centres where important urban routes meet. Which of the three urban models that you have studied comes to mind here?*

Retail businesses

Large department stores are found in the CBD. They attract many customers and their owners can afford to pay high rents (except in times of economic recession). Shops are at street level because window displays attract customers in from the street. City centre shops need a high cash turnover because of the cost of the rent that they are paying.

Offices

Banks, insurance companies, building societies, and legal and accountancy firms are also located in the CBD. Banks and mortgage companies are found at street level because they have many customers. However, firms that conduct much of their business by mail, email and over the internet do not require offices on the ground floor. That is why legal, accountancy and consultancy companies may be found on the upper floors of buildings in the CBD. They cannot match the rent that retailers can afford to pay for ground floor space because they have fewer customers.

Offices are located further away from the city centre, where rents are lower, than retail stores.

Manufacturers

Manufacturers cannot afford to pay the high rent that retailers and office companies pay in the city centre because manufacturers require a lot of space. Today, manufacturers tend to locate on the perimeter of the city, where land is much cheaper, the bid rent is far lower and sites are much larger than in the city centre.

Truck access is important for manufacturers for obvious reasons. Therefore, they are located close to ring roads such as the M50 in Dublin and the Galway ring road. Some manufacturers prefer to locate on greenfield sites beyond the urban fringe where there is room for future expansion.

Geofact

Medical devices companies in Galway are located on the ring road outside the city.

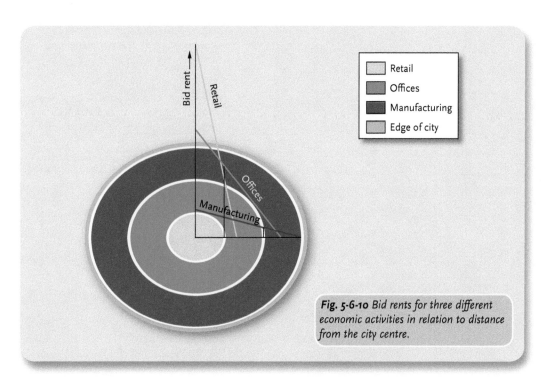

Fig. 5-6-10 *Bid rents for three different economic activities in relation to distance from the city centre.*

ELECTIVE 5 – THE HUMAN ENVIRONMENT

LAND USE CHANGES AS URBAN CENTRES GROW

Cities grow over time as the urban population of a country grows due to natural increase and inward migration from rural areas. As cities expand, land use within the city changes over time and space. Examples include the following.

■ Residential developments invade agricultural land on the urban fringe.

■ Transport networks expand to meet increased demand.

■ Shopping centres are built on the urban fringe.

■ Industrial estates are built on zoned land and the CBD expands into the inner city and areas of urban decay close to it.

These developments lead to changed land use.

Shopping centres on the urban fringe

Urban centres today have ring roads to cater for motorists and trucks that do not wish to travel through a city or town. Developers have used the lands close to ring roads to build out-of-town shopping centres. There are many such centres in the US and they are also found on this side of the Atlantic. Because of their size, shopping centres on the urban fringe involve a major change in land use, from agricultural land use to shops and car parks. Examples include the Liffey Valley and Dundrum Shopping Centres in the Dublin area.

Questions

1. The photograph below shows evidence of zoning in West Dublin. Give three examples.
2. Explain three ways in which land use here changed as Dublin grew outwards.

Liffey Valley is a sprawling shopping development located at the junction of the M50 and the M4. While it is easily reached by car, that very fact brings a high cost to the environment in terms of pollution. The Quarryvale site on which it is built was the subject of a planning tribunal for several years.

Transport land use

As cities expand outwards, land must be made available for road and light rail transport. Commuters travel inwards to the CBD to work every day. While some cities, such as Paris and London, have underground rail networks, many cities do not. Roads require a great deal of space. Dublin has a six-lane ring road – the M50 – whose purpose was to exclude through-traffic from the city centre. However, the M50 is used as a commuter route by many commuters. The M50 occupies a lot of former agricultural land on Dublin's urban fringe.

Dublin also has two Luas lines, which have extended into the outer suburbs. Sandyford is an important station that serves the Luas Green Line. The station has a large car park that provides park-and-ride facilities for commuters into the CBD. The Red Line has park-and-ride facilities at the Red Cow Interchange on the city's western fringe. These park-and-ride facilities were farmland only a generation ago.

THE IMPACT OF EXPANDING CITIES ON THE RURAL LANDSCAPE

As cities expand, built-up areas encroach into nearby villages, agricultural land and rural countryside where fields are surrounded by trees and hedges. One way to limit or control this is by using **greenbelts**, such as those found in Britain since the 1930s. This is land that is set aside around cities and in which development is strictly controlled. Greenbelts put a limit to urban sprawl. Greenbelts prevent cities from absorbing surrounding villages and prevent towns from merging together. They preserve the natural countryside.

Greenbelts are important to the environmental health of a region. Trees in the greenbelt act as sponges that absorb pollutants and release oxygen.

Greenbelts – a link with nature

Greenbelts give city dwellers links with nature. People who live in the urban jungle may become disconnected from nature and from wildlife. Greenbelts provide evidence on the urban doorstep of ecosystems and of wildlife. Greenbelts have farms and garden allotments where city dwellers can see farm animals and vegetables growing and observe the changing seasons. Paths through greenbelt woodland outside the city are a haven of peace and renewal for urban dwellers. Greenbelts also absorb heavy rain and may prevent flooding in urban residential estates.

'Trees are the ultimate urban multi-taskers.' – *Gary Moll* in American Forests

Question
Can you suggest three tasks that trees perform in the urban environment?

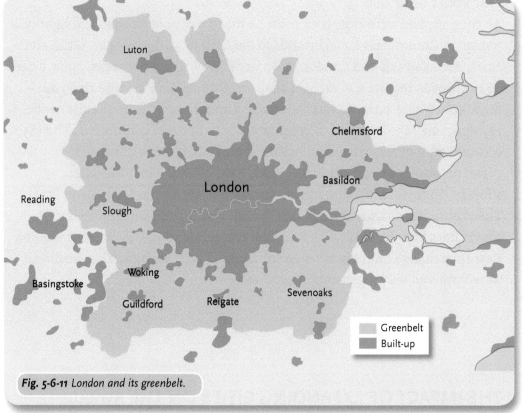

Fig. 5-6-11 *London and its greenbelt.*

Geofact

An unfortunate result of the economic downturn of 2008 is the number of unfinished **ghost estates** that have been partly built around Irish cities, towns and villages. These are in a state of limbo, where the natural world has been bulldozed and replaced by half-finished sites, some of which are falling into a semi-derelict state.

Question

Can you give two reasons for the existence of ghost estates in the Republic of Ireland?

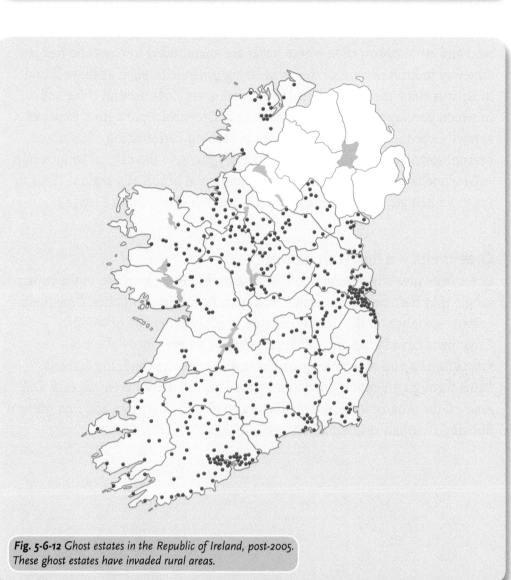

Fig. 5-6-12 *Ghost estates in the Republic of Ireland, post-2005. These ghost estates have invaded rural areas.*

The destruction of the cultural landscape

Urban expansion changes the cultural landscape of rural areas around cities. When land is rezoned for development, the bulldozers move in and obliterate hedgerows and wildlife. Bulldozers remove farmhouses and change the character of an area. A landscape that developed over hundreds of years is obliterated in the space of a few days. The names of rural townlands may be changed and developers use street names that may have no link at all to the original cultural landscape. These names may be borrowed from abroad or even named after a developer's own family.

The cultural landscape also includes historic sites. As cities expand into the countryside, ring roads and motorways are often built around them. This can lead to the destruction or partial destruction of historic ruins. This occurred at Carrickmines in South Dublin as the M50 was being completed. We will examine the Carrickmines heritage issue on page 126.

Link

You will have the opportunity to examine heritage issues on pages 146–148.

Fig. 5-6-13 *The expansion of cities leads to the destruction of the cultural and natural landscape.*

Question

State three ways in which the rural landscape is overrun in Fig. 5-6-13.

CASE STUDY

The Carrickmines medieval site

The M50, Dublin's ring road, was nearing completion as the 21st century began. The plans for the final southern section revealed that the route would pass through part of the historic site of Carrickmines. This led to a study of the site by a team of archaeologists.

The study found that the site dated back to 12th-century Dublin. Viking families who had remained in Dublin after the Battle of Clontarf lived there. The site included the remains of a castle and other fortified buildings. The dig revealed the remains of a medieval village and castle at the edge of the Pale.

These revelations led to a temporary halt to the completion of the M50. Opponents of the project used the courts to try to prevent the destruction of this ancient monument. However, the minister concerned used the National Monuments Amendment Act 2004 to allow the road to be finished, as its completion was deemed to be in the national interest.

The motorway was then completed. The former site is now largely **preserved by record** – in photographs and video recordings and in museums. Half of the archaeological site is covered by motorway. The little that remains of the medieval site has been described as a 'motorway ornament in the middle of a spaghetti junction'.

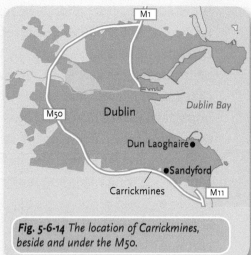

Fig. 5·6·14 *The location of Carrickmines, beside and under the M50.*

Definition

THE PALE: The area around Dublin under British rule where English was spoken from the 13th century onwards.

Carrickmines archaeological site.

Questions

1. State two arguments that people who wanted to preserve Carrickmines by record only would have used.
2. Name two options that could have been considered to preserve the Carrickmines heritage.
3. Can you suggest three benefits that designated greenbelts would bring to Ireland?

Leaving Cert Exam Questions

1 **Land use models**

OL

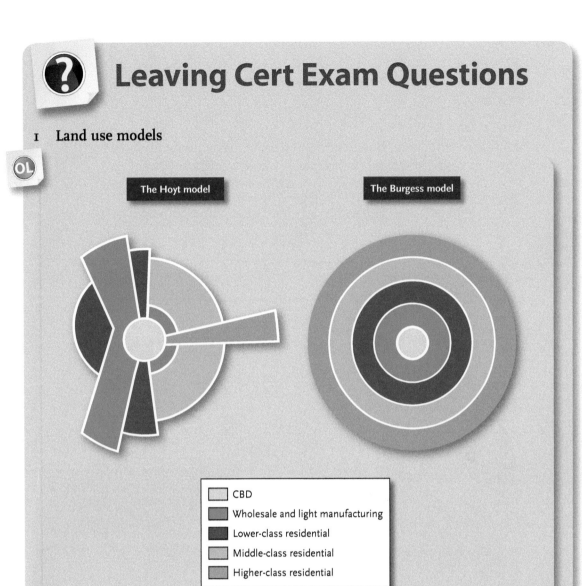

Fig. 5-6-15 *Land use models.*

Examine the two urban land use models from Hoyt and Burgess shown in Fig. 5-6-15. Explain **two** differences between the two models. (40 marks)

2 **Greenbelts**

OL

A park such as this is an example of a land use zone within a city. Explain fully **two** reasons why it is important to preserve greenbelts such as this within towns and/or cities. (30 marks)

A winter scene in an urban park.

3 Dynamics of settlement

Describe and explain the land use zones in **any** city you have studied. (30 marks)

4 Urban expansion

'As cities expand, they impact on surrounding rural areas.' Discuss this statement with reference to examples you have studied. (30 marks)

5 Urban land use

With reference to **one** example you have studied, describe and explain changing land use in urban areas. (30 marks)

6 Urban land use

Examine the relevance of **one** of the land use models in Fig. 5-6-16 as it applies to land use zones in a city you have studied. (30 marks)

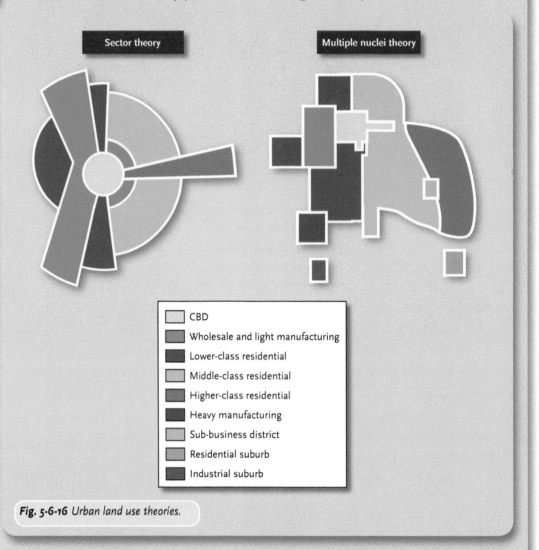

Fig. 5-6-16 Urban land use theories.

7 Changing land use

Different activities compete for space in urban areas. As a result, different land use zones develop. Referring to examples you have studied, examine how these land use zones change as urban centres grow. (30 marks)

8 Changing land use patterns

Describe and explain the changing land use patterns in an urban area you have studied. (30 marks)

Urban growth – problems and issues

Urban traffic management is very challenging today. Traffic congestion affects people's quality of life. The challenge of getting to and from work at the same time as everyone else is a major issue for planners and commuters alike.

Learning objectives

After studying this chapter, you should be able to understand:

- that urban areas face traffic congestion and other environmental challenges
- that areas of urban decay can be successfully renewed
- that urban strategies can be used to deal with urban sprawl and increasing urban populations
- that cities in the developing world face major challenges related to rapidly increasing populations
- that the cities of the future must be sustainable.

TRAFFIC CONGESTION – AN URBAN PROBLEM

American, Canadian and Australian cities grew outwards in the 20th century. In general, cities in these continents have long, wide, straight streets, ideal for cars. However, European cities are much older. Streets in many Old World cities of Europe are narrower and were designed for horse transport in the 19th century. When cars and trucks were introduced onto these streets, traffic congestion occurred.

In Ireland, increasing prosperity in the last 40 years has seen vehicle numbers increase. Poor public transport networks also led people to turn to car transport for commuting. Irish people leaped from the family with no car to the two-car family in one generation. Many third-level students now have cars. Because of this rapid increase in car ownership, city planners have been playing catch-up as they struggle to cope with traffic congestion.

Geofact

Car ownership increased from just under 1 million in 1995 to about 2.5 million in 2012 in the Republic of Ireland.

The Dublin Commuter Count

Every November, the Dublin Transportation Office conducts a count of commuter movements across the Royal and Grand Canal bridges into Dublin city centre at 33 locations during the hours 7 a.m. to 10 a.m.

Year	Cars (including taxis)	Goods vehicles	Buses	Bicycles	Motorcycles	Pedestrians
1997	73,561	3,283	1,459	5,628	1,816	16,679
2011	60,607	1,176	1,688	6,870	1,656	15,092

Table 5-7-1 How Dubliners got to work, November 1997 and 2011.

Questions

Examine Table 5-7-1 and answer the following questions.

1. Suggest one reason for the reduction in goods vehicles entering the city centre across the canals.
2. Suggest two reasons for the reduced number of cars entering the city centre in 2011.
3. Name one mode of public transport in Dublin that is not included in the above list of transport modes.

The DART crossing the Liffey beside the Custom House.

Geofact

It has been suggested by some city authorities that cars with four people or more should be allowed to use bus lanes. What do you think of that?

The impact of traffic congestion in cities

Traffic congestion has **a social impact**. People's schedules are thrown out of gear. People miss appointments and become stressed because of the time that they waste in traffic. Commuting parents are often tired when they get home and feel guilty about missing time with their children.

Traffic congestion has **an economic impact**. Truck deliveries to shops and factories are delayed. Fuel costs are higher when traffic congestion occurs and eat into people's weekly budget. Traffic congestion adds to air pollution and can lead to a rise in chest infections and days lost because of that.

TRAFFIC MANAGEMENT

With more than half of the world's population living in cities, it is more important than ever that cities have healthy environments for people. Heavy traffic pollution interferes with health. The aim of good traffic management

Traffic management in urban streets. Describe the three examples of traffic management shown here.

includes improvements in the flow of traffic, but it must also reduce pollution and stress for the sake of people's health.

Traffic management steps

■ One-way streets.

■ A ban on parking on all busy urban routes by the use of double yellow lines along kerbs.

■ A hefty parking charge for kerbside parking in the city centre to discourage motorists from driving into the city centre.

■ Flyovers or underpasses on key junctions so that traffic lights can be eliminated.

■ Tunnels such as Dublin Port Tunnel that eliminate heavy traffic from the city centre.

■ An electronic congestion charging system where motorists pay to drive through the city at busy times.

■ Ring roads that allow through-traffic to bypass urban centres.

■ Park-and-ride facilities that allow out-of-town commuters to use public transport in the city centre.

Geofact

29.4 million: The number of passengers who travelled on the Luas in 2012.
119 million: The number of passengers who travelled on Dublin Bus in 2010.

Geofact

Connolly Station, one of Dublin's most important railway stations, was opened in 1844, at a time when the country was very poor.

The Brisbane CBD, with a two-tier motorway over the Brisbane River.

Question

Do you think the traffic solution used in Brisbane (roads over a river) would find favour in Dublin? Explain your answer.

Link

Transport services in Dublin, *Today's World 1*, pages 285–7, and in Paris, page 323.

PUBLIC TRANSPORT – THE WAY TO GO

The best way to help traffic flow **is to greatly reduce it** by making public transport more attractive. Drivers must be weaned away from the wheel. Public transport includes:

- underground metro systems such as those in London and Paris
- light rail such as Luas
- suburban rail such as the DART
- a bus network running on Quality Bus Corridors that is fast, reliable and efficient.

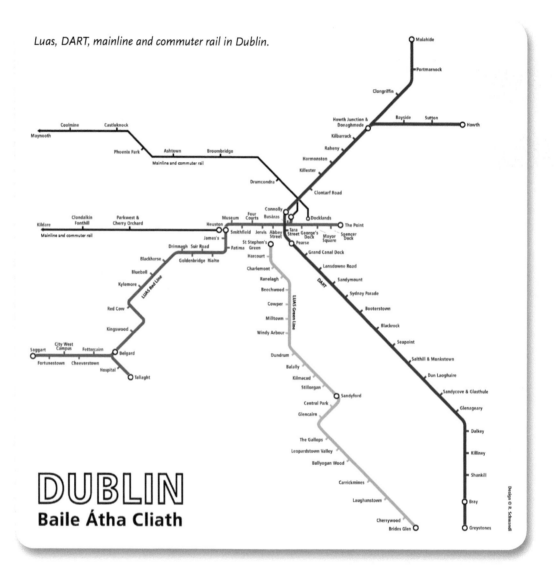

Luas, DART, mainline and commuter rail in Dublin.

Link

Transport services in Dublin, *Today's World 1*, pages 285–7.

European citizens use public transport much more than in the US or Australia because European cities are built differently. European cities have **high-density multi-storey apartments** with tram lines and buses close by. Their public transport systems are efficient and cheap because many people use them. This means that investment is available to modernise them and maintain their attractiveness. In Ireland, economic challenges have meant that very little funding is now available for spending on public transport such as Metro North in Dublin.

We will now examine how Curitiba in southern Brazil has led the way in urban bus transport.

Low-density suburbs in the Killiney-Dalkey area of South Dublin, with Dun Laoghaire in the background. Irish cities, including Dublin, have low-density housing. Irish planners did not link urban growth to public transport. As a result, people have to travel quite a distance to the bus stop if they are not living on a bus thoroughfare. On a wet morning, it is tempting to use the car.

CASE STUDY

Curitiba, Brazil

Geofact
The population of greater Curitiba – 3.3 million – is three times the population of Dublin city and county.

Link
The Brazilian region, *Today's World 1*, Chapter 21.

Fig. 5-7-1 The location of Curitiba in south-east Brazil.

Curitiba has developed a model of urban transport that overcomes most of the challenges that are faced in traffic management all over the world. City planners in Curitiba devised an **urban master plan** in 1965. Under this plan, urban growth was to be integrated with public transport. Zoning laws were put in place to direct residential and commercial development along transportation routes. Therefore, as the city grew outwards, residential districts, public transport routes and traffic management **were all developed together**. (Apart from Adamstown, built alongside mainline rail in West Dublin, this has not happened in Irish cities.)

CASE STUDY

Buses

Bus transport was given the highest priority. There are many categories of buses, each of which is colour coded:

- **express buses** in designated bus lanes along five main arteries
- **feeder buses** in the districts between the main arteries that ferry passengers to the main bus arteries
- **inter-district buses** in designated bus lanes on other important streets.

The bus fleet today has more than 1,900 buses. Buses carry 2.2 million passengers a day in Curitiba. At this time, 75% of commuters in Curitiba use public transport to get to work.

High usage means that no government subsidies are necessary to maintain bus services. The elderly and people with disabilities – 15% of all passengers – travel free. It is no wonder they all use it because a standard fare can bring passengers on a journey of 70 km. The quality of buses continues to improve and most are air conditioned.

Jaime Lerner, mayor of Curitiba in the 1970s. Jaime Lerner was largely responsible for the development of Curitiba as a sustainable city.

Geofact

In Curitiba, sheep graze in the parks to keep the grass down. This is more environmentally friendly than petrol mowers.

Passengers buy their tickets at automatic ticket machines. Ten private bus companies operate the system. A semi-state company pays the bus companies according to the length of the routes that they travel in addition to the number of passengers that they carry. Therefore, bus companies have an incentive to cover as much of the city as possible.

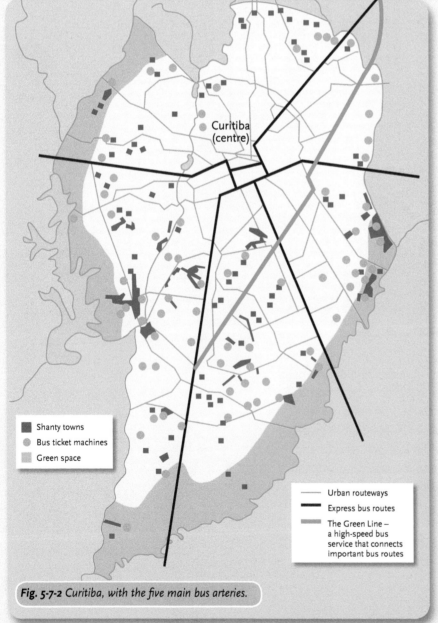

Curitiba (centre)

Shanty towns
Bus ticket machines
Green space

Urban routeways
Express bus routes
The Green Line – a high-speed bus service that connects important bus routes

Fig. 5-7-2 *Curitiba, with the five main bus arteries.*

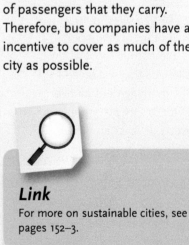

Link

For more on sustainable cities, see pages 152–3.

CASE STUDY

The environmental payback

Because of successful public transport, car use is far lower than it is in other cities in Brazil. Curitiba's air pollution levels are 30% below the level of other large cities in Brazil. The atmosphere in the city is visibly cleaner that in São Paulo or Rio de Janeiro. Residents in the shanty towns of Curitiba are given bus tickets in return for bringing their recycling waste to recycling centres. Therefore, the city integrates high bus use with keeping the city clean. That is an example of **lateral thinking**.

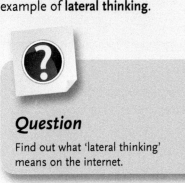

Question

Find out what 'lateral thinking' means on the internet.

An articulated bus in Curitiba on a designated bus lane.

URBAN SPRAWL – AN URBAN PROBLEM

Urban sprawl is a feature of the modern world. It is very evident in the US. The American lifestyle has been built around the car since the early years of the 20th century. Families began to move to the suburbs in cities across the US because the car gave people the option to commute to work. The most extreme example of sprawl exists in the Los Angeles area in southern California, which extends over an area the size of Co. Clare.

When sprawl takes place, many people abandon the city for the suburbs. This has a **doughnut effect**. Those who remain in the city are often poorer than those who move to the suburbs. The city centre begins to experience **inner-city decline** and its population may be reduced or impoverished. As wealthy people leave, migrants move into the inner city.

Definition

URBAN SPRAWL is the uncontrolled spread of urban areas into the surrounding countryside.

Fig. 5-7-3 The doughnut effect empties the city centre of people as factories and residents move to the perimeter of the city.

TIVE 5 – THE HUMAN ENVIRONMENT

Urban sprawl in Ireland

In recent years, the European Environmental Agency has expressed surprise at the extent of urban sprawl in the Republic of Ireland. We have a modern economy and society, but when it comes to urban sprawl, we have managed to make incredible mistakes in the last 20 years.

Urban sprawl is not just confined to the major cities of the Republic. Sprawl, in the form of low-density housing estates (including ghost estates), commercial developments and roads, affects large and small towns in counties across the state.

Urban sprawl in Douglas/Carrigaline in Co. Cork.

Geofact

If Dublin had the same population density per km² as Paris, the city would occupy a mere one-sixth of its present area.

Geofact

Satellite photography of Ireland clearly reveals the extent of urban sprawl in Ireland.

Europeans are astonished at the low population density that exists in Irish cities. Paris has a population density of 23,000 per km², but Dublin's population density is a mere 4,000 per km². Other Irish cities have even lower densities than Dublin.

The causes of urban sprawl in the Republic of Ireland

- Many young couples were unable to buy homes in Irish cities because of rapid inflation in the price of Irish homes during the boom years of 1995 to 2008. Homes in towns and villages outside the cities of Dublin, Cork and Limerick were considerably cheaper, so they moved to those towns and villages.

- Large areas of land around cities and towns were zoned for residential and commercial purposes by county and city councils. When land was rezoned, planning divisions within local councils had little option but to grant planning permission when builders applied for it.

- The rapid development of motorways, especially in the Dublin commuter belt, meant that people persuaded themselves that they could live further afield and commute to work in the Dublin region every day.

- Ghost estates have also contributed to urban sprawl. In some cases, estates were built in places where there was little demand for homes. This was the case in the Upper Shannon Rural Renewal Scheme, where urban sprawl has produced a number of ghost estates outside towns and villages in Cavan, Longford, Leitrim, Roscommon and Sligo.

'Planning failures facilitated a boom that led to an oversupply of 100,000 homes.' – Quote in an *Irish Times* editorial referring to the building frenzy of the boom years in Ireland up to 2008

Definition

ARTIFICIAL LAND USE: Land that has been changed from farmland or natural cover to built-up areas with houses, roads, footpaths and other forms of built development. See Fig. 5-7-4.

The consequences of urban sprawl

- Urban sprawl has led to a great increase in built-up areas in the Republic. These built-up surfaces increased by **65%** in the years 1995 to 2008.

- Urban sprawl led to a shift in population growth outwards from Dublin towards the **commuter belt counties** of the Midland and the Border regions. The 2011 census found that Laois had the fastest-growing population of any county (up by 20% in five years), followed by Cavan and Fingal (both up by 14%) and Longford and Meath (both up by 13%).

- Urban sprawl leads to long commuting times behind the wheel of the car. The number of commuting hours in Ireland is twice the European average. Commuting time in Ireland is also **30% more than the US average** and could be among the highest in the world.

- Sprawl leads to a high use of fossil fuels among commuters in Ireland. This in turn leads to additional emissions of heat-trapping gases in the atmosphere and leads to global warming.

- The cost of urban sprawl to the rural landscape is very high. Large areas of rural landscape are lost. Habitats such as hedges are uprooted. Wildlife such as nesting birds, badgers and foxes are displaced. Former farms are paved over with roads and footpaths.

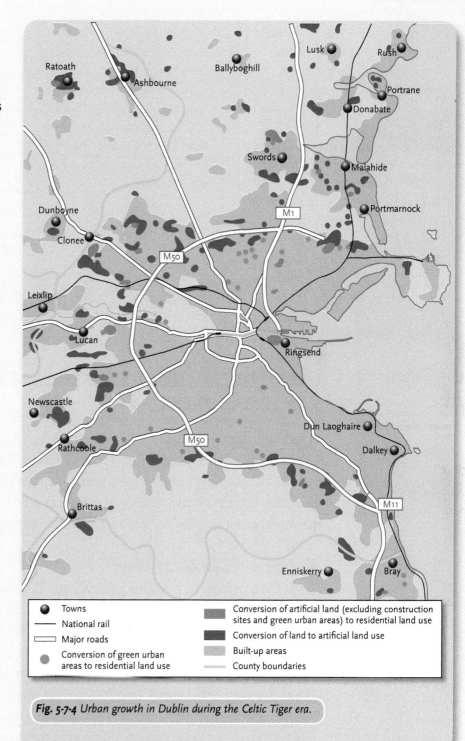

Towns

National rail

Major roads

Conversion of green urban areas to residential land use

Conversion of artificial land (excluding construction sites and green urban areas) to residential land use

Conversion of land to artificial land use

Built-up areas

County boundaries

Fig. 5-7-4 *Urban growth in Dublin during the Celtic Tiger era.*

- Natural drainage patterns are upset. During the boom years estates were built on **river floodplains**. Run-off from paved surfaces in times of heavy rain led to flooding of homes and severe hardship for families.

- The cost of services is higher in areas of urban sprawl than in compact urban areas. Sprawling estates require more roads, water pipes, sewage pipes and electricity cables than high-density estates.

CASE STUDY

Conclusion

Due to the recession that began in late 2008, the Irish landscape that was close to urban centres, ravaged during the boom, is getting a break. It is not possible to undo the mistakes of the past. However, as a nation, we can decide on a new way to build our cities. We must seriously examine the following steps:

■ That cities and towns should be built from the inside outwards with **in-fill developments**.

■ That **high-density housing** similar to the Parisian model is the way to go.

■ That public transport developments such as light rail and suburban rail should be integrated with future housing developments. In this way, urban sprawl, traffic congestion, air quality and quality of life can be tackled together. We can learn from Curitiba, Copenhagen and other cities that have pursued this strategy.

Questions

1. What do you think is the meaning of in-fill developments?
2. Can you attempt to explain why developers and planners did not pursue the above policies during the building frenzy?

URBAN DECAY AND THE ABSENCE OF COMMUNITY – AN URBAN PROBLEM

What is urban decay?

Urban decay occurs when a part of the city becomes dilapidated and derelict as businesses and well-off families move away from it. Urban decay generally, but not always, occurs in the inner city. Urban decay is linked to unemployment and the decline of inner-city communities.

Why does urban decay occur?

Cities were smaller in previous generations. City centres were vibrant places where craft shops and industries were located. Low-paid workers lived in the city centre in nearby streets. Population densities were high. Members of extended families lived close to each other and looked out for each other. With the collapse of jobs due to industrial decline or changes in port activities – as in the case of inner-city Dublin – people begin to move away. Buildings become unoccupied and derelict.

However, urban decay is also found in impoverished and neglected communities where public housing policy failed. This occured in Ballymun in Dublin's north side.

Characteristics of areas that suffer from urban decay

■ **High unemployment occurs.** This is very damaging for young adults, who may become long-term unemployed.

■ Many people in areas of urban decay are **poorly educated**. This makes it even more unlikely that they will get a job.

■ Areas of urban decay have **high levels of social housing**. These areas do not have a good social mix and can become deprived areas very quickly.

■ **Drugs, crime and violence** become a problem in the area.

■ **People begin to move out** of the area if they can afford to do so because of the derelict appearance of the area. Parents want to raise their children in a safer and more wholesome environment.

■ **Communities in deprived areas become fragmented.** Many households are composed of single-parent families and some teenagers become difficult to control. They roam around housing estates at night and some become sucked into the cycle of drugs and violence.

CASE STUDY

Ballymun in Dublin's north side

How did Ballymun come about?

In the 1960s, inner-city Dublin had very poor housing. The city authorities devised an urban strategy to improve this situation. This strategy involved the surprising decision to move inner-city residents to newly built high-rise blocks in Ballymun, on the northern periphery of the city. Similar strategies had been put in place in British cities, but social problems had arisen there within a short time. Tenants began to move into the Ballymun flats in 1966.

Ballymun – a socially deprived area

High-rise living in Ballymun was not successful. Lifts often broke down. Stairs and corridors were poorly maintained. The quality of the construction left a lot to be desired. Insulation was very poor and the flats were cold in winter.

Young families from the inner city were uprooted from their neighbourhood and transplanted several kilometres away. Their **social and family supports** – grandparents, uncles and aunts –

were several kilometres away in the inner city. The young residents felt isolated in Ballymun.

Geofact

In 1998, 80% of Ballymun was made up of social housing compared to a national average of 10%.

Indications of **social deprivation** came to the surface in Ballymun over the years. The area had high unemployment, many people were unskilled and teenagers left school early. Therefore, the cycle of poverty began to repeat itself because early school leavers had fewer employment opportunities. The area became a black spot for drugs and crime. Many flats were vacant and vandalised.

Strategy for renewal

Ballymun Regeneration Ltd (BRL) was established in 1997. BRL produced a master plan for the area. At all stages, BRL involved the local people in discussion. They had a sense that the mistakes of

Link

The Dublin region, *Today's World 1*, pages 277–90.

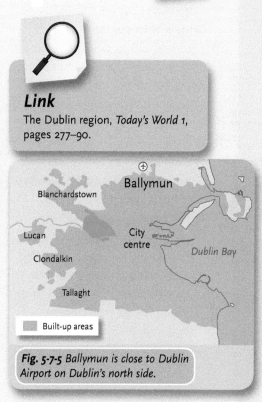

Fig. 5-7-5 Ballymun is close to Dublin Airport on Dublin's north side.

the past would not be repeated. Residents got a sense that they mattered and that they could help to create the type of town that they wanted. Their views became part of the plan for regeneration.

It was fortunate that the economic boom of the Celtic Tiger years made money available (more than €2 billion) to regenerate the area. The plan for Ballymun envisages a town of 30,000 eventually.

CASE STUDY

The main features of the new Ballymun include the following.

■ The old tower blocks have been demolished and new homes ranging from one to four floors have replaced them. The new homes are attractive, well built with modern materials and are well insulated.

■ A mix of social and private housing has been given priority. It is hoped that when the regeneration is complete, privately owned housing will account for 56% of the total homes.

■ Main Street is the new town centre, with activities similar to town centres across the country. Banks, offices, shops and public service buildings line Main Street.

■ Neighbourhoods with corner shops, crèches, parks and playgrounds are found around the new Ballymun.

■ The town is well served with good bus transport into Dublin city centre. It is beside the M50 and close to the airport. Ikea, located close to Ballymun town, has provided employment opportunities.

Part of the new Ballymun.

■ Much attention is being paid to the social regeneration of the new town. Adult education, up-skilling and training are vital. While this is ongoing, the economic recession has affected the Ballymun community like everywhere else. Long-term unemployment continues to be a major problem in the town. The technological park that was to be built beside the town has not happened.

■ Community activities such as sport are encouraged. A state-of-the-art leisure centre and swimming pool are open. With these facilities available, people no longer feel neglected and they put time and effort into maintaining the good appearance of the area. Much attention is paid to litter collection and to recycling.

The advantages of a social mix in housing:
■ it adds demographic balance to an area that enriches people's lives
■ it promotes tolerance of social difference
■ it broadens the educational influences on children
■ it provides exposure to alternative ways of life.

Question
Explain the advantages of a mix of social and private housing.

ENVIRONMENTAL QUALITY IN CITIES – AN URBAN PROBLEM

Air quality

Air quality is a concern for everybody because of its impact on people's health. For instance, in 1962, a smog event in London led to the deaths of at least 4,000 people. As many as 100,000 people developed severe respiratory infections.

Respiratory or chest conditions have increased in recent decades in Ireland among both children and adults. Air pollution has a role in this. Chest conditions cause children to lose time at school and adults to be absent from work.

The EPA's reports are a valuable source of information on air pollution in Ireland. The 2010 report states that air quality in the Republic of Ireland is generally good and is among the best in Europe. Ireland's air quality meets all EU standards. This is due to:

■ prevailing Atlantic winds
■ relatively few large cities
■ the absence of widespread heavy industry such as iron and steel smelting.

Dublin at twilight.

However, the EPA states that air traffic emissions remain a threat to air quality in Irish cities. Traffic emissions include **nitrogen dioxide** and **particulate matter (PM$_{10}$)**. These remain a concern in Dublin and Cork city centres and are reaching EU limits in those cities. While emissions from each car have been greatly reduced due to better engine technology, the increase in the number of vehicles in recent years threatens air quality.

Geofact
The Environmental Protection Agency (EPA) was established in 1993 as the Republic's environmental watchdog.

Definition
SMOG: A combination of smoke and fog.

Question
Can you identify two sources of pollution visible in the photograph of Dublin?

Source: EPA.

Location	1997	2003	2009
Wood Quay	74	14	1
Rathmines	9	27	1

Table 5-7-2 *Air quality – number of days with PM$_{10}$ greater than 50 µg/m³ in two locations in Dublin.*

Emissions from coal

Traditionally, bituminous coal, which gives off high emissions of particulate matter, has been burned in Ireland. In winter, even in small Irish towns, the burning of bituminous coal in domestic fires causes air pollution when foggy conditions combine with still air.

A ban on the use of bituminous coal was introduced in Dublin in 1990. This ban was later extended to Cork, Limerick, Galway, Waterford, Sligo and Wexford. In August 2011, the ban on the sale of bituminous coal was extended to Ennis, Clonmel, Carlow and Athlone because of high levels of air pollution in those towns. Smokeless coal, wood pellets and peat briquettes can be used by domestic consumers instead. A further regulation requires that all coal sold has to have a sulfur content of no more than 0.7%. However, small towns continue to sell bituminous coal throughout the country.

Traffic solutions to air pollution

We have already seen that urban sprawl has occurred in Irish cities and towns. Housing developments have made many people dependent on cars because housing was generally not integrated with public transport. That means that the car is the most feasible way that many people have of getting to work. Furthermore, the building of motorways, particularly in the Dublin area, actually encourages people to stay behind the wheel.

However, some positive developments have helped to separate people from their cars and reduce air pollution. These include the following.

- Public transport such as buses, the DART and the Luas in Dublin provide an alternative to the car for many commuters.
- Park-and-ride facilities in commuter towns and around Dublin persuade some commuters to combine car transport with public transport.
- Heavy goods vehicles are now banned from Dublin's city centre.

Geofact
The total number of registered vehicles in Ireland increased by 134% over the period 1990 to 2009.

Geofact
The EPA has 27 air monitoring stations in the Republic.

Geofact
More than one-third of the people of Copenhagen commute to work by bicycle.

The Dublin Bikes bicycle rental scheme has proved to be very popular with many people in the city centre.

Dublin Bus now provides real-time schedules to commuters.

■ Gas-fired central heating releases carbon dioxide only and is available in many cities and towns in the country.

■ Electric cars, with no engine pollution, are likely to become a common sight in Irish streets in the coming years.

■ Bicycle lanes are being extended in several cities and towns. A tax exemption is now available for bikers who commute to work by bicycle. 40% of Dubliners have a commuting journey of less than 5 km, an ideal distance for people who wish to use a bike. The bike rental scheme in Dublin has proved to be a winner with the public.

Question

Explain how real-time information displayed at bus stops helps commuters.

An e-car recharging at a charge point.

The challenge of waste in the urban environment

Waste management is a major issue today because we generate so much of it – **three-quarters of a tonne** of municipal waste per person per annum. In Ireland, most waste was dumped in landfill sites until the beginning of this century. In the long term, **landfill is unsustainable** because we will run out of landfill sites in Ireland and in other countries in a short time. According to a report published in 2011, half of the landfill sites in Ireland will be full by 2014. In recent years, recycling of waste – **a sustainable form of waste management** – has been growing.

Quantity	3,103,820 tonnes
National landfill rate	62%
National recovery rate (recycling)	37.5%

Source: EPA.

Table 5-7-3 *Disposal and recovery of managed municipal waste in the Republic of Ireland, 2008.*

Many of our EU partners dispose of a high percentage of waste through **incineration** and waste-to-energy plants, which they see as an additional option in sustainable waste management. However, in Ireland some members of the public are opposed to incineration. Some communities have been accused of being unduly influenced by the NIMBY and BANANA syndromes.

Definitions

NIMBY: Not in my back yard.

BANANA: Build absolutely nothing anywhere near anyone.

Geofact

There are 249 licensed landfill sites in the Republic.

Definition

WASTE-TO-ENERGY INCINERATION: In the incineration process, the heat produced by incineration is used to generate energy and heating for nearby homes and offices.

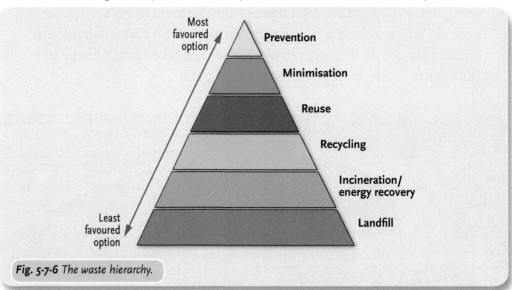

Fig. 5-7-6 *The waste hierarchy.*

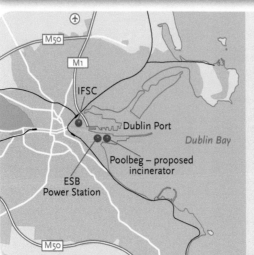

Fig. 5-7-7 *Energy recovery, i.e. waste-to-energy incineration, is part of the waste pyramid. However, it is one of the options least favoured by many environmentalists, despite its widespread use in Europe.*

A waste-to-energy incinerator for Poolbeg, Dublin Bay?

In 2007, planning permission was granted by An Bord Pleanála for a waste-to-energy incinerator in Poolbeg, Dublin, to handle much of the capital's waste. The planned incinerator had generated much controversy over many years.

Arguments for the project

- Under an EU directive, Ireland must significantly reduce the quantity of landfilled waste or the government will face heavy fines.
- Waste-to-energy incinerators are commonplace in highly advanced countries such as Germany, the Netherlands and Austria. Many incinerators are built in urban regions in these countries.
- Dublin City Council has run out of space for landfill. The Arthurstown landfill site just over the county border in Kildare closed at the end of 2010. Dublin City and South Dublin waste had to be hauled to the **Drehid site in Co. Kildare** and to

The Poolbeg area at the left in Dublin Port.

Fig. 5-7-8 The location of the Drehid and Ballynagran landfill sites.

Ballynagran in Co. Wicklow in 2011.

- Long-haul disposal of Dublin waste is unsustainable. Dublin should look after its own waste.
- The plant will divert much of Dublin's waste from landfill and save three hectares of landfill each year.
- The plant is compatible with nearby activities in Poolbeg that include a power station, a sewage treatment plant, oil storage and port activities.
- Waste-to-energy incineration does just what it says. With a capacity for treating 600,000 tonnes of waste every year, the Poolbeg operation will provide power and heating for thousands of homes nearby. This will reduce the burning of fossil fuels and lower the level of CO_2 emissions in the capital.
- There are already several small incinerators operating in the

Republic. The Food Safety Authority has recorded no increase in dioxin levels in foods produced near those sites. The EPA – the Republic's environmental watchdog – states that, properly managed, incinerators do not have an adverse effect on human health.

Arguments against the project

Residents in nearby areas have opposed the project since it was first suggested in 1999. Several politicians and environmental groups also oppose it. Their main arguments include the following.

- Incineration is one of the least favoured options in the waste hierarchy pyramid and can divert public attention and investment away from recycling.
- Reducing, reusing and recycling waste can be greatly expanded through raising people's awareness. This reduces the need for an incinerator.

145

- Mechanical and biological treatment of waste – additional sorting of waste for recycling and composting – will further reduce the volume of waste for landfill.
- The 2013 target of 35% recycling of municipal waste was actually exceeded five years ahead of target in 2008 and this figure will increase.
- Trucks entering and leaving the plant every day will increase traffic, noise and air pollution.

- The proposed waste-to-energy incinerator will be the size of Croke Park and will have a negative visual effect.
- The plant may be too big for the amount of waste available for incineration because recycling will reduce the available waste.

Question

Now that you have read the arguments for and against, what is your position on the incinerator? Explain your answer.

An Indian cyclist in Delhi with a large load of recycling material.

Question

Explain how heritage contributes to your town's identity and character.

Geofact

1948: The year An Taisce was founded.

HERITAGE ISSUES IN URBAN AREAS

Those involved in heritage issues in Ireland claim that as a nation, we are not as aware of our heritage as other European countries. It was not until the 1960s that heritage issues became important here. Over the last few decades, several organisations, such as An Taisce, the Irish Georgian Society and the Dublin Civic Trust, have brought heritage issues to the fore in Ireland.

The Heritage Act 1995

Partly because of pressure from heritage organisations, the 1995 Heritage Act put heritage issues on a more secure footing. This Act established the **Heritage Council**. The Council promotes knowledge of and pride in our national heritage. It is concerned with the conservation and care of the nation's heritage.

Under this Act, each local authority in the Republic was obliged to compile a register of protected structures. All towns with medieval cores have now been surveyed. Local authorities must take heritage into account in all urban plans for the future. **Heritage officers** are employed by many local authorities to ensure the nation's heritage is protected.

The O2 in Dublin's docklands. The old CIÉ Point Depot is now part of one of the country's best-known concert venues. It is one of the busiest concert venues in the world.

Geofact
For more than 50 years the Irish Georgian Society has rescued and restored historic buildings throughout Ireland.

'The best way to preserve a historic building is to put it to a modern use.' – Jim Higgins, heritage officer, Galway city

The Heritage Act was passed just in time, as the building boom linked to the Celtic Tiger was about to take off. Because of the Heritage Act, many buildings in Irish towns and cities have been sensitively restored. Heritage buildings are also of great interest to tourists.

CASE STUDY

Heritage battles in recent decades

Hume Street, Dublin

In 1970, a property company was granted planning permission to demolish several Georgian houses in Hume Street in order to build an office block. However, the occupation of the houses by a group of students, including Marian Finucane and Ruairí Quinn, forced the demolition to stop. This became known as the Battle for Hume Street and was waged over several months. The campaign failed as security staff

Georgian buildings in Hume Street, Dublin. Identify three features of this architecture.

eventually dragged the students away and the houses were demolished.

The affair captured the imagination of the nation and led to much debate about the importance of heritage in the culture of Ireland. It brought heritage issues to centre stage and won a new respect for heritage campaigners. In spite of the loss of eight houses in Hume Street, the protesters' action caused developers to think twice about heritage. Partly because of the Hume Street protests, much of Georgian Dublin survives.

Geofact
Some people in Ireland saw Georgian houses as a relic of British rule in Ireland.

Wood Quay, Dublin
In 1968, Dublin Corporation (Dublin City Council) commissioned plans for new civic offices beside Christchurch Cathedral. When foundation work began, the remains of Viking Dublin were revealed. Experts claimed that the site was unique, with many artefacts from the Viking era of early Dublin. 'Save Wood Quay' became the catch-cry of the campaigners. However, in spite of years of protest, the Corporation got its way and the civic offices took shape in 1981. The artefacts were stored in the National Museum – preserved by record.

Carrickmines
The Carrickmines historic site in South Dublin became the victim of progress as the M50 was completed (see page 126 for details).

Questions
1. Can you name the heritage buildings in your town or city? What are these buildings used for today?
2. Suggest one reason why Georgian buildings are an important part of Irish heritage.

Dublin City Council offices in Wood Quay, Dublin city centre, with Christchurch Cathedral close by.

CITIES IN THE DEVELOPING WORLD

In the developing world, cities are growing very rapidly indeed. The factors that are responsible for this include:

■ high rates of natural increase, i.e. higher birth rates than death rates
■ the migration of large numbers of people from the countryside to the city because of push and pull factors.

Some of the largest cities in the world are now in the developing world. These are truly mega-cities, most of which struggle to provide a decent life for their people. In fact, there are two cities in these giant urban regions: one composed of relatively wealthy people and the other composed of very poor people, many of whom live in shanty towns. An examination of São Paulo in Brazil will highlight life in a typical city in the developing world.

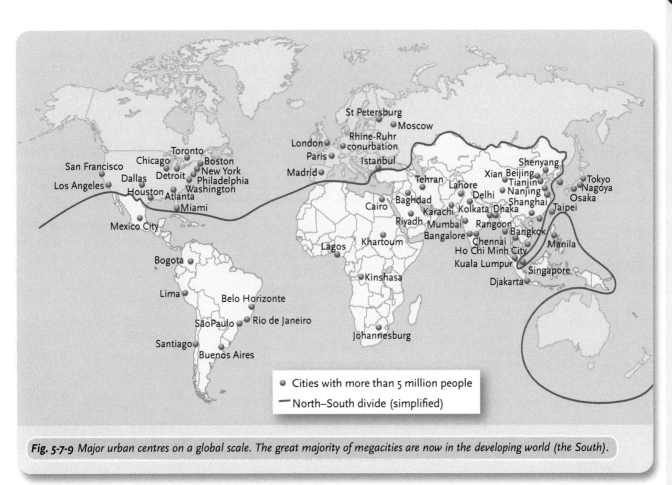

Fig. 5-7-9 *Major urban centres on a global scale. The great majority of megacities are now in the developing world (the South).*

CASE STUDY

São Paulo

São Paulo in Brazil is the largest city in the Southern Hemisphere and has grown very rapidly. The population of greater São Paulo is in the region of 20 million. The city's rapid growth has occurred because of inward migration from the countryside and because of high birth rates. As birth rates have declined in recent years, population growth in São Paulo is now much slower than in the past.

The city faces many problems. These include income inequality, a major housing crisis and traffic challenges.

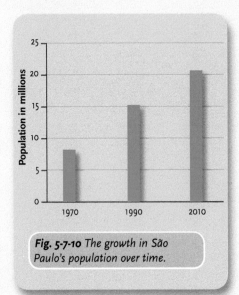

Fig. 5-7-10 *The growth in São Paulo's population over time.*

Link

Revise the development of São Paulo in *Today's World 1*, page 365.

Income inequality

São Paulo has very wealthy people and extremely poor people. In 2002, a report stated that Moema, the wealthiest district, has a **HDI** score that is very close to that of Spain. On the other hand, Marsilac, one of the poorest districts, has a **HDI** score similar to Sierra Leone, one of the world's poorest countries. In Marsilac, people die younger, have much lower levels of literacy and have much lower incomes than wealthier residents of the city.

São Paulo is the economic powerhouse of Brazil. Therefore, the city has many wealthy industrialists, bankers, owners of chain stores and plastic surgeons. These people live in condominiums or in gated communities in wealthy suburbs. On the other hand, migrants who arrive in the city possessing only the clothes on their backs find it very difficult to

Geofact

The well-to-do of São Paulo, and indeed in all of Brazil's east coast cities, are obsessed with their appearance. Plastic surgeons enjoy huge status and income.

lift themselves out of poverty. The poor live in shanty towns, as we will see below.

Crime is a major problem because poor people live so close to the wealthy. Since they are the targets of criminals, many wealthy people are driven around in armoured vehicles or take to the air in helicopters. The city has the largest number of helicopters in the world after New York and Tokyo.

Geofact

Residents of favelas are known as favelados in Brazil.

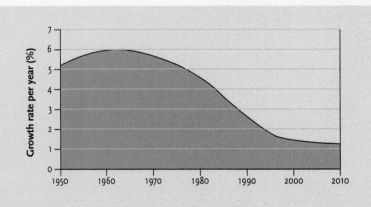

Fig. 5-7-11 *Population growth rate in greater São Paulo over time.*

Definition

HDI: The Human Development Index, developed by the UN, measures life expectancy, literacy rates and income levels to rate the well-being of people in most of the countries of the world.

The housing problem – favelas

The rapid growth of the city has led to a housing crisis in São Paulo. The city has several shanty towns, known as favelas, where at least 2 million of the poorest people live. Inward migrants with no place else to go live in the densely populated favelas. Heliopolis and Paraisopolis – close to the CBD – are two of the best-known favelas. Many favelas are without basic services such as piped water, electricity and sewage.

Favela residents have few legal rights. They have often been forcibly moved on by wealthy landowners who employed strong-arm tactics to do so. The result is that permanent favelas have grown in difficult locations such as hill slopes, areas prone to flooding and beside landfill sites.

However, poor people live in favelas because homes – flimsy buildings made of plastic, waste timber and galvanised metal – are cheap to rent or to build. Favelas may also be close to where they work and residents pay no property taxes.

Crime

Crime is a major problem in the city generally and also in the favelas because of poverty, poor street lighting and overcrowding. Police enter some favelas only when heavily armed. Police corruption is a problem. Local criminals are a threat to favela residents. Drug gangs protect their turf in the favelas by violent means and life is very cheap. Parts of the city are violent and have high murder rates. However, the murder rate has declined sharply in recent years. One explanation is that because of the reduction in the

A favela in São Paulo.

birth rate over recent decades, the numbers of 15- to 24-year-old males – the age group most likely to turn to petty crime – has declined.

Some improvements have occurred in favelas in recent years. As favela communities developed, favela removal by the authorities gave way to favela upgrade. Basic services such as electricity, water and sewage are coming, if slowly. During his term of office in the years 2002 to 2010, President Lula placed favela improvements high on his agenda.

Link
Urban traffic problems, pages 129–30.

Traffic in São Paulo

São Paulo is among the five worst cities in the world for traffic congestion, along with New Delhi, Mexico City, Beijing and Lagos. The city has more than 6 million cars as well as trucks and delivery vans. **The city does not have ring roads** so traffic has to go through the city. Traffic flows are interrupted for an average of four hours a day. Congestion delays delivery trucks and causes long commuter times for workers jammed into overcrowded buses.

Apart from the fear of kidnapping, congestion is another reason why businesspeople use rented helicopters to keep appointments. Motorcycle couriers called **motoboys** are employed by businesspeople to carry packages and parcels around the city. These couriers give a whole new meaning to the term 'road warriors'.

CASE STUDY

Public transport is poorly developed, in contrast with Curitiba (see pages 133–5). The metro system has only three lines running on 61 km of track. Metro lines are being extended. Trains are very overcrowded. Buses are numerous and widely used. However, while there are bus lanes, gridlock halts buses as well as cars.

Some traffic solutions have worked in other cities.
- Mexico City has a programme of a weekday without a car for all car users.
- Several cities, such as London, have congestion charges through the city centre, which reduce traffic by up to 30%. These have yet to be tried in São Paulo.

- The long-term solutions for São Paulo include the development of ring roads, investment in a greatly lengthened metro network and a Curitiba-style bus network.

Geofact
Time magazine reported in 2008 that 1,000 new cars were taking to the streets of São Paulo every day.

Geofact
On 9 May 2008, 266 km of traffic were at a standstill on São Paulo's streets because of traffic congestion.

Exam focus
Identify three challenges facing São Paulo. Write down five SRPs on each of the three challenges.

Definition
SUSTAINABLE CITIES provide for the needs of the present generation without jeopardising the needs of future generations.

THE FUTURE OF URBANISM

Many cities have grown very quickly in the past few generations as the population of the world expanded rapidly. Growth in some cities, especially in the developing world, has been chaotic. The challenge of providing services such as water, sewage and public transport has overwhelmed cities in poor countries.

The population of the world may reach 10 billion people over the next several decades. Cities in the developing world will continue to grow because most of these additional people will be housed in cities. It is therefore very important that the quality of life for urban dwellers is improved. One option that urban planners must consider is moving cities in the direction of **sustainability**.

Sustainable cities

A sustainable city does not allow today's growth to be achieved at tomorrow's expense. Cities must use less of the world's resources by switching to public transport and to the highest level of recycling of resources. A sustainable city avoids urban sprawl by encouraging growth from the city centre outwards rather than giving planning permission for large suburban housing and shopping developments on the edge of the city.

Allotments in vegetable gardens help urban dwellers to stay in touch with nature and to grow their own vegetables.

The characteristics of more sustainable cities include the following:
- a smaller ecological footprint through a reduction in fossil fuel use and in air pollution
- wide use of cheap, frequent and safe public transport that is energy efficient
- safe cycle paths for cyclists
- green spaces for city dwellers
- mixed use neighbourhoods that combine living, working and shopping
- affordable housing for the less well off
- the active involvement of communities in urban decision-making
- sustainable building practices, with homes that are well insulated
- the preservation of heritage buildings
- elimination of urban sprawl with compact residential development from the centre outwards
- reduce, reuse and recycle waste.

These steps greatly improve the quality of life in cities. Cities in Europe have put many of the above steps into practice. City centre streets have been pedestrianised, street furniture has been added, footpaths widened and green spaces created. These steps create a village atmosphere among the communities who live in city centres. Such changes are evident in Zurich, Stockholm, Heidelberg, Copenhagen, Reykjavik and other cities.

We have seen that Curitiba has become a model for cities in its urban transportation planning. Bogota, the capital of Colombia, well known for many of the wrong reasons, such as drugs cartels, has also pioneered bicycle lanes and street festivals for its inhabitants, with much success.

Exam focus

Choose three characteristics of sustainable cities and write down five SRPs on how each contributes to sustainability.

Question

Explain the term 'ecological footprint'.

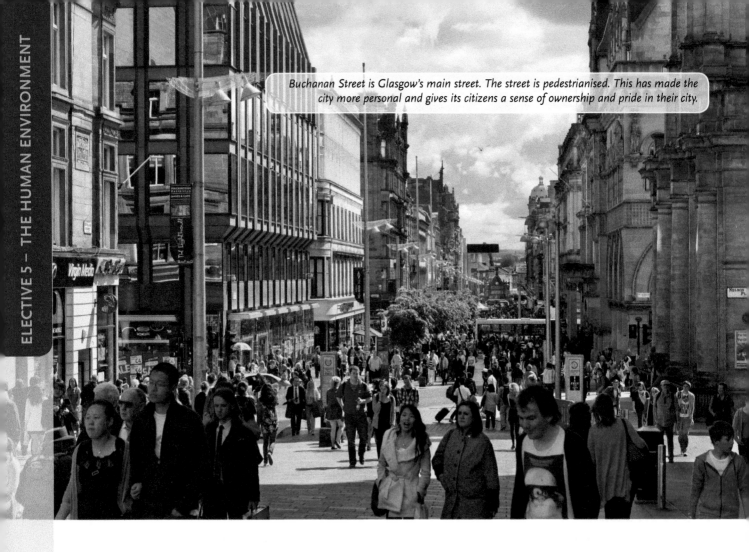

Buchanan Street is Glasgow's main street. The street is pedestrianised. This has made the city more personal and gives its citizens a sense of ownership and pride in their city.

? Leaving Cert Exam Questions

1 **Transport in urban areas**

   (i) Name **one** traffic problem experienced by cities that are growing rapidly.

   (ii) Name **one** city that has such a problem.

   (iii) Name **two** reasons why this problem has developed.

   (iv) Explain **one** solution to this problem. (40 marks)

2 **Growth of cities in the developing world**

   (i) Name **one** city in the developing world that has grown rapidly.

   (ii) State **one** reason why this city has grown rapidly.

   (iii) Describe **one** problem caused by this rapid growth.

   (iv) Explain **one** solution to this problem. (30 marks)

3 **Traffic congestion**

   (i) Explain **two** causes of traffic congestion in any city studied by you.

   (ii) Explain in detail **one** solution to this traffic congestion. (30 marks)

4 Traffic congestion

Below is a camera image taken by Dublin City Council showing traffic at Donnybrook. Most modern towns and cities suffer from traffic congestion.

Urban traffic in Donnybrook.

02/03/07   09:50:26

(i) Explain **two** causes of traffic congestion in any city studied by you. Clearly state the name of the city in your answer.

(ii) Examine in detail **one** solution to this traffic congestion. (30 marks)

5 Urban studies

Many cities in the developing world are expanding rapidly because of inward migration from the countryside.

(i) Name **one** expanding city in the developing world studied by you.

(ii) Explain **two** problems faced by this city because of its growing population. (30 marks)

6 Urban problems

Using examples that you have studied, suggest how urban problems in the developing world differ from urban problems in the developed world. (40 marks)

7 Urban sprawl

Below is a photograph of a shanty town in Manila in the Philippines.
Explain **two** reasons why shanty towns such as this grow near cities in the developing world. (30 marks)

Part of a shanty town in Manila.

8 Urban sprawl

(i) Explain the term 'urban sprawl'.

(ii) Explain **two** causes and **one** problem resulting from urban sprawl in any city studied by you. (30 marks)

9 Urban sprawl

(i) Explain **two** causes of urban sprawl in any city you have studied.

(ii) Explain **two** problems caused by this urban sprawl. (40 marks)

10 Urban problems

(i) Name a developed or a developing city that you have studied.

(ii) Explain **two** problems arising from the growth of the city named in part (i).

(iii) Describe **two** solutions to these problems. (40 marks)

11 Urban problems

(i) Explain the term 'traffic congestion'.

(ii) Explain **two** methods used to overcome traffic congestion. Use an example you have studied in your answer. (30 marks)

12 Developing world cities

'Problems can develop as urban centres grow.' Discuss this statement with reference to **one** developing city you have studied. (30 marks)

13 Urban growth

The rapid growth of cities in the developing world has led to social and economic problems. Examine **two** of these problems with reference to examples you have studied. (30 marks)

14 Urban growth

The growth of urban centres may lead to the development of problems. Examine any **two** of these problems with reference to examples that you have studied. (30 marks)

15 Urbanisation

'Authorities in developing world cities have attempted to overcome the problem of rapid urban growth.' Examine this statement with reference to example(s) that you have studied. (30 marks)

16 Problems in cities

With reference to **one** example you have studied, examine the effectiveness of urban planning strategies in dealing with planning problems. (30 marks)

17 Urban centres

'Cities are places of opportunity but also have problems.' Examine this statement with reference to a city or cities of your choice. (30 marks)

18 Urban future

Examine **two** of the problems created by the continued pace of urban growth in a region you have studied. (30 marks)

Today's World 3
OPTION 7

Soils

7.1

OPTION 7 – GEOECOLOGY

INTRODUCTION

Soil is a layer of natural materials on the Earth's surface that is capable of supporting plant growth.

COMPOSITION OF SOIL

Soil is composed of a variety of materials. Some come from the actions of weather on rock and some come from living sources.

The four main materials are:

- mineral particles
- organic matter
- air
- water.

Roughly half of a soil's volume is made up of mineral particles and organic matter (solids). The remaining half is made up of varying amounts of air and water that fill the pore spaces.

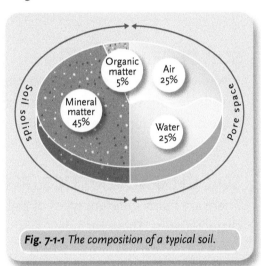

Fig. 7-1-1 *The composition of a typical soil.*

Mineral particles

Mineral particles include stones, sand, silt and clay (see Soil texture, pages 160–2). These come from **rock that has been broken down** by weathering and erosion over long periods of time. They may have been deposited in situ or transported by rivers, waves or ice.

The size of the particles depends on the **parent material**. For example, particles of clay are very small and fine, while grains that come from sandstone are larger and coarse.

Some minerals are soluble, so they dissolve in water. These can then be absorbed by plants, providing them with nourishment.

Learning objectives

After studying this chapter, you should be able to understand:

- the composition of soils
- the factors that influence the formation of soil
- the processes that operate within soil
- the global pattern of soils
- the development of brown earths in Ireland
- how humans alter soil characteristics.

Geofact

Only 25% of the Earth's surface is made up of soil. Just 10% of that soil can support the growth of food.

Organic matter

Organic material consists of the remains of plants and animals as well as living creatures.

When plant material such as leaves, needles, bark and twigs falls to the ground, it is known as **plant litter**. Living creatures in the soil include very small (micro) organisms, such as bacteria and fungi, as well as larger creatures, such as earthworms, mites and slugs.

As the plant litter and the remains of dead creatures begin to decay, they are broken down further by the micro-organisms to form a thick, jelly-like, dark-coloured substance called **humus**. This is rich in nutrients and helps to fertilise the soil as well as bind the soil particles together.

Larger creatures, such as earthworms, help to mix the humus into the soil particles and also loosen the soil, enabling water and air to pass through.

Air and water

Air and water are found in the pores (spaces) between the particles of soil.

The proportions can vary greatly, depending on the soil type and climate. Loose sandy soils have much more pore space than tightly packed clay soils.

In desert regions, the percentage of water in the soil is very low. Other soils are waterlogged and have an almost complete absence of air in the pores.

Air supplies oxygen and nitrogen to the soil, which are essential for plant growth. Water is also essential for plant growth, as it contains dissolved minerals and nutrients that are absorbed by the plants' roots.

SOIL PROFILE

If you look at a cross-section down through a body of soil (in a soil pit or on a roadside cut), you will see various layers, called **horizons**. Taken together, these horizons form the **soil profile**.

SOIL CHARACTERISTICS (PROPERTIES)

There are many different types of soil and each one has unique characteristics. These include:

- texture
- structure
- pH value
- organic matter
- moisture
- colour.

Soil texture

Soil texture is a term used to describe the way a soil 'feels'. Texture depends on the proportion of sand, silt and clay particles in the soil.

- **Sand** particles are the largest and coarsest particles. They feel gritty.
- **Silt** particles are medium sized. They feel soft and silky.

■ **Clay** particles are the smallest and smoothest particles. They feel sticky.

Texture influences the ability of a soil to hold water and retain nutrients and the ease with which roots can penetrate the soil.

Sandy soils are dominated by large particles with some silt and clay. The particles are loose, with large pores between them. This allows water to drain away freely and irrigation may be needed. Nutrients can be leached out of the soil, so fertilisers must be applied regularly.

Silty soils fall between clay and sand in terms of particle size. They are generally quite fertile and will support a wide range of plants. The smaller pore spaces help retain more moisture. When wet, they tend to become heavy and poorly drained, but not to the same extent as clay.

Clay soils have very small particles that tend to stick together. They are capable of retaining water and can become heavy. When they are wet, clay soils become waterlogged. The soil tends to be very sticky and is difficult to cultivate. When they are dry, clay soils shrink and crack. This makes it difficult for plant roots and water to penetrate the ground.

Loam soil is regarded as the perfect soil. It is a blend of roughly equal amounts of sand, silt and clay. While it retains some moisture, it is free draining and easy to dig. It also retains its nutrients, producing a very fertile soil that is suited to farming and gardening.

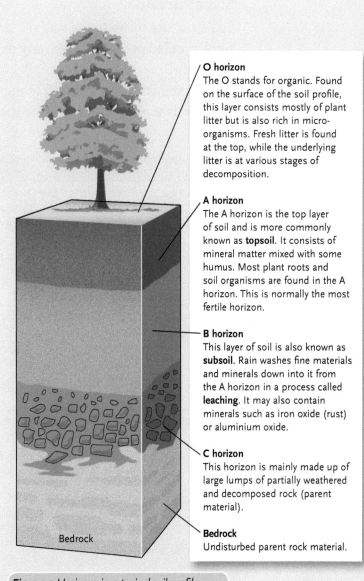

O horizon
The O stands for organic. Found on the surface of the soil profile, this layer consists mostly of plant litter but is also rich in micro-organisms. Fresh litter is found at the top, while the underlying litter is at various stages of decomposition.

A horizon
The A horizon is the top layer of soil and is more commonly known as **topsoil**. It consists of mineral matter mixed with some humus. Most plant roots and soil organisms are found in the A horizon. This is normally the most fertile horizon.

B horizon
This layer of soil is also known as **subsoil**. Rain washes fine materials and minerals down into it from the A horizon in a process called **leaching**. It may also contain minerals such as iron oxide (rust) or aluminium oxide.

C horizon
This horizon is mainly made up of large lumps of partially weathered and decomposed rock (parent material).

Bedrock
Undisturbed parent rock material.

Fig. 7-1-2 *Horizons in a typical soil profile.*

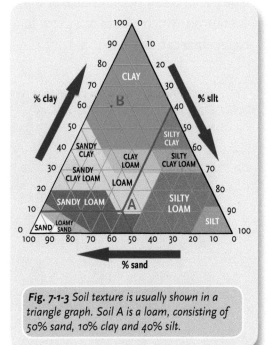

Fig. 7-1-3 *Soil texture is usually shown in a triangle graph. Soil A is a loam, consisting of 50% sand, 10% clay and 40% silt.*

Questions

1. What percentages of sand, clay and silt make up the soil at B in Fig. 7-1-3?
2. What type of soil is made up of 60% sand, 30% clay and 10% silt?

Soil structure

Soil structure refers to the way soil grains are bound together into small clumps called **peds**. The peds vary in size and shape to give the soil different structures.

Good soil structure allows free movement of water and air. Soil structure also affects the space available for roots, seeds and living organisms.

Ped type	Description	Shape
Crumb	Small, rounded grains, similar to breadcrumbs. Found near surface where roots have been growing. Excellent for drainage and air movement.	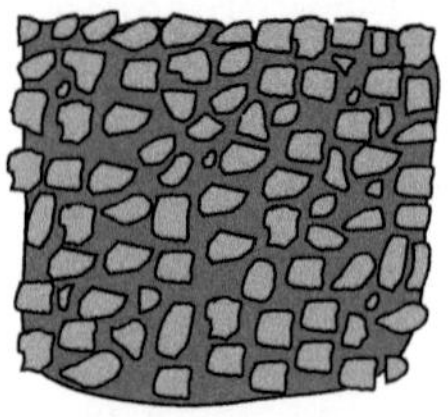
Platy	Thin, flat particles that often overlap. Usually found in compacted soil. These impede roots and hold up movement of water.	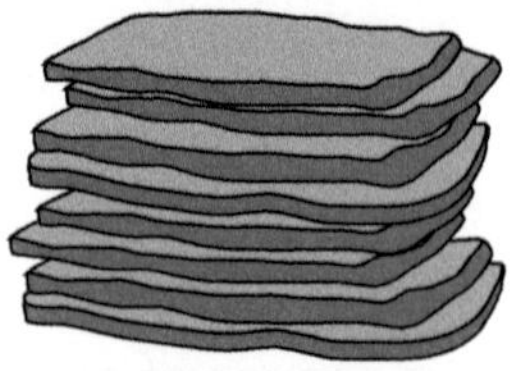
Blocky	Cube-shaped particles that fit very tightly together. Few pore spaces for roots and air to pass through.	

Table 7-1-1 *Different ped shapes.*

pH value of soil

The pH of a soil is a measure of the degree to which it is **acid** or **alkaline**. It controls which plants can grow in a particular soil and also what living organisms can survive in it.

Geofact

The best agricultural soil is slightly acidic, with a pH of around 6.5. This is the level at which most nutrients are available in the soil.

Alkaline soils
Alkaline soils have a **high pH level** (above 7). They are limey and contain high levels of calcium. They develop on chalk or limestone regions. They are also common in regions with desert or drought.

Neutral soils   Neutral soils have a pH level of 7.

Acidic soils
Acidic soils have a **low pH level** (below 7). These soils have been heavily leached by rainfall and lack minerals. The more acidic the soil is, the fewer living organisms there are in the soil. Acidic soils are usually infertile and crushed limestone must be added to reduce the level of acidity.

10
9.0
8.5
8.0
7.5
7.0
6.5
6.0
5.5
5.0
4.0
3.0

Fig. 7-1-4 *The pH of soil.*

Humus content

Humus is the organic matter in soils that is formed from decaying **organic matter** such as fallen leaves, grasses and animal waste.

Bacteria and fungi in the soil help to break down this organic matter. Soil organisms such as earthworms and insects also digest the organic matter to form humus. These are also responsible for mixing and aerating the soil. When they die, their remains add more humus to the soil.

Humus particles can make soil look dark brown or black. They also improve soil structure because they bind the grains of soil together to form peds. This helps to reduce soil erosion.

Fertile soils are rich in humus. The humus is important because it is rich in nutrients such as carbon and nitrogen. It also enables the soil to store moisture.

Plant litter and insects.

Questions

1. How is humus formed?
2. Describe three effects that moisture content has on soils.

Soil moisture

Moisture content is an important factor in determining how well the soils support vegetation. Moisture enables the plant roots to receive nutrients in solution. It also disperses the nutrients through the soil.

- The amount of moisture that can be retained in soil is influenced by the texture and structure of the soil.
- Sandy soils are often very dry. They have very little ability to hold water, as it quickly drains away through the big pore spaces between the grains.
- Clay and silt soils have small pores. These enable the soil to retain moisture for a long time. However, these soils may become waterlogged in periods of heavy rainfall.
- Loam soils, with their crumb structure, tend to be well drained but still retain enough moisture to remain fertile.

The amount of moisture retained by a soil is also influenced by the amount of precipitation that falls and whether the underlying rock is permeable or impermeable.

Soil colour

Colour is the most obvious feature of a soil. It can tell us about some of the properties of a soil as well as about the processes that occur beneath the surface.

Brown and black soils owe their dark colour to the presence of humus. The exact colour varies with the amount of humus present and its stage of breakdown. Soils that are rich in humus are very fertile.

Grey soils are often described as 'washed out' because humus and nutrients have been leached out of them by rainfall. Many grey soils have poor drainage or suffer from waterlogged conditions. These soils are naturally infertile.

Red soils owe their rusty tinge to the presence of iron oxide in the soil. They develop in regions with a warm, moist, tropical or equatorial climate. The iron in the soil breaks down and rusts, giving the soil its reddish colour. Red soils can be low in nutrients and organic matter.

FACTORS AFFECTING SOIL FORMATION

The type of soil that is found in a region depends on a number of factors and how they interact with one another:

- climate
- parent material
- topography
- soil organisms
- time.

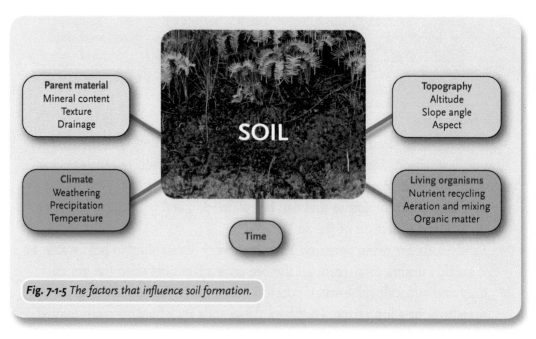

Fig. 7-1-5 *The factors that influence soil formation.*

Climate

Climate is the most important factor influencing soil formation. The two main climatic influences on soil are **temperature** and **precipitation**.

- In regions that have a **hot climate**, chemical weathering is rapid. This creates great depths of soil.

- Bacteria thrive, so vegetation is rapidly decomposed into humus.
- In regions that have a **cold climate**, there is much less biological activity, so the formation of humus is very slow. Weathering is limited to freeze-thaw, producing angular particles.
- In regions with **wet climates**, heavy rainfall causes leaching, washing nutrients out of the soil. Many soils become waterlogged.
- In regions with **dry climates**, drought results in the upward movement of groundwater. This can draw salt and calcium to the surface. (See Salinisation, page 170, and Calcification, page 171.)

Parent material

Parent material is the source of the mineral matter in the soil. This may be a **solid rock** that has been broken down by weathering or **sediments** that were deposited by glacial, fluvial or wind action. The majority of Irish soils have developed on glacial deposits.

Many soil properties are determined by the type of rock that the parent material came from.

- Soils that develop from **sandstone** are sandy and free draining.
- Soils that develop from **shale** have a high clay content and tend to be badly drained.
- Soils that develop from **limestone** do not weather very well into soil-forming particles. While the soils that develop are rich in calcium, they are thin, dry and poorly developed.
- Soils that develop from **igneous** and **metamorphic** rocks are very slow to weather and tend to be acidic.

Topography

Soil formation is influenced by **relief**, **altitude** and **aspect** and these factors are interlinked.

- Soils in flat **upland** areas are more likely to be waterlogged and leached due to the wet conditions.
- **Upland** areas are colder, so there is very little activity by animals and micro-organisms. As a result, the dead vegetation is not converted to humus but builds up as peat.
- Where the land **slopes**, soil erosion is usually quicker than the formation of new soil beneath. As a result, soils are thinner. Slopes also encourage run-off, so soils here are better drained.
- Soils tend to accumulate on flat, **low-lying** areas. The weather is warmer and activity by animals and micro-organisms converts dead organic matter to humus.
- **South-facing** slopes in the northern hemisphere are warmer and drier than **north-facing** slopes. Thus, different soils may develop on both sides of the slope.

Questions

1. Explain the influence of the following on soil:
   - temperature
   - precipitation.
2. How does parent material influence soil characteristics?

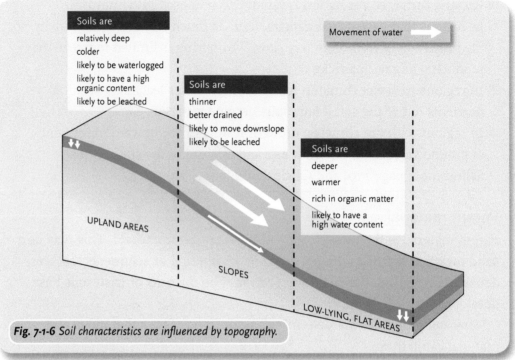

Fig. 7-1-6 *Soil characteristics are influenced by topography.*

Soil organisms

Soil is home to large numbers of plants, animals and micro-organisms. Living organisms in the soil include plant roots, animals, insects, fungi and bacteria.

■ Plant roots help to **bind** loose soil particles and prise open compacted soil.

■ The plants themselves provide a **protective cover** to the soil, helping to reduce soil erosion.

■ Plants return **nutrients** to the soil after they die and decompose.

■ Worms and termites **aerate**, **mix** and **drain** the soil by burrowing through it. Burrowing by animals (mice, rabbits, etc.) also helps.

Geofact

One spoonful of topsoil may contain up to 50 million bacteria.

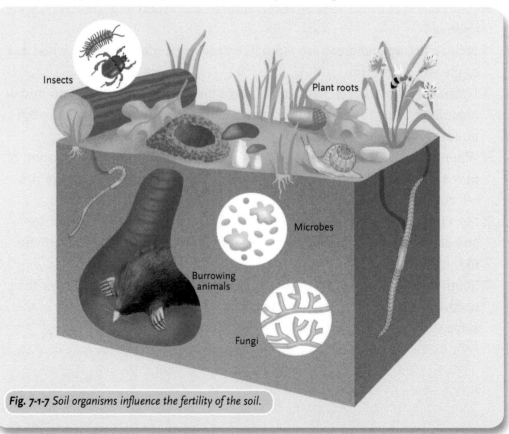

Fig. 7-1-7 *Soil organisms influence the fertility of the soil.*

- When these creatures die, their decomposed bodies add **nutrients** to the soil.
- Bacteria and fungi in the soil help to break down organic matter into **humus** (humification). (See pages 168–9).

Time

Time does not help to form soil. However, it does affect the properties of the soil.

- Soils take a long time to form – perhaps up to 400 years per centimetre of depth.
- The soil profile of a young soil is not well developed, unlike that of an older soil with its clear horizons.
- Older soils tend to be strongly weathered.
- Most Irish soils are relatively young because they are largely post-glacial.

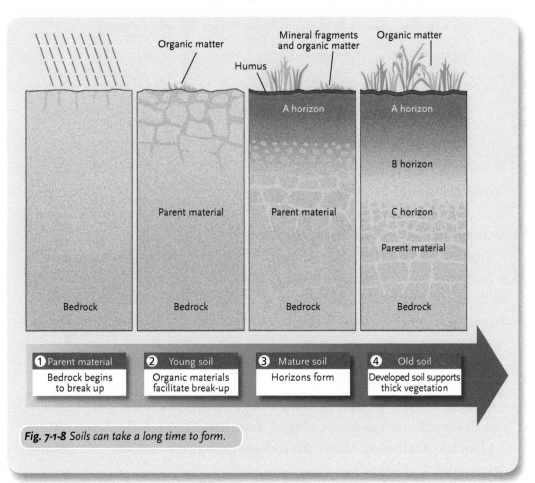

Fig. 7-1-8 Soils can take a long time to form.

Geofact

It can take up to 12,000 years for sufficient soil to form to allow agriculture to take place.

PROCESSES OF SOIL FORMATION

No two soils have the exact same characteristics. This is because a number of processes operate within the soil. These processes work within the five factors listed above (climate, parent material, topography, soil organisms and time). The processes are:

- weathering and erosion
- humification
- leaching
- podzolisation
- laterisation
- salinisation
- calcification.

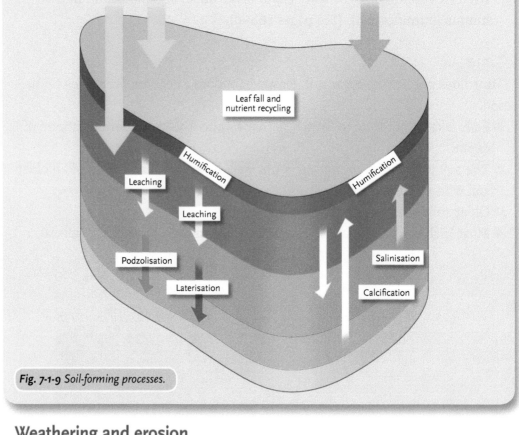

Fig. 7-1-9 Soil-forming processes.

Question

Explain how each of the following affect soil formation:

- erosion
- mechanical weathering
- chemical weathering.

Weathering and erosion

Most of the tiny particles that make up our soils started out as solid rock until broken down by weathering and erosion.

Erosion breaks down solid rock (bedrock) to produce the parent material of many of our soils. It produces particles that vary in size, from boulders to tiny particles of clay. These are then transported from their place of origin and deposited. They include alluvium (rivers), boulder clay (glaciation) and loess (wind).

Mechanical weathering includes freeze-thaw and exfoliation. Rocks are broken into particles of scree, but the characteristics of the minerals are not changed. Through heating and cooling, expansion and contraction, the particles break down to grains of sand (from sandstone) or clay (from shale).

Chemical weathering causes the rocks to decompose and also changes the characteristics of the minerals:

- **Carbonation** occurs when rainwater reacts with the calcium carbonate in limestone, dissolving it and removing it in solution.
- **Hydrolysis** occurs when rainwater breaks down granite, causing the feldspar in the rock to change into kaolin clay.
- **Oxidation** occurs when oxygen in the atmosphere reacts with iron in the soil and rock. The iron is oxidised (rusts), causing rocks to crumble more easily and giving the soil a reddish-brown colour.

Humification

Humification is important, as it increases the fertility of the soil. It occurs when organic matter is broken down and decomposes to form **humus**.

Organic matter consists of plant litter as well as the waste products and the remains of the many creatures living in it. The humus is then washed down into the soil by rainfall or mixed into the soil by animals and micro-organisms living there.

Humus releases **nutrients** into the soil in soluble form so that they can be absorbed by plant roots. These nutrients include nitrogen and calcium. Humus also increases soil's ability to retain water. It has a gel-like texture that holds particles together and gives a crumb structure to the soil.

Humification occurs very rapidly in hot, humid climates. In temperate climate zones, such as in Ireland, the process is much slower, taking about 10 years. Humification practically ceases in arctic climates.

Leaching

Leaching is the removal of soluble material, including nutrients, from soil by water. It is most common on steep slopes and upland areas with heavy rainfall.

When rainfall exceeds evaporation, there is free downward movement of water through the pores in the soil. Soluble minerals and organic matter are **leached** or moved down through the soil profile.

Limited leaching is important, as it washes humus into the soil, increasing its fertility. Where there is excessive leaching, nutrients are washed out of the A horizon and deposited at a lower level, often beyond the reach of plant roots. Thus, the soil is robbed of its nutrients and may become **infertile**.

Pesticides and fertilisers, such as nitrates, may also be leached out of the soil. This may result in the contamination of groundwater.

Questions

1. List two impacts of leaching on soil formation.
2. Explain the terms 'podzolisation' and 'hardpan'.

Podzolisation

Podzolisation is an extreme form of leaching. It is most common in regions where the vegetation is coniferous forest or peat and where there is very high annual precipitation.

Rainwater becomes more acidic as it passes through the bed of organic matter on the surface. The acidic rainwater is then capable of dissolving and removing almost all the minerals and nutrients in the soil. Having been bleached of all its coloured minerals, with the exception of the more resistant quartz, the A horizon has an **ash-grey colour**.

The minerals are then deposited in the B horizon, which becomes darker in colour. When iron oxide (rust) is one of these minerals, it gives the soil a reddish colour. It also cements grains of soil together to form a **hardpan**. Hardpan hampers drainage, makes cultivation difficult and may lead to **waterlogging**.

A podzol soil profile, with an upper dark humus layer with plant roots and a white, ash-like leached layer below.

Laterisation

Laterisation is a severe form of leaching that is associated with tropical and equatorial regions. Here, temperatures are high, precipitation is heavy and there is an abundance of plant litter on the ground.

Chemical weathering occurs at a rapid rate due to the hot, humid conditions. Rocks are rapidly broken down to great depths, resulting in very deep soil.

All the minerals in the soil, with the exception of iron oxide and aluminium oxide, decompose and quickly dissolve into solution. The heavy rainfall then **leaches** the dissolved minerals deep into the ground. The rapid leaching means that horizons are poorly developed and the soil does not retain its fertility.

The iron undergoes oxidation (rusting) when it is exposed to the atmosphere. This gives the soil its reddish-rusty appearance. This distinctive soil is known as **latosol** (see pages 189–90).

Salinisation

Salinisation is the accumulation of **soluble salts** close to the surface of the soil. Salinisation occurs in hot desert and semi-desert regions where precipitation is low and **evaporation** is high.

Groundwater naturally contains salt. It is drawn up through the soil by capillary action. The high rate of evaporation draws the moisture into the atmosphere but leaves the soluble salts behind in the upper layer of soil. Over time, the level of salts in the soil increases. The salts then solidify, forming a hard, toxic (poisonous) crust.

Salinisation can also be caused by **irrigation**. It raises the level of groundwater, bringing salts closer to the surface. When the plants absorb the water or when it is evaporated, the dissolved salts are left behind in the soil. If the level of salt in the soil becomes too high, the soil becomes poisonous and plants die.

Salinisation in a semi-desert landscape in Australia. Note the loss of vegetation.

Question

Explain the terms 'leaching' and 'evaporation'.

Calcification

Calcification is the accumulation of **calcium carbonate** near the surface of the soil.

Calcification usually occurs under grassland vegetation, for example in the interior of continents (prairies and steppes). It is associated with regions that have low rainfall, where the rate of evaporation is higher than the rate of precipitation.

Calcium carbonate is drawn upwards towards the surface by capillary action and plant roots. The calcium carbonate then builds up in the A horizon, creating a fertile soil that is rich in nutrients and ideal for grass growth. When the grasses die and decompose, the calcium carbonate is returned to the soil.

CLASSIFYING SOILS

All soils can be classified into one of **three groups**: zonal, intrazonal and azonal soils.

Zonal soils occupy **large regions** of the Earth's surface where the climate has been stable for a long period of time. They are by far the most important and widespread of the three orders. They are mature soils with distinctive soil profiles and well-developed horizons. They include the following:

Zonal soil	Description
Brown earths	These are the soils of regions with a cool temperate maritime climate, including Ireland (see pages 173–4).
Latosols	These are the soils of regions with a tropical or equatorial climate, including Brazil (see pages 189–90).

Table 7-1-2 Zonal soils occupy large zones of the Earth's surface.

Intrazonal soils develop when **local factors** (such as relief, parent material or drainage) have a stronger influence than vegetation and climate. These factors can be enough to change the characteristics of the zonal soil. This leads to the development of intrazonal soils, including the following:

Intrazonal soil	Local influence
Gleys	These soils have a high clay content and limited pore spaces, thus impeding free drainage. They may become waterlogged and suffer from lack of oxygen.
Peat	These soils result from extreme waterlogging of both the surface vegetation and underlying material. Peat soils are the upper portion of peat bog deposits.

Table 7-1-3 Intrazonal soils have developed where local factors have had an influence.

Azonal soils are of recent origin. Soil-forming processes have not had much time to operate. These are immature soils that have poorly developed soil profiles. They include the following:

Azonal soil	Cause of immaturity
Regosols	These are soils that have developed on materials deposited by wind (loess, volcanic ash and sand dunes), rivers (alluvium) or ice (glacial till).
Lithosols	These soils consist of partly weathered rock fragments and are usually found on steep slopes. Mass movement and erosion are too rapid to allow for soil development.

Table 7-1-4 Azonal soils are newly formed soils that have not yet matured or developed horizons.

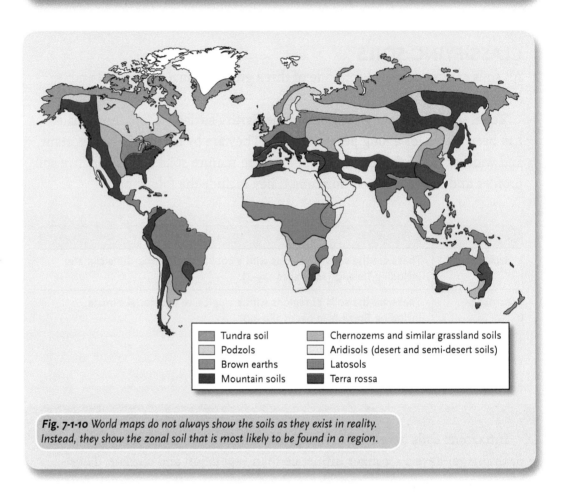

Tundra soil — Chernozems and similar grassland soils
Podzols — Aridisols (desert and semi-desert soils)
Brown earths — Latosols
Mountain soils — Terra rossa

Fig. 7-1-10 World maps do not always show the soils as they exist in reality. Instead, they show the zonal soil that is most likely to be found in a region.

Zonal soil	Climate	Vegetation
Latosols	Tropical/equatorial	Tropical rainforest
Aridisols	Desert	Desert
Terra rossa/red-brown soil	Warm temperate maritime	Mediterranean
Brown earths	Cool temperate maritime	Mixed deciduous forest
Chernozems	Continental	Prairies/steppes
Podzols	Boreal (subarctic)	Coniferous forest (taiga)
Tundra/arctic brown	Tundra	Tundra

Table 7-1-5 The main zonal soils with their associated climate type and vegetation.

IRISH BROWN EARTH SOILS

Brown earth is the most common soil type in Ireland. It developed in response to Ireland's cool temperate maritime climate and natural vegetation cover of deciduous forest. The main parent material is boulder clay, deposited during the last Ice Age. However, there are some variations due to local conditions.

Mineral particles make up the main component of brown soils. Most of the particles developed from glacial till deposited at the end of the last glacial period.

Brown soils tend to be **loamy**. The crumb structure means that the soil particles are loosely packed. This helps the movement of air and water in the soil. Brown earths do not develop a hardpan. As a result, they are free draining.

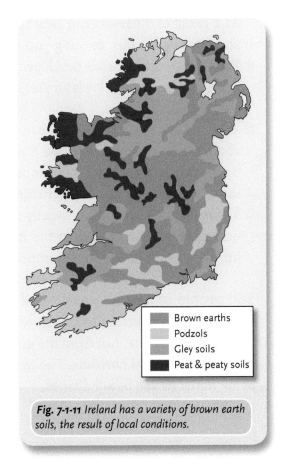

Brown earths
Podzols
Gley soils
Peat & peaty soils

Fig. 7-1-11 *Ireland has a variety of brown earth soils, the result of local conditions.*

The soils originally developed on **deciduous forests** with thick undergrowth. These supplied a heavy leaf fall and other plant litter for the soil. This litter is rich in nutrients and organic matter. The warm climate ensures that biological activity takes place for up to nine months of the year. Brown earths contain a huge number of earthworms and **micro-organisms**, such as bacteria and fungi. These help to break down the organic matter (**humification**) and the remains of dead creatures to provide a supply of rich, dark **humus** to the soil. They also draw the humus down and mix it with the mineral particles, where it releases its nutrients. Humus also helps to give the soil its distinctive colour and makes it crumbly.

Most Irish brown earths have a pH value that is between 5 and 7, making them **slightly acidic**. This range allows the soil to support a wide variety of plant life and bacterial activity. However, the addition of ground limestone over the years means that some of the soils are slightly alkaline.

The moderate amount of rain that falls also washes nutrients into the soil. More importantly, it means that **leaching is limited**. This, together with the mixing and burrowing actions, means that the boundary between the horizons is not always clear.

Most of the deciduous woodland has been cut down and the land is now used for **agriculture**. Brown earths have a **natural fertility** and are easy to work throughout the year. They are capable of supporting both pasture and tillage production.

Geofact
About two-thirds of the land area of Ireland is covered by some type of brown earth.

Question
List four characteristics of brown earth soil.

OPTION 7 – GEOECOLOGY

As a result of differences in local conditions, there are some variations in Irish brown earth soils, creating pockets of intrazonal soils.

■ **Podzol** brown earth soils developed where boulder clay covered the limestone bedrock in lowland areas. They have undergone slight leaching and are paler in colour.

■ **Acidic** brown earth soils developed in areas that are 500 metres or more above sea level. They developed from parent materials that were low in lime, such as granite and sandstone. The acidity can be cancelled out by the addition of ground lime (crushed limestone).

■ **Shallow** brown earth soils, usually no more than 50 cm deep, are found on limestone landscapes such as the Burren. While they are fertile and rich in limestone, their lack of depth impedes agriculture.

Soil profile of a brown earth soil

A soil profile is a vertical section down through the soil. It shows a number of horizontal layers that run from the ground surface to the parent rock. These layers are called **soil horizons**. The major horizons are lettered O, A, B and C. Some horizons can be subdivided.

Question

Explain the terms 'soil profile', 'horizon' and 'litter'.

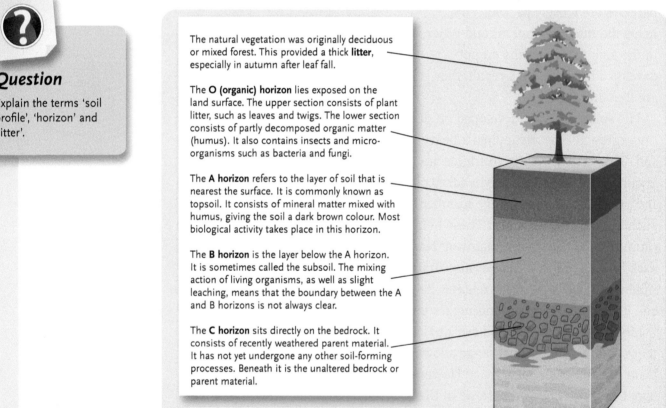

The natural vegetation was originally deciduous or mixed forest. This provided a thick **litter**, especially in autumn after leaf fall.

The **O (organic) horizon** lies exposed on the land surface. The upper section consists of plant litter, such as leaves and twigs. The lower section consists of partly decomposed organic matter (humus). It also contains insects and micro-organisms such as bacteria and fungi.

The **A horizon** refers to the layer of soil that is nearest the surface. It is commonly known as topsoil. It consists of mineral matter mixed with humus, giving the soil a dark brown colour. Most biological activity takes place in this horizon.

The **B horizon** is the layer below the A horizon. It is sometimes called the subsoil. The mixing action of living organisms, as well as slight leaching, means that the boundary between the A and B horizons is not always clear.

The **C horizon** sits directly on the bedrock. It consists of recently weathered parent material. It has not yet undergone any other soil-forming processes. Beneath it is the unaltered bedrock or parent material.

Bedrock

Fig. 7-1-12 *A soil profile consists of a series of layers called horizons.*

HUMAN INTERFERENCE WITH SOIL CHARACTERISTICS

Worldwide, up to 10 million hectares of soil lose some of their fertility annually. When the loss of soil fertility is at its most extreme, **desertification** may occur. This is usually as a result of both **environmental problems** and **human interference**. This is a problem in many parts of the world, but none more so than in the **Sahel**.

Irish brown earths are fertile and support a range of farming types.

THE SAHEL

The Sahel is a belt of semi-arid land about 3 million square kilometres in area that runs for 4,000 km east to west across Africa. It is the transitional zone between the arid Sahara Desert to the north and the slightly tropical areas of Central Africa to the south. It occupies parts of several countries, including Mali, Burkina Faso, Chad and Sudan.

Questions

1. Name the three countries that have the biggest land areas within the Sahel.

2. Which country has the largest share of its land area within the Sahel?

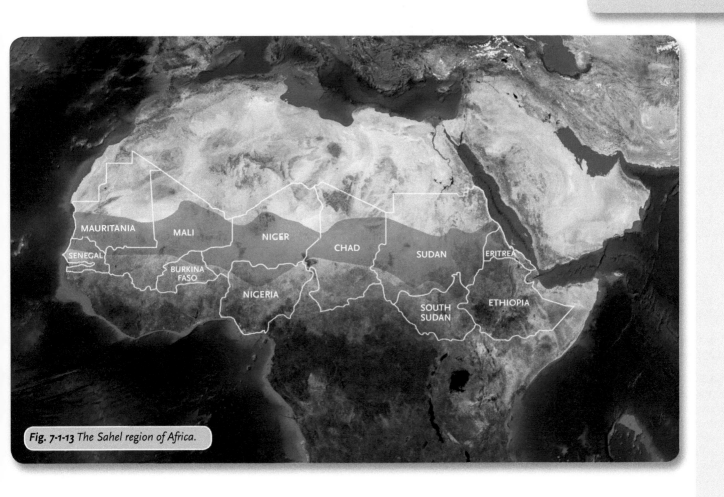

Fig. 7-1-13 *The Sahel region of Africa.*

Climate in the Sahel

The climate in the Sahel swings between extreme heat and more temperate conditions, with rain only falling in four or five months of the year, usually between May and October when the growing season gets underway. However, over the past 40 years, rainfall has dramatically decreased and has also become less reliable.

Whether the climatic patterns of the Sahel are caused by global warming or are a result of the cycle of naturally occurring rainfall patterns is a matter of debate. Either way, most climate models for the Sahel predict even drier conditions for the future.

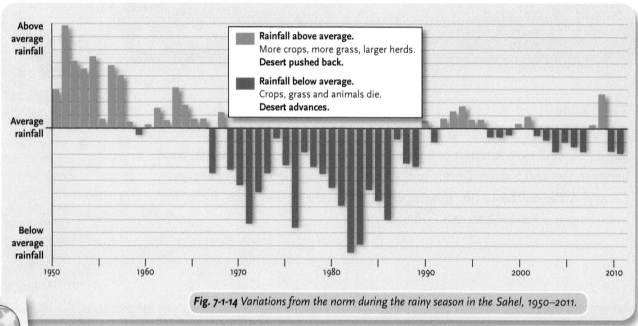

Fig. 7-1-14 *Variations from the norm during the rainy season in the Sahel, 1950–2011.*

Geofact

Sahel comes from an Arabic word meaning 'shore' or 'coast'. This refers to the appearance of the vegetation of the Sahel as a shoreline marking the edge of the Sahara Desert.

Definition

DESERTIFICATION is the spread of desert conditions into new lands, turning productive land to wasteland through overuse and mismanagement.

Population of the Sahel

There is rapid population growth in the region. The growth rate is about 3% per annum, resulting in a doubling of the population approximately every 20 years. Thus, most parts of the Sahel are now overpopulated.

Overpopulation occurs when a region has so many people living in it that it is unable to provide them with resources such as food and fuel. Overpopulation not only impacts on the standard of living, but also on the environment.

Desertification in the Sahel

In the latter part of the 20th century, desert conditions advanced southwards into the Sahel by between 5 and 10 kilometres per year. This spread of desert conditions is known as **desertification**.

Desertification does not just refer to the expansion of existing deserts. It also refers to the formation of areas where soil fertility and vegetation cover have been damaged. When vegetation cover is lost, the unprotected soil is blown away by the winds, resulting in **soil erosion**. This can turn productive land into non-productive desert.

Desertification results from a combination of **climatic change** (mainly drought) and **human activities**. These activities include:

- overgrazing
- overcropping
- deforestation.

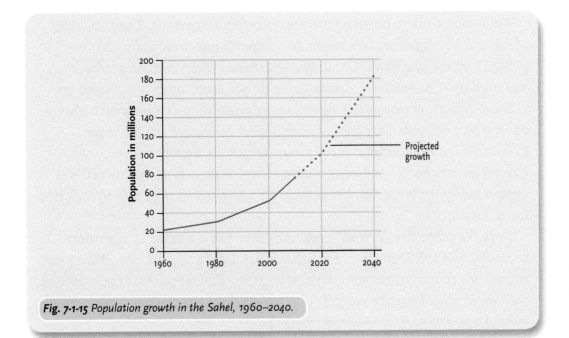

Fig. 7-1-15 *Population growth in the Sahel, 1960–2040.*

Geofacts

Desertification threatens the livelihoods of some of the poorest and most vulnerable populations on the planet.

Desertification occurs on all continents except Antarctica.

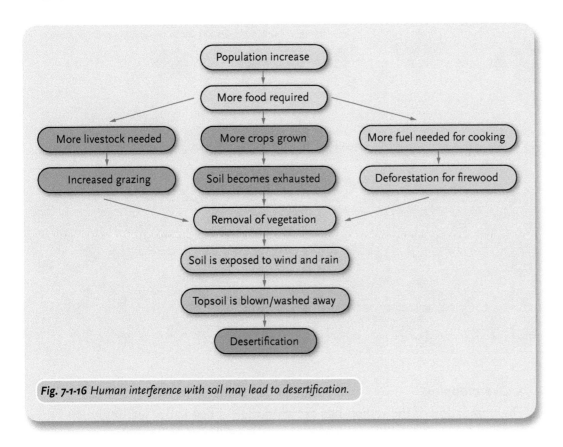

Fig. 7-1-16 *Human interference with soil may lead to desertification.*

Geofact
Overgrazing is not confined to the Sahel. It is a problem in many regions, a number of which do not have arid climates.

1. Overgrazing

The ownership of livestock, particularly cattle, was seen as a symbol of wealth and social status in many of the tribes in the Sahel. At the same time, the number of farmers in the region was growing. The increase in cattle and goat numbers led to increased competition for land among **nomadic herders**. The land was grazed beyond the point where it could renew itself. Many herders moved their animals onto marginal grazing areas. Young trees and shrubs were also grazed and damaged by the animals.

Wells were sunk to provide for better watering of animals. The availability of water encouraged herders to remain longer in one area, adding to the pressure on the grassland. Groundwater that had taken centuries to build up was used up. The level of the water table dropped and many wells dried up.

Some African governments viewed nomadic herding as a backward system and encouraged **sedentary** (settled) farming in its place. Farmers began to fence in land and graze it more intensively. Soils were not left to rest (**fallow**) for any period and were unable to renew their fertility. The soil was compacted by the large number of animals and rains were unable to soak into the ground.

Once the protective layer of vegetation cover was damaged, **soil erosion** occurred. The soil of much of the Sahel is dry, light and sand like. It does not contain much humus to bind particles together. The topsoil was easily eroded both by wind and surface run-off from the occasional torrential downpour, leaving only the harder, rockier subsoil.

The increase in cattle numbers has led to overgrazing and soil erosion.

2. Overcropping

The population of the region has grown rapidly since 1960, leading to an increased demand for food. Herding was gradually replaced by the growing of **food crops**. As a result, the area devoted to crops has trebled in the last 50 years.

Dry croplands need time to recover from growing crops when no fertiliser is used. This recovery time is called a **fallow year**. The increasing demand for food meant that the fallow year was abandoned. When the land is replanted too soon, fertility declines and yields decrease rapidly.

Animal manure had always been used to fertilise the land. Due to the shortage of wood, the dried manure was used as a fuel instead of as a **fertiliser**. Farmers began to purchase and use chemical fertilisers, but then had to sell their crops to pay their debts.

A greater area of land now had to be cultivated to maintain the same return. Farmers began to clear and use areas of **marginal land**, removing the vegetation and planting crops in its place. Marginal land is not very fertile to begin with, so this land soon lost its nutrients, leading to crop failure. The loss of vegetation cover also robs the soil of its source, however small, of humus.

Many governments in the region were unable to pay their **international debts** to Western banks, so they encouraged farmers to grow **cash crops** in order to raise money to pay off the debts. These crops included groundnuts, cotton and millet. The growing of the same crop in the same place year after year is called **monoculture**. It rapidly exhausts the soil of its nutrients and the soil gradually becomes infertile.

Overcropping has now reduced soil fertility and robbed the land of its vegetation cover. Some land is abandoned. Soil erosion follows, either by wind or surface run-off during occasional heavy rains.

3. Deforestation

Deforestation is the large-scale clearing of forest and then using the land for a non-forest purpose. Forests are cleared in order to provide extra land for agriculture by the **slash-and-burn** method. They are also cut to provide wood for house construction and especially fuel for cooking and heating.

The forest cover is important because trees slow down the wind. Their roots also help to bind soil particles and they absorb moisture in periods of heavy rainfall. Their leaf fall adds nutrients to the soil, increasing its fertility.

The demand for wood is so great that trees are cut down 30 times faster than they are replaced. Even young trees, small bushes and scrub vegetation have been cut down. People simply do not have the resources to replant the trees. In some cases, where trees have been planted as shelter belts, poachers have cut down the newly planted trees.

As the population of the region grew, so did the demand for **firewood**. When trees closer to settlements have been cut down, women often have to walk miles each day to collect firewood and carry it home in the heat of the sun. In Niger, the exploitation of trees for fuel has proved more profitable than traditional agriculture. Firewood for the larger towns is collected up to 200 km away.

The removal of the forest cover exposes the soil, which is quickly dried out and burned by the sun. Winds erode the soil, carrying it off in dust storms.

Definitions

MONOCULTURE occurs when the same crop is planted in the same field year after year with no crop rotation.

SLASH AND BURN involves cutting down trees and then burning their stumps and any remaining vegetation. The ashes are mixed with the soil as a fertiliser.

Geofact

Every year, half a million hectares of trees are cleared in Mali alone. Over 80% of the energy used in the country comes from wood.

Deforestation partly caused by making charcoal for cooking fuel from bush wood.

Definition

APPROPRIATE TECHNOLOGY:
- meets people's needs
- uses local skills and materials
- is affordable
- promotes self-sufficiency
- helps protect the environment.

SOIL CONSERVATION IN THE SAHEL

Soil is a sustainable resource, but only if it is managed properly. Measures are being taken to both reduce soil erosion and reclaim land where soil erosion has already taken place. Great emphasis is placed on the use of **appropriate technology**.

Stone lines (bunds)

This involves placing lines of **small stones** across slopes to reduce run-off. It is used in Burkina Faso, a country that receives occasional heavy downpours. The lines take up less than 2% of the ground space, yet they can increase yields by over 50%, and even more in drier years.

This method of soil conservation is very effective when the slopes are gentle. Most stone lines run continuously across the slope, parallel with the contours. Others are crescent shaped and overlap one another. Both systems

Stone lines (bunds) are built to prevent erosion. The lines, like very low dykes, slow down rain running off the land and dam it back uphill, giving it time to soak in and nourish root crops.

work in the same way. They trap most of the rainfall, giving the water time to soak into the ground and nourish root crops. They also top up the water table and reduce soil erosion.

The bunds trap soil, seeds and organic matter such as leaves instead of allowing them to be removed by wind and rain. These materials can then be raked back across the fields. The trapped organic material will eventually turn to humus and increase soil fertility.

Bunds are cheap and easy to build and use freely available local materials. The work is done during the dry season when labour is not needed for farming.

Strip cropping and shelter belt combination

This involves planting one or two species of tree interspersed with two or three different crops. Generally, the crops are planted in strips of equal width.

The trees are permanent, but the crops are grown in a three- or four-year rotation or cycle. The cycle also includes a fallow year (no crops) when the soil is allowed to rest.

Trees such as the acacia or tamarind are ideal because they also produce food. The crops are arranged so that a close-growing crop (such as groundnuts) is alternated with a mid-height crop (millet) and a very tall plant (maize).

Geofact
One negative aspect of strip cropping is that one crop may tend to harbour plant diseases and pests that are harmful to the other crops.

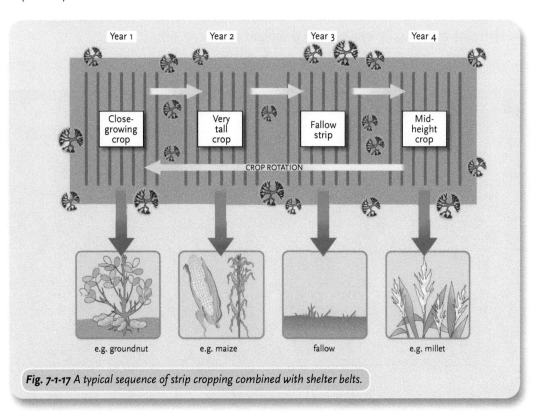

Fig. 7-1-17 *A typical sequence of strip cropping combined with shelter belts.*

The benefits of strip cropping include the following:
- The trees break most of the force of the wind and protect the strips of crops as well as providing a source of food.
- The trees may be trimmed or thinned to provide firewood.
- The taller crops reduce wind speed, thus reducing soil erosion.

■ There is a smaller width of exposed soil in the fallow year and this is further protected by higher crops.

■ Run-off is limited and soil erosion following heavy rains is reduced.

■ More rainwater seeps into the ground.

■ The soil will not become exhausted, as each crop absorbs different nutrients and minerals from the ground.

■ Food yields increase overall.

■ Soil erosion is halted and soil fertility increases.

Zai holes

Zai holes are planting pits that are dug through hard, crusted soil. This technique has been used by farmers in other semi-arid regions for centuries. Now it has been adapted to the new climate conditions of the Sahel. It is a very simple and low-tech improvement for these farmers. The only tool that is needed is a hoe or spade.

Pits are dug during the dry season from November until May. The number of pits can be as high as 10,000 per hectare, with the size varying according to the type of soil and the crop that is to be planted.

After digging the pits, the farmers add a compost of leaves and stems, topped with manure if available. They then put a small covering of soil over it. The pits also capture windblown soil, leaves and litter. Termites are attracted to the organic matter. By digesting it, the termites also make nutrients more easily available to the plant roots.

Fruit trees being planted in zai pits in Mali.

When the first rainfall of the season arrives, water is trapped in the pits and it soaks into the ground. Seeds are then planted in the middle of each pit and the pit is filled with soil. Depending on the size of the hole, the crops grown vary from trees to cereals and vegetables. In some cases, a mixture of all three types is planted.

The advantages of zai holes are that they:

■ capture rain and surface run-off water

■ concentrate both nutrients and water precisely where they are needed

■ protect seeds and organic matter against being washed away

■ increase yields and give a guaranteed supply of food

■ restore soil fertility

■ lead to a reduction in soil erosion.

Leaving Cert Exam Questions

All questions are worth 80 marks.

The characteristics or properties of soils

1   Describe and explain the characteristics of any **one** soil type studied by you.

Factors that influence soil formation

1   Examine the factors that influence soil characteristics.

2   With reference to **one** soil type you have studied, examine how parent material, climate and organic matter influence the soil.

Processes of soil formation

1   Soil characteristics are affected by their immediate environment and by a combination of processes operating in that environment. Examine any **three** soil processes that affect soil characteristics.

2   Examine **two** of the natural processes that influence soil formation.

3   Explain how weathering, leaching and podzolisation impact on the characteristics of soil.

Global soil types

1   Examine the general composition and characteristics of any **one** soil type that you have studied.

Human interference with soil characteristics

1   Discuss how human activities can accelerate soil erosion.

2   Examine how overcropping/overgrazing and desertification can affect soils.

3   Examine **two** ways in which human activities have impacted on soils.

7.2

Biomes

INTRODUCTION

A biome is a large area on the Earth's surface where climate, soil, natural vegetation and animal life (fauna) are inter-related. Each biome gets its name from the dominant vegetation found within it. For instance, much of Brazil forms part of the **tropical rainforest** biome.

Learning objectives

After studying this chapter, you should be able to understand:

- the factors that influence the development of biomes

- the characteristics of the tropical rainforest biome

- how humans alter biomes.

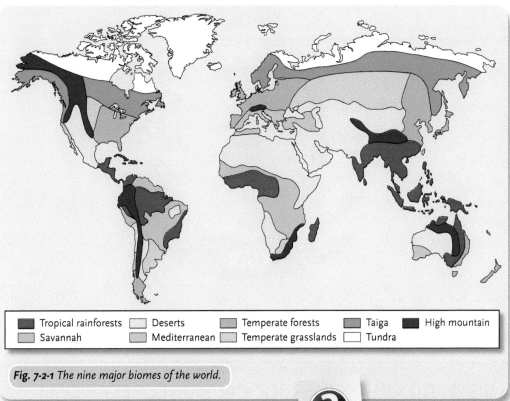

| Tropical rainforests | Deserts | Temperate forests | Taiga | High mountain |
| Savannah | Mediterranean | Temperate grasslands | Tundra | |

Fig. 7-2-1 *The nine major biomes of the world.*

Activity

Identify the type of biome at each of the following locations: (a) Ireland (b) New Zealand (c) Egypt (d) Norway.

Geofact

Ireland is within the **temperate deciduous forest** biome. Even though Ireland now has very little forest cover, this was the natural vegetation of the country until it was cut down to make way for agriculture.

FACTORS THAT INFLUENCE BIOMES

Four main factors combine to produce and control each biome: climate, soils, vegetation and animal life.

- **Climate** is perhaps the most important aspect of a biome because it determines what kind of soil will develop there as well as what vegetation and animal life can live in the region. The main influences are temperature and precipitation.
- **Soils** are very important because they influence the type of vegetation that will grow in a particular region. Plant growth is affected by the depth, texture, structure and organic content of the soil. Soils in turn are influenced by the climate of the region as well as by the parent rock.
- **Vegetation** growth is influenced by the climate and soil characteristics. Vegetation in turn influences the animal life as well as soils (characteristics and fertility).
- **Animal life** must be able to adapt to the conditions of climate and vegetation of a biome in order to survive. Animal life in turn can affect the vegetation cover positively by fertilising it or negatively by overgrazing.

Geofact

- Over one-third of the world's trees grow in the tropical rainforests.
- Tropical rainforests are home to about half of all living things on the planet.
- Tropical rainforests are also called nature's medicine cabinets.

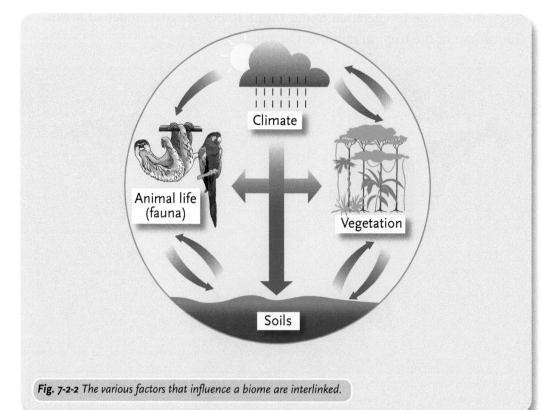

Fig. 7-2-2 *The various factors that influence a biome are interlinked.*

Link

Human activities may also influence and alter biomes (see pages 193–201).

DISTRIBUTION OF THE TROPICAL RAINFOREST BIOME

Tropical rainforests lie in the tropics, i.e. between the Tropic of Cancer and Tropic of Capricorn.

Central America and South America

The majority of tropical rainforests are found here, with the largest intact tropical rainforest in the world located in the Amazon Basin.

Africa

The largest zones of forest are located in central and western Africa. The island of Madagascar has the world's greatest diversity of plant and animal life, probably due to its remoteness from the mainland.

Australasia

The main stretches of forest are found in western India, Bangladesh, Malaysia and the islands of Java and Borneo. The smallest belt of tropical rainforest is found in north-east Australia.

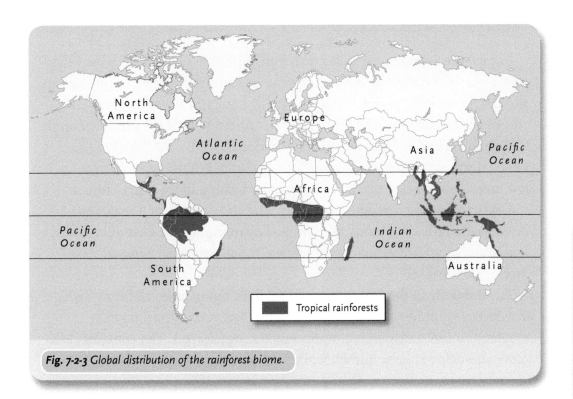

Fig. 7-2-3 *Global distribution of the rainforest biome.*

Geofact

Roughly 80% of the food we eat originally came from tropical rainforests. Without rainforests, we wouldn't have the seeds that produce coffee and chocolate. Other rainforest foods include chicle (chewing gum), bananas, black pepper and nuts.

CHARACTERISTICS OF THE AMAZON RAINFOREST BIOME

Climate

The **tropical climate** of the Amazon rainforest is like that of any other typical tropical rainforest. It is hot, wet and humid all year round.

On average, the **temperature** in the tropical rainforest is about 27°C. There is very little daily or seasonal variation in temperature throughout the year. In fact, the difference between the day and night temperatures (diurnal range) is greater than the difference between any of the seasons.

In this region, sunlight strikes the Earth at a very high angle. The higher in the sky the sun is, the greater the heat received from it. This results in intense solar energy hitting the ground. This intensity is also due to the consistent day length for regions on or near the equator: about 12 hours a day, 365 days per year.

OPTION 7 – GEOECOLOGY

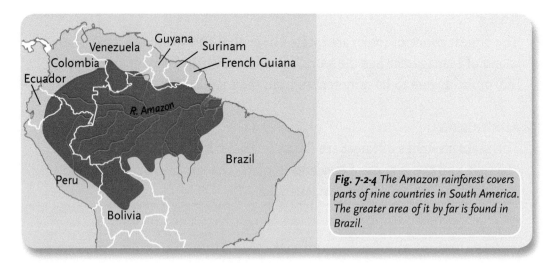

Fig. 7-2-4 *The Amazon rainforest covers parts of nine countries in South America. The greater area of it by far is found in Brazil.*

Question

Name four countries in South America where Amazon rainforest is found.

Geofact

Tropical rainforests with a cloud cover, such as in the Amazon Basin, are known as **selvas**.

Annual **precipitation** exceeds 2,000 mm, with rain falling throughout the whole year in the region. Two seasons can be identified: the very rainy season and the not-so-rainy season. There are up to 200 rainy days each year, with afternoons characterised by heavy showers. About 50% of the precipitation in the rainforest comes from its own evaporation.

The north-east trade winds and south-east trade winds converge in a low pressure zone close to the equator. Solar heating in the region forces the warm air to rise through convection. The air is cooled as it rises and condensation occurs. Clouds form in the late morning and early afternoon hours, and by mid-afternoon, convectional thunderstorms form and precipitation begins.

The **humidity** in the Amazon rainforest does not usually fall below 80%. The intense humidity is due to the moisture that comes from rainfall, evaporation and transpiration (water loss through leaves). The constant cloud cover also helps to keep humidity high.

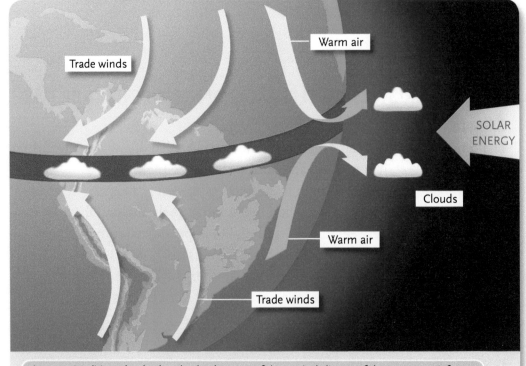

Fig. 7-2-5 *Conditions that lead to the development of the tropical climate of the Amazon rainforest.*

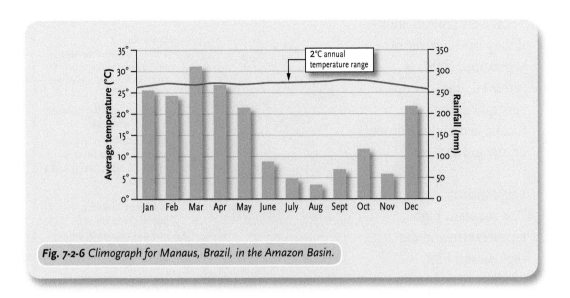

Fig. 7-2-6 *Climograph for Manaus, Brazil, in the Amazon Basin.*

Afternoon tropical rainstorm in the Amazon Basin. Note the dense cloud cover.

Question

Name (a) three months of the wet season and (b) three months of the not-so-wet season.

Soil

Tropical red soils, or **latosols**, make up the zonal soil that has developed beneath tropical rainforests. Latosols are often up to 30 metres deep as a result of intensive weathering of the underlying rock. They are **infertile** soils that are very low in nutrients, yet they can support a luxuriant growth of forest due to the nutrient-rich top layer.

Latosols are **red** or **yellow** in colour from the presence of iron oxide (rust) or aluminium oxide in the soil. Leaching is so intense that all other minerals have been removed.

The texture of latosols varies (clay, silt, sand, loam) because the parent rock varies so much. For the same reason, soil structure could be crumb, platy or blocky.

Question

List three characteristics of latosols.

Latosols are wet soils if they have a cover of vegetation. If this is removed, they dry up very quickly and can form a cement-like crust on the ground.

Vegetation

The constant high temperature and the regular and high rainfall create humid conditions. Added to 12 hours of daily sunshine, these conditions are ideal for the rapid growth of vegetation. The tropical rainforest biome has the widest range of vegetation (**biodiversity**) of all biomes.

The growing season lasts all year. Thus, there are flowers and fruit all year round. Even though many trees are deciduous, the forest has an evergreen appearance because trees lose their leaves at different times of the year.

Rainforests consist of a number of **layers**. These have developed as plants adapt to their environment, be it competing for sunlight or surviving on the dark forest floor.

Rainforest vegetation has **adapted** to its environment in a number of ways in order to survive.

- Trees have developed a **shallow root system** because all the nutrients are found close to the surface.
- **Buttress roots** form an aboveground root system to prevent the emergent trees from

Geofact

Latosols are a good source of materials for brick making and road construction.

Question

List three ways in which vegetation has adapted to rainforest climate conditions.

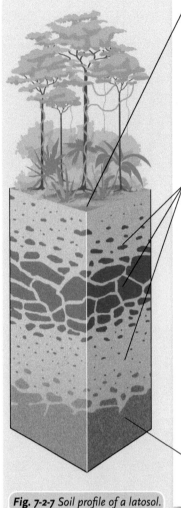

O horizon
There is a thick **litter layer**, with a continuous supply of litter from falling leaves and branches.

There is a very thin but very fertile **humus** layer.

Decomposition of organic matter, aided by bacterial activity, is rapid, taking just a few days.

A, B and C horizons
Soil horizons are not very distinct due to the continuous abundance of **mixing agents**.

There is a great depth of soil as a result of extreme weathering (including laterisation; see page 170).

The soil has a **red colour** due to the presence of iron oxide (rust), which remains in the soil after other minerals have been removed by leaching.

Nutrients rarely reach these lower layers. If they do, they are rapidly leached downwards, leaving the soil infertile.

Bedrock
The bedrock is also subject to rapid **chemical weathering**.

Fig. 7-2-7 *Soil profile of a latosol.*

*Road cutting through virgin rainforest as the forest in the foreground is cleared for agriculture. Note the **red soils**.*

being blown down by winds as well as to increase the surface area over which the trees can draw their nutrients.

■ The tallest trees have **small leathery leaves** and waxy bark to cope with wind and sunshine.

■ Leaves in the canopy have holes or drip tips to shed the heavy rainfall.

■ Plants in the dark understory have large leaves to capture as much light energy as they can.

■ **Lianas** have their roots in the ground but climb high into the tree canopy to reach available sunlight by wrapping around trees for support.

Animal life

The rainforest is home to a rich variety of animal life. Colourful and unusual animals dwell in all five layers of the forest. All types of creatures are represented, from tiny insects to large mammals.

The plants of the canopy have a very high yield of fruit, seeds and flowers. This attracts a wide variety of birds both to the canopy and to the emergent layer, including **eagles**, **toucans** and members of the **parrot** family.

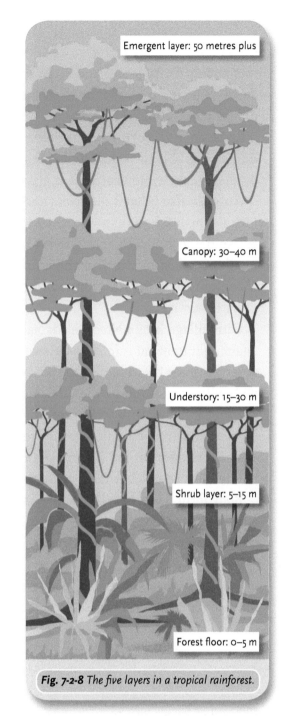

Emergent layer: 50 metres plus

Canopy: 30–40 m

Understory: 15–30 m

Shrub layer: 5–15 m

Forest floor: 0–5 m

Fig. 7-2-8 *The five layers in a tropical rainforest.*

Understory and forest floor, with its fallen vegetation in a state of decay. Note the buttress roots on the bigger trees.

Some animals find most or all of their food high in the trees of the canopy so that they will rarely, if ever, need to go to the rainforest floor. The **sloth** eats mainly fruits, leaves and bugs, spending most of its time hanging upside down. Other animals that dwell in the canopy include a wide variety of **monkeys** and **squirrels**.

Large animals such as the **jaguar** inhabit the forest floor. An excellent hunter, it is able to swim, climb trees or run after its prey. Other forest floor dwellers include the **anaconda**, a giant snake, and the **anteater**.

Animals also inhabit the rivers and marshes of the rainforest. These include the **black caiman**, a large crocodile, and **piranha** fish. The rainforest is also home to **insects** (butterflies and beetles), **arachnids** (spiders and ticks), **reptiles** (snakes and lizards) and **amphibians** (frogs and toads).

Animal life in the Amazon rainforest has **adapted** to its environment in order to survive.

Camouflage is one effective adaptation. The jaguar has a spotted coat, enabling it to blend into the shadows in the background. Sloths move very slowly, making them harder to spot. Stick insects and frogs blend in very well with fallen vegetation on the valley floor.

Some animals try to **scare predators** by convincing them that they are bigger and fiercer than they really are. Many butterflies have large 'eye' designs on their wings. This makes them look like the head of a very large animal instead of a harmless butterfly.

Body form has evolved for some animals. Monkeys have muscular tails that allow them to hang from trees. They have also developed long arms to enable them to swing between trees and avoid ground predators. The flying squirrel has flaps of skin linking its front and back legs that allow it to glide between trees. The beak of the toucan is strong enough to crack nuts, but being so long, it also enables it to lose some body heat.

Question

List three ways animal life has adapted to conditions in the rainforest.

Adult eagle of the Brazilian rainforest.

The flying squirrel cannot actually fly, but glides from tree to tree on the folds of skin between its front and back legs. It is nocturnal, emerging at night to feed on a varied diet including fruit, leaves, insects, eggs and small animals.

HOW HUMAN ACTIVITIES ALTER BIOMES

The Brazilian government decided to open up the rainforest to take advantage of its vast resources in the early 1970s. Many multinational companies (MNCs) also took advantage of opportunities that became available to them.

As long as traditional lifestyles remained in place, the human impact on the rainforest biome was minimal. However, over the last 200 years, with rapid population growth, the rate of change has been very fast. Today there are few parts of the rainforest where there is a truly natural environment unaltered by humans.

The Amazon rainforest has been altered by human activities that include:

■ deforestation
■ intensive agriculture
■ permanent settlement
■ industrialisation.

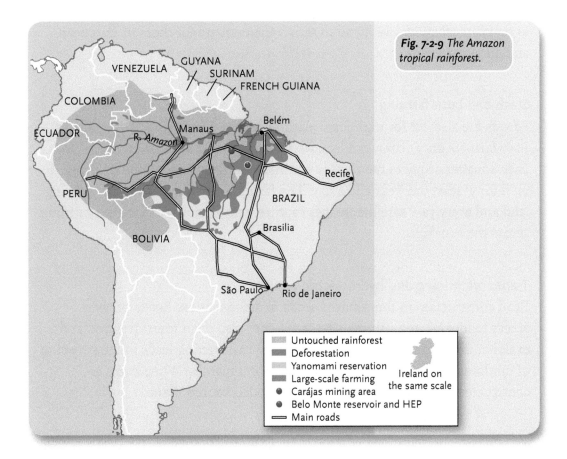

Fig. 7-2-9 *The Amazon tropical rainforest.*

Legend:
- Untouched rainforest
- Deforestation
- Yanomami reservation
- Large-scale farming
- ● Carájas mining area
- ● Belo Monte reservoir and HEP
- ══ Main roads

Ireland on the same scale

Question

Examine Fig. 7-2-9 showing tropical rainforest areas and name:
■ two rivers
■ two cities
■ one tribal zone
■ one mining zone.

Deforestation

During the past 40 years, about 20% of the Amazon rainforest has been cut down. The destruction of rainforests often occurs because of the short-term economic benefits that are involved. These include the following:

The global demand for timber

There is an ever-increasing demand for timber for building, furniture and paper products as the world's population increases by more than 70 million per year. The rapid growth of developing economies, especially in Asia, will also increase the demand for hardwoods.

Many unwanted trees are destroyed in the logging operation. The Brazilian government estimates that more than three-quarters of all logging is illegal.

The expansion of grazing land

Vast areas of rainforest have been cleared to make way for grazing cattle to fill the world's increasing demand for meat. Today, Brazil is the world's largest producer and exporter of beef. Most is large-scale ranching, with about 80 million head of cattle being reared at any given time. The Brazilian Amazon now has more than 550,000 square kilometres of pasture, an area larger than France.

The demand for crops

Vast areas of the Amazon rainforest are being converted into plantations to grow cash crops such as soybeans, coconuts and palm oil. These are exported to repay international debt and to satisfy the demand for them in European and other markets.

Slash-and-burn farming

Forests are also cut for traditional slash-and-burn farming by native peoples. Poor farmers are encouraged by government policies to settle on forest lands. Each squatter acquires the right to continue using a piece of land by living on it for at least one year and a day. The farmers typically use fire for clearing land and every year satellite images capture tens of thousands of fires burning across the Amazon.

Transport, mining and hydroelectric power

Road construction in the Amazon leads to deforestation. Roads provide access to logging and mining sites while they also open forest frontier land to exploitation by poor landless farmers. Open-cast mining leads to the stripping of rainforest over mineral deposits by large companies. When dams are constructed, vast areas of rainforest are flooded behind them.

Question

List the causes of deforestation in order of importance.

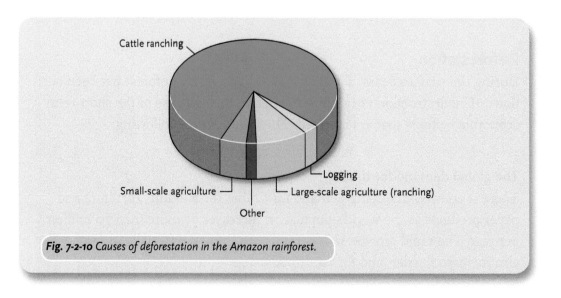

Fig. 7-2-10 Causes of deforestation in the Amazon rainforest.

Fig. 7-2-11 *The rate of deforestation has decreased rapidly since 2004. Satellite monitoring now pinpoints forest clearance, and illegal logging is heavily penalised. Permits for clear cutting are now difficult to obtain.*

Deforestation rate
Projection of future deforestation

Question

What area of rainforest was destroyed in (a) 2004 and (b) 2010? Suggest a reason for each.

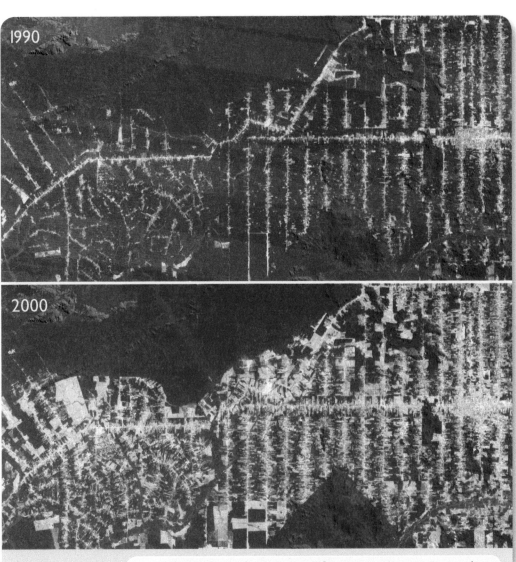

Deforestation in the Amazon rainforest, *comparing 1990 (top) and 2000 (bottom) satellite images. Main roads take loggers into the centre of the rainforest, with minor roads branching off to provide access to trees for logging.*

OPTION 7 – GEOECOLOGY

Impacts of deforestation

Deforestation leads to the **loss of plant, animal and insect species** – a decline in biodiversity. Plant and animal species are interdependent. For instance, many plants depend on birds and insects for pollination. When forest habitats are destroyed, whole species disappear. At least 25% of pharmaceutical ingredients are sourced in forests. These include aspirin, quinine and curare. To date, only 1% of the world's plant species have been tested for their medicinal value. As species disappear, we are losing a valuable treasure chest of ingredients in the fight against disease.

Deforestation contributes to **climate change**. Trees are a major carbon store of CO_2, which they absorb and convert into oxygen. However, as trees are logged, burned for fuel or cleared for farming, the CO_2 is then released into the atmosphere. This contributes to **global warming**, with up to 20% of all global CO_2 emissions caused by deforestation. Therefore, deforestation in Brazil has global consequences.

The Amazon produces half its own rainfall through the moisture it releases into the atmosphere (evapotranspiration). If enough of that rain is eliminated through deforestation, the remaining trees dry out and die. Deforestation in the Amazon region has also been found to severely reduce rainfall in Texas and northern Mexico during the spring and summer seasons, when water is crucial for agricultural productivity.

Deforestation leads to **soil erosion** and **soil infertility**. Trees provide a protective barrier against heavy rain, especially on hillsides. When trees are cut, the protective barrier is lost. Heavy rain and wind erosion remove the unprotected topsoil. Landslides and mudslides are also a problem.

The absence of leaf fall soil means that the soil loses its source of nutrients from plant litter and it soon loses fertility. Without trees to soak up the rainfall, severe leaching occurs. Exposed clay is baked into a hard, infertile soil called laterite. A once-forested area is turned into a barren landscape in a few short years.

There has also been a reduction in the population of **native people** (see page 198).

Intensive agriculture

Cattle ranching

Cattle ranching is the biggest cause of deforestation in the Amazon and nearly 80% of deforested areas in Brazil are now used for pasture. Many MNCs bought large areas of forest that they turned into cattle ranches. Often they did not save and sell the valuable hardwood timbers, burning them instead to speed up the land clearance process.

The cattle industry has ballooned since the 1970s, giving Brazil the largest commercial cattle herd in the world. The country also tops the world's beef export market and the government plans to double its share of the market by 2018. This push by the Brazilian government for the industry to expand on such a massive scale throws its plans for reducing deforestation into serious doubt.

Geofact

Brazil has more amphibian, bird, mammal, reptile and plant species than any other country.

Geofact

Cattle ranching has the highest rates of slave labour in Brazil – over 3,000 people held as slaves were freed from ranches in 2010.

Cash crops

Cash crops are important to help the Brazilian government pay its international debts. The soybean is one such crop and has become one of the most important contributors to deforestation in the rainforest. A new variety of soybean has been developed by Brazilian scientists to flourish in the rainforest climate. Brazil is now on the verge of replacing the US as the world's leading exporter of soybeans.

In areas where soils and landscape are suitable for soybean cultivation, rainforest lands are typically cleared for cattle ranching, then sold on to soybean producers some two to three years later. The cattle ranchers then move into frontier areas, thus increasing deforestation.

■ Large-scale agriculture is typically quite **destructive of native ecosystems**. The clearing of the forest devastates animal, bird and insect life.

■ The availability of cheap land in the Amazon means that farmers tend to **abandon areas** after a few years of production. It is cheaper to open up the forest for fresh land than to recover pastures or use artificial fertilisers on a regular basis. This leads to further deforestation. In the first year of pasture, each animal needs one hectare to support it. This rises to 2.5 hectares after three years of grazing.

■ Amazon soil is actually rather poor. The vegetation is lush only because it feeds itself with all the organic matter provided by dead plants and animals. Once this cycle is broken by agriculture, the soil becomes infertile in a few years and **soil erosion** is likely.

■ When soil erosion occurs, the soil is washed into rivers, where it may be deposited on the riverbed. This causes river levels to rise and **flood** low-lying areas, further damaging the ecosystem.

Geofact

For every 1/4 lb hamburger consumed from rainforest beef, about 6 square metres of rainforest was cleared.

A small island of rainforest remains in the midst of a soybean plantation.

Permanent settlement

There has been a huge **reduction in local tribes** living in the region. From an estimated 2 to 6 million, there are now fewer than 350,000 native people living in the forests. It is estimated that about 100 tribes have disappeared altogether.

■ The Yanomami are one such tribe that was traditionally considered to be isolated, having contact only with other small local tribes. They depended on the rainforest, using slash-and-burn farming methods to grow bananas, gather fruit and hunt animals and fish.

■ Many Yanomami have been forced off the land to make way for new developments. Their rights and traditions were ignored by the government, loggers and miners. Some have been murdered for resisting the newcomers.

■ Up to 25% of the native population has been wiped out by diseases such as malaria, the common cold and measles – diseases brought to the region by loggers and miners. The Yanomami had never been exposed to these diseases and they had no natural immunity to them.

■ The Brazilian government still refuses to recognise tribal land ownership, despite having signed an international agreement guaranteeing it. The culture and way of life of the Yanomami have been destroyed and many now live in poverty.

Question

List three reasons why the population of local tribes has decreased.

Yanos are communal houses. They are built in clearings in the forest and look like giant doughnuts from the air. The Yanomami use palm leaves to make an enormous thatched roof that is supported by timber poles made from forest trees. Each family has its own area with a fireplace and somewhere to hang their hammocks. Although each family is separated from the next by the poles that hold up the yano, they all face the common open space in the middle.

Manaus was founded as a small **river port** at the confluence of the Amazon and Negro rivers. It has now developed into a major trading and industrial centre for central Amazonia. Its original growth was due to the rubber industry. The Brazilian government has now designated it as a growth pole and duty-free zone. Its industries include cars, ship building, chemical production, electronics and petroleum refining. It has a population of almost 2 million people, having grown tenfold over the last 20 years. This growth has impacted negatively on the rainforest biome.

■ The continued growth of the city has led to the clearing of vast areas of forest for housing and firewood.

■ Rapid population growth has led to an increased demand for food. This has led to further deforestation in the region surrounding the city, as ranching and other food producers respond to the demand.

■ Manaus does not have a waste treatment plant. Most of the sewage and waste water flows into the River Negro without any treatment, thus causing pollution. This pollution impacts negatively on river life and riverside vegetation.

■ The suburbs of Manaus are home to many favelas, especially in the floodplain area, with houses built on stilts over streams of open-air sewage.

Two views of Manaus, a city built at the confluence of the Amazon and Negro rivers in the heart of the rainforest.

Industrialisation

Mining

Deposits of minerals known to exist in the Amazon Basin include diamonds, iron ore, bauxite, tin, copper, lead and gold. The Brazilian gold rush began in 1980 when gold was discovered in Pará state. At least 250,000 people moved into the area and worked for low wages in crowded gold mines. Gold mining continues in the region today.

■ Most of the mines use open-cast mining techniques. Apart from forest destruction in the area immediately surrounding a mine, associated road-building leads to deforestation and also encourages more settlers to move in.

■ Environmental practices have been lax. Mercury and cyanide, which are used in the mining process, are toxic compounds. These materials have been spilled on land and washed into the region's rivers. Land and water in the immediate area have been polluted. Mercury concentrations increase up the food chain, causing problems for fish, animals and humans.

■ Tens of thousands of miners have illegally entered the area. Indigenous peoples (e.g. the Yanomami) have been forced to abandon their traditional villages and have also been affected by murder and disease.

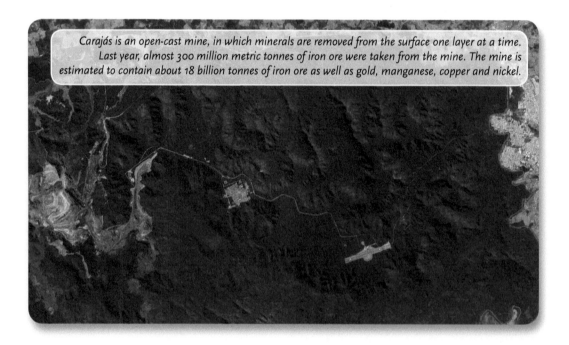

Carajás is an open-cast mine, in which minerals are removed from the surface one layer at a time. Last year, almost 300 million metric tonnes of iron ore were taken from the mine. The mine is estimated to contain about 18 billion tonnes of iron ore as well as gold, manganese, copper and nickel.

Hydroelectric power (HEP)

Hydroelectric power currently accounts for more than 75% of Brazil's electric energy generation, but less than half the potential HEP has been tapped. The government plans to develop 48 new HEP plants by 2020. Most of that capacity is set to come from 18 new dams in the Amazon River Basin.

■ A typical dam site is a valley of rainforest, inhabited by Indians, who farm the land and depend on the river for washing, drinking and fishing. After the dam is built, the land slowly floods, destroying the entire valley's forest as well as endangering animal and plant species.

■ Thousands of people are uprooted and forced to move elsewhere against their will. Their culture and way of life are destroyed.

■ Hydroelectric dams produce huge amounts of carbon dioxide and methane gas. Carbon dioxide is tied up in trees and other plants. It is released when the reservoir is initially flooded and the plants rot. As the trees and plants rot, there is a build-up of methane gas. This is later released into the atmosphere and leads to climate change.

Geofact

The Belo Monte Dam, currently under construction, will lead to the displacement of between 20,000 and 40,000 indigenous Indians as well as the loss of 1,500 square kilometres of rainforest.

Blast furnaces

Brazil's Carajás region is home to almost 50 blast furnaces. The blast furnaces produce pig iron, the main raw material for steel. The furnaces largely depend on illegal camps that cut and burn rainforest for charcoal. The charcoal is preferred to coke because it is cheaper. Most of the pig iron is exported to the US and from there to major car manufacturers like Ford, General Motors, BMW, Nissan and Mercedes.

■ The illegal charcoal companies use what is effectively slave labour and also cause major air pollution.

■ Laws that state that 80% of the forest must be left intact are ignored. Around three-quarters of the region's forests have been lost already, the bulk of it since pig iron production began in the mid-1980s.

■ With forest running out in the region, loggers are now illegally entering indigenous lands and conservation areas. Some indigenous tribes have already lost much of their land to the illegal loggers.

■ Atmospheric pollution results from various stages of the process, e.g. carbon dioxide (greenhouse effect), carbon monoxide (poisonous) and sulfur dioxide (acid rain).

Geofact

The amount of charcoal needed to produce 25 tonnes of pig iron consumes one hectare of virgin forest.

Leaving Cert Exam Questions

All questions are worth 80 marks.

Characteristics of a biome

1 Examine the characteristics of any **one** biome that you have studied under **three** of the following headings:
   ■ climate
   ■ soils
   ■ flora
   ■ fauna.

2 Describe and explain the main characteristics of **one** biome that you have studied.

3 Examine the influence of climate on the characteristics of **one** biome that you have studied.

4 Examine the main characteristics of a biome that you have studied.

Adapting to biomes

1 Describe how plant and animal life adapt to soil and climatic conditions in a biome you have studied.

Altering biomes

1 Examine how any **three** of the activities listed below can impact on biomes:
   - early settlement and clearing of forests
   - the felling of tropical rainforests
   - intensive agricultural practice
   - industrial development.

2 'The development of economic activities can alter biomes.' Discuss this statement with reference to appropriate examples you have studied.

3 Assess how biomes have been altered by human activity.

4 Assess the impact of human activity on a biome you have studied.

5 Examine **two** ways in which human activities have altered the natural characteristics of a biome you have studied.

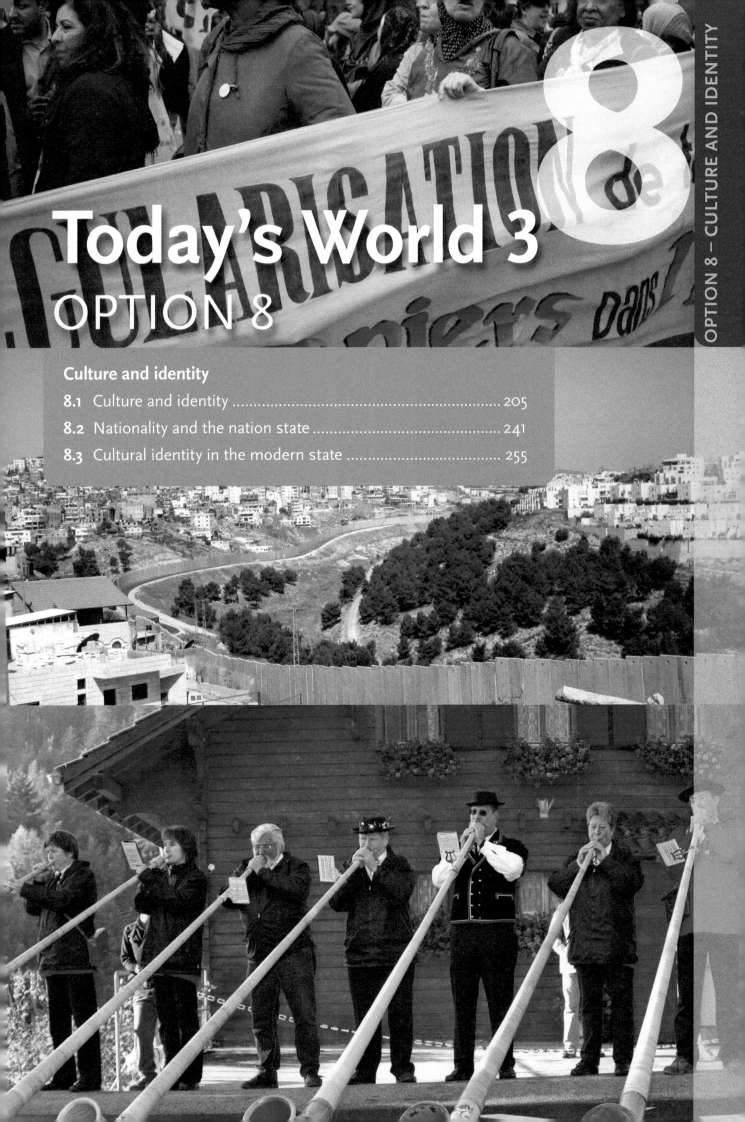

Today's World 3
OPTION 8

Culture and identity

Culture and identity

8.1

There is only one race – the human race. Scientists now recognise that all humans come from one gene pool with identical characteristics and abilities. The word 'race' is not a sorting category and race is studied here as a celebration of the diversity of all the people of the Earth.

Learning objectives

After studying this chapter, you should be able to understand:

■ the meaning of the term 'race' and the distribution of racial groups on Earth

■ the role of migration in how the distribution of racial groups in recent centuries has changed

■ the distribution of the world's major religions and languages

■ the importance of culture in Ireland and France.

THE RACES OF HUMANKIND

Biologically, humans are one species. Race refers to the physical variations in the appearance of human beings. These variations include skin colour, facial features, hair and stature. These features are passed on genetically from generation to generation.

Over thousands of generations, people adapted to the climatic environment in which they lived. People living in tropical regions have had to cope with strong rays from the sun since the dawn of humankind. People in tropical lands have a pigment called melanin in their skin. This gives skin a dark colour and protects it from the sun's rays.

People who live in middle and higher latitudes are paler because they have less melanin in their skin. They do not need it because the sun's rays are weaker. Skin colour is therefore a biological adaptation to the environment.

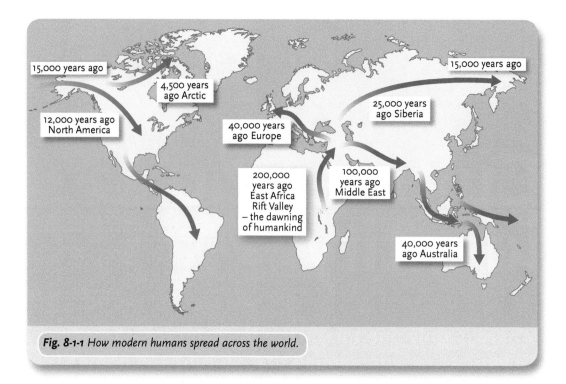

Fig. 8-1-1 *How modern humans spread across the world.*

Geofact

Many scientists now claim that humankind originated in the Rift Valley of East Africa. Some 100,000 years ago, humans walked out of Africa and into Eurasia.

A multicultural tutorial group in a British university.

RACIAL GROUPS

The great majority of racial groups belong to three races: Caucasian, East Asian and African.

Caucasian

Caucasians are also known as Indo-Europeans. This is the most widespread and numerous race. Caucasians inhabit Europe, India, South-west Asia and North Africa. Migration due to the European discovery of the Americas by Columbus in 1492 has caused Caucasians to spread to North and South America, Australia, New Zealand and South Africa.

A Caucasian family.

East Asian

This is the next most numerous race. This race is found in East, South-east and Central Asia. East Asians crossed the Bering Straits from Asia to the Americas many thousands of years ago and made their way across the vast American continents. These were the people who lived there when Europeans colonised the Americas after Columbus. The Aztecs, Incas, Sioux, Apaches and Seminole tribes were members of the East Asian race.

A Chinese family. The Chinese belong to the East Asian race.

African

This is the least numerous race of the three main races of people. The African race is mainly found in Sub-Saharan Africa. European slave traders captured millions of Africans and transported them to the American continents in the 18th and 19th centuries. The descendants of former slaves are now found in Brazil, in the Caribbean islands and in the US. In the US, they are known as African-Americans and make up about 12% of the population of the US. The population of African migrants to European countries has grown in recent decades.

A group of young people in Nairobi, Kenya.

Other groups

There are other widely dispersed groups of people who are not members of the three main racial groups. These include Australian Aborigines and the Kalahari Bushmen in South-west Africa.

Link
Population movements, pages 45–70.

CHANGES IN RACIAL PATTERNS THROUGH MIGRATION

Multiracial societies did not exist before the European discoveries of the New World. Before the European discoveries, the American continents were populated by tribes who had crossed the Bering Straits from East Asia thousands of years before. After Christopher Columbus reached the Caribbean islands in 1492, Europeans began to cross the Atlantic in increasing numbers. Over the next several centuries, racial patterns were changed.

We will now examine three aspects of migration that changed traditional racial patterns:

- colonisation
- the slave trade
- migration from former colonies to Europe.

Colonisation

Spanish and Portuguese colonists colonised the region now known as Latin America. The Spanish colonists settled in the Andean countries and in Central America while the Portuguese settled in Brazil. In the course of their colonisation, the Spanish destroyed the Aztec and Inca civilisations and enslaved those native people who survived.

British and French colonists settled in North America. Many people went to British colonies in what is now the east coast of the US to escape religious persecution in Britain and in mainland Europe. The French settled in the province of Quebec in Canada. The US declared its independence from Britain in 1776.

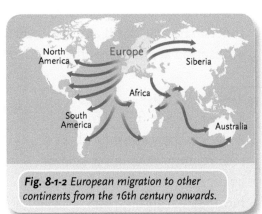

Fig. 8-1-2 *European migration to other continents from the 16th century onwards.*

As in Latin America, native tribes suffered badly in European colonies in North America:

■ Native people had no immunity to measles, smallpox or even the common cold.

■ Many native people, especially in North America, had a weakness for alcohol. Alcohol combined with guns in native hands decimated many tribes.

■ During the building of the railways in the 19th century, hunters such as Buffalo Bill wiped out the buffalo herds, the food of many Indian tribes of the plains.

■ By the end of the 19th century, native people were largely confined to reservations and replaced by Caucasians.

Question

Why, do you think, are Central and South America called Latin America?

An artist's impression of the European colonisation of the western region of the US and Canada.

Question

How do you think Native Americans would have responded to this impression of European colonisation?

Australia, inhabited by Aborigines 40,000 years ago, became a penal colony of Britain at the end of the 18th century. However, the **carrying capacity** of Australia in terms of human settlement was low because of drought. Even today, it has only 22 million people. The Aborigines, who were treated cruelly by European settlers, are largely in the margins of society in Australia.

In the late 19th century, the scramble for Africa brought European settlers to many parts of Africa. The British colonised East Africa while the French concentrated on North and West Africa. Therefore, the Caucasian race is now widespread across the world.

The slave trade

The slave trade from Africa to the Americas grew significantly in the 18th century, although it existed before that. The countries involved included Portugal, Spain, France, the Netherlands and Britain. The slave trade was an example of **involuntary or forced migration**. It continued into the early decades of the 19th century. It was a profitable business. At least 12 million African men, women and children were

Fig. 8-1-3 *The Atlantic slave trade.*

transported as slaves across the Atlantic. Nearly 2 million died en route.

Slaves were seen as a commodity that could be bought and sold. They were forced to work in plantations as slave workers tending cotton, sugar cane, tobacco and cocoa.

An artist's impression of slaves bound below deck on the Atlantic crossing (Bermuda Maritime Museum).

Geofact

Vermont was the first American state to abolish slavery in 1777. Denmark followed suit in 1803.

The result was that millions of people of the African race found themselves in the Americas – in eastern Brazil and Surinam; in Caribbean islands such as Jamaica, Haiti and Trinidad; and in the southern states of the US, such as Alabama and Mississippi. Even after slaves won their freedom in the second half of the 19th century, they were discriminated against in education and jobs, especially in the US.

An engraving of slaves in a sugar cane plantation in the Caribbean.

While there is a great deal of racial mixing between Caucasians and people of African descent in Brazil and the Caribbean islands, intermarriage between the races is far less prevalent in the US. In the US, people of mixed race account for a little over 2% of the population. In Brazil, the figure is 39%.

Migration from former colonies to Europe

The French and British empires began to collapse around 1950. Colonies became independent in South Asia, Africa and the West Indies.

Over the last 50 years, native people from former colonies have made their way to Britain, France and the Netherlands. They did so for **push and pull** reasons. They wanted to escape poverty in their homelands and to seek a better life in Europe. In addition, many former colonies, such as Jamaica and Trinidad, joined the British Commonwealth. This made it easier for people from those countries to migrate to Britain.

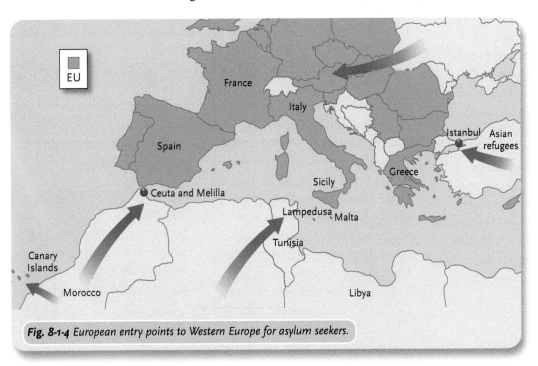

Fig. 8-1-4 *European entry points to Western Europe for asylum seekers.*

In addition, tens of thousands of asylum seekers from Africa and Asia have reached Europe in the last two decades. Therefore, while people of African and Asian origin are racial minorities in Europe, most countries in Western Europe are now home to people of Asian and African origin. Many European countries have therefore become multiracial societies.

The result of colonisation and migration was that many societies became **multiracial**.

CASE STUDY

France – a multiracial society

France has believed in the principles of liberty, equality and fraternity since the French Revolution of 1789. Therefore, the state does not collect statistics on the racial or ethnic origins of its people. As a result, we do not know how many people of ethnic minority live in France. However, it is widely accepted that the number is at least **5 million** out of a total population of about 63 million in mainland France (2012 estimate).

A demonstration in Paris by immigrants in 2010 in support of equality for migrants.

The growth of minorities in France

As the French economy expanded in the 1960s, the French government encouraged people from the former colonies of Morocco, Tunisia and Algeria to work in France. Thousands of workers took up the offer of a move to France. These people worked in menial and poorly paid jobs that the French did not want to do. They were joined by migrants from Senegal, Mauritania and other former French colonies. Many immigrants found themselves living in ghettoes in French cities, in many cases in high-rise apartments on the margins of society.

Over time, these workers began to bring their families to France. As the economy ceased to expand in the 1970s and unemployment rose in France, the French were surprised that these migrants did not want to return home. Migrants had become accustomed to life in France. They had their families and friends with them and their children saw France as their home. Mosques had been built in Muslim neighbourhoods.

Growing unrest among minorities

Unrest was growing under the surface among minority groups. Migrant communities in Paris, Marseille and Lyon began to harbour resentment because of poverty, unemployment and marginalisation. Migrant communities did not see any real steps being taken to integrate them into mainstream French society. Migrants claimed that the French expression of *Black, Blanc, Beur* was meaningless. Migrants felt alienated in their adopted country.

Definition

BLACK, BLANC, BEUR: Black, White and Arab.

Furthermore, as with minorities in other countries, there was not a single representative of North African origin in Parliament in 2010. Job applicants with French family names get three times as many interviews and job offers as minority applicants with the same qualifications.

Recent riots

These resentments boiled over in recent years, especially in November 2005, when riots in a number of French cities led to a declaration of a state of emergency. Arson attacks on cars and other property damage shocked French society out of its complacency in

Xenophobia in France

Many French people are resentful of the presence of people of foreign origin in France. They claim that French culture is under threat from people of foreign origin. People who feel this way give political support to the French National Front, a right-wing anti-immigration party.

relation to minority groups.

The future

President Sarkozy, himself the son of immigrant parents from Hungary and president during the years 2007 to 2012, provided a fresh approach to the challenge of the integration of immigrants. He began to appoint ministers from minority backgrounds to important posts in the government.

Companies are now using affirmative action in hiring workers from minority groups. The largest companies in France have signed up to a **Business Diversity Charter**. Companies must now publish an annual account of the steps they have taken to promote diversity in the workplace.

However, in the 2012 presidential election, Marine Le Pen, the leader of the National Front, which has traditionally been opposed to inward migration, received 17.9% of the vote in the first round. The challenge of the assimilation of migrants into mainstream French society has some way to go.

Yasid Sabeg, appointed as Commissioner for Equality and Equal Opportunity, said, 'We cannot allow France to become an apartheid state.'

Link

Inward migration in France, *Today's World 1*, pages 325–6.

Activity

Check out the work of Yasid Sabeg on the internet.

Racially mixed societies

As we have seen, the European discoveries of the New World led to contacts between different races. As people of different races came into contact with each other, children of mixed race were born. This led to mixed race societies. This is evident in the US, for instance. Brazil has millions of racially mixed people.

CASE STUDY

Brazil – a racially mixed society

Native people

Native tribes lived in Brazil for thousands of years before the Portuguese colonised Brazil. Many native people died as they came into contact with European diseases such as smallpox, measles and the common cold – infections to which they had no immunity.

African slaves

The Portuguese began to introduce African slaves to the country in the 16th century. From the 16th to the 19th century, 4 million African slaves were brought forcibly to Brazil from West Africa. These slaves were put to work on plantations in Brazil growing coffee, sugar cane and cotton.

European colonists

European colonists have migrated to Brazil for 500 years. These include Portuguese, German, Italian, Spanish and Lebanese migrants.

From the intermixing of these races came the modern Brazilians. Racially, Brazil is a melting pot. All over Brazil, the physical traits of Caucasians, Africans and native people are found in many combinations. Skin colour, facial characteristics and hair reflect the mixed racial ancestry of millions of modern Brazilians.

Brazilians distinguish between people of mixed race. The main categories of racially mixed people in Brazil are:

- **Mestizos:** People of European and native tribal ancestry.
- **Mulattos:** People of European and African ancestry.
- **Cafuzos:** People of African and native ancestry.

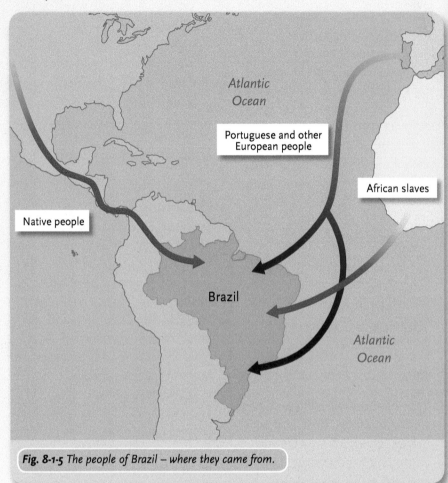

Fig. 8-1-5 *The people of Brazil – where they came from.*

Race relations today

Brazil finally abolished slavery in 1888, considerably later than the US. However, Brazil does not have the bitter racial divisions that have been evident in many parts of the US throughout the 20th century. This is partly because almost four in 10 Brazilians are of mixed race. Brazilian society is much more of a melting pot than that of some other multiracial societies.

However, Brazilians are as status conscious as people in every society. While status in Brazil is linked to wealth and level of education rather than colour, Brazil is not a colour-blind society. African-Brazilians are more likely to be found in menial jobs and are more likely to live in slums than white Brazilians.

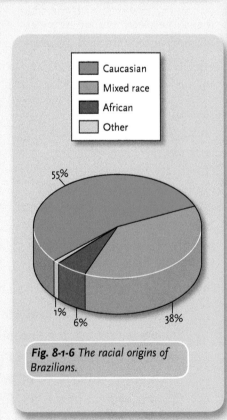

Fig. 8-1-6 *The racial origins of Brazilians.*

CASE STUDY

African-Brazilians die younger, are more likely to go to jail and have a lower ratio in third-level education than white Brazilians. It is also undoubtedly true that the interests of native people in the Amazon Basin have been routinely ignored for generations. These factors strongly suggest that Brazil is not an equal society in terms of race.

Politics and race in Brazil

Caucasians play a dominant role in Brazilian politics. From the president to state governors and members of Parliament, the top positions in politics are occupied almost totally by white people. People of African and of mixed race backgrounds are on the margins of politics. That means that they have very little influence on change that could bring about a more equal society.

The key to change is education. Education gives people an awareness that change is possible. When mixed race and African-Brazilians take their place in the corridors of political power, only then will racial inequalities be addressed.

Many Brazilians of African or mixed race ancestry have been very successful in the sporting arena. Sport is a strong unifying force in Brazil. Brazilians of every race and colour take great pride in Brazil's sporting achievements.

Link
Race in Brazil, *Today's World 1*, pages 361–3.

RACIAL CONFLICT

Racial conflict has occurred in many regions of the world. As the Indo-European race colonised the Americas and later Africa and Australia, their desire for land and gold brought them into conflict with native peoples who formed a different race of people. You will be aware from your Junior Cert history course that the Aztec and Inca nations were destroyed by Spanish conquistadores. Racial conflict also occurred in the more recent history of the US. We will now examine this.

Link
The slave trade, pages 210–1.

CASE STUDY

Racial conflict in the US

The slave trade brought more than 12 million slaves to the New World from Africa. Even though the importation of slaves was banned in the US in 1807, up to 4 million African-Americans remained in slavery in the cotton fields of southern states such as Alabama and Louisiana. It was not until 1863 that President Lincoln signed the emancipation of slaves into law.

Geofact
To Kill a Mockingbird, Harper Lee's novel of injustice against an African-American, is well known in Irish schools.

Even after the defeat of the southern **Confederate states** in the American Civil War of the 1860s, African-Americans remained in dire poverty for generations. For almost 100 years after the civil war, African-Americans suffered discrimination because of the **Jim Crow laws**, mainly in the 11 former Confederate states. These laws included the segregation of public schools, public places and public transportation and the segregation of restrooms, restaurants and drinking fountains for whites and blacks. African-Americans were in effect excluded from voting because of difficult literacy tests. The US military was also segregated.

In addition, the Ku Klux Klan, a white supremacy movement in southern states such as Mississippi and Alabama, made sure that these laws were enforced and committed crimes of violence and lynching against black Americans.

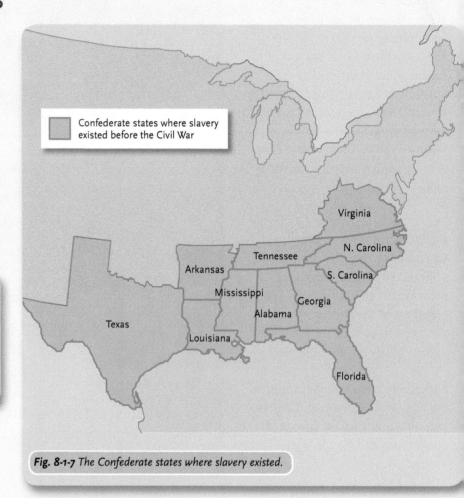

Confederate states where slavery existed before the Civil War

Virginia

N. Carolina

Tennessee

S. Carolina

Arkansas

Mississippi

Georgia

Alabama

Texas

Louisiana

Florida

Fig. 8-1-7 The Confederate states where slavery existed.

The civil rights movement
This movement began in earnest in the 1950s. The struggle over several years saw heightened racial tensions. Key events in the struggle included:

■ Rosa Parks's refusal to give up her seat on a bus to a white passenger
■ the Montgomery Bus Boycott in Alabama by African-Americans

A protest in Little Rock, Arkansas, in 1959 against the admission of African-American pupils to a high school.

CASE STUDY

James Meredith entering the University of Mississippi in 1962.

- the ruling of the US Supreme Court in 1955 that white and black children should be able to go to the same schools
- the Little Rock affair*
- the emergence of Martin Luther King and his 'I Have a Dream' speech
- the support of President Kennedy for black Americans' civil rights
- James Meredith entered the University of Alabama**
- the Civil Rights Act of 1964, which gave equal voting rights to all Americans, irrespective of creed or colour
- the assassination of Martin Luther King in 1968.

Radical views

Martin Luther King was a moderate leader who believed in peaceful protest. However, even before his assassination in 1968, more radical voices within the African-American community were emerging.

*Little Rock, Arkansas
Nine African-American teenagers turned up at an all-white school in Little Rock for their first day at school in 1957. The governor ordered soldiers to block them from entering. President Eisenhower had to send in federal troops to protect the students. However, local police and white parents tried to block the students' entry. Eight of the nine attended school all year, escorted by armed federal troops. During that time, they were bullied and spat at. Racial tension in many states was very high.

**James Meredith – a pioneering student
In 1962, James Meredith became the first black student to enter the University of Mississippi. The university governor and white students tried to prevent his entry, but President Kennedy ordered 400 federal marshals and 3,000 troops to ensure that his right to university education was honoured. In 1963, a similar event occurred at the University of Alabama.

Activity

Have a look at Martin Luther King's 'I Have a Dream' speech on the internet.

Martin Luther King, Jr. His death in 1968 led to riots and protests in many US cities.

CASE STUDY

The Black Panthers in particular believed in militant tactics to achieve their goals. These sentiments led to race riots in black ghettoes, many of which were hotbeds of frustration and unrest.

Recent decades

The tensions of the 1960s gradually receded. Over time, the civil rights movement gave way to the controversy over US involvement in Vietnam. Over the years, many African-Americans became better educated and more involved in politics. However, racial harmony is still a challenge for the country. African-Americans are seriously under-represented in politics. They are more likely to be in jail, to finish school earlier and to be unemployed. They are less likely to have college degrees than whites. Ghettos of African-Americans in cities such as Detroit have high levels of poverty. Many neighbourhoods are blighted by drugs. African-American incomes are the lowest in the US.

In 1992, four white policemen were acquitted in a trial in California even though they were recorded on film beating a black man, Rodney King. The riots that followed were very destructive and led to the deaths of 51 people in California.

However, the election of **Barack Obama** to the White House in 2008 and his re-election in 2012 represents a great leap forward for African-Americans and for racial harmony in the States. History is likely to record his election as a key moment in African-Americans' long road to equality.

Geofact

Papua New Guinea, with 6.9 million people, has 830 languages.

Geofact

The language spoken by the greatest number of people is Mandarin Chinese, with over 1.2 billion speakers.

Definition

A **DIALECT** is a regional variation of a language. In the Irish language, the Donegal dialect is different in many ways to the Kerry dialect.

LANGUAGE AS A CULTURAL INDICATOR

There are at least 3,000 languages in the world. Some languages, such as Mandarin Chinese, Spanish and English, are spoken by hundreds of millions of people, while some are spoken by only a few hundred people. Many languages have become extinct in recent times. Examples include the languages of North American native tribes. The languages of some tribes of the Amazon Basin are also endangered because of the small number of speakers.

Language is a very important part of culture. Pádraig Mac Piarais recognised this in his dictum *Gan teanga gan tír* (Without a language, without a country). A common language gives people a sense of identity. The founding fathers of the state of Israel in the middle of the 20th century recognised this. As Jews from many parts of Europe began to enter the new Jewish state, the ancient language of Hebrew was restored as the daily language of the country. A common language gave Israeli people a sense of unity and identity as they struggled to preserve the state of Israel in a region hostile to them. Hebrew is therefore a strong cultural indicator in Israel, surrounded as it is by people who speak Arabic.

Language families

Languages are grouped into language families. A family of languages is descended from a common or parent language. For instance, Latin is the parent language from which Romance languages such as Italian, French and Spanish grew.

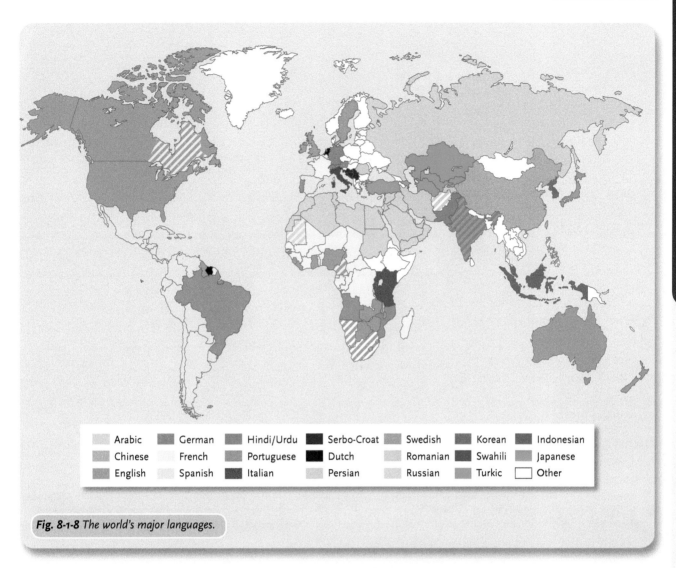

Fig. 8-1-8 *The world's major languages.*

Celtic languages are a family of languages. These languages, spoken in Brittany and in parts of Britain and Ireland, come from a Celtic parent language that Celtic people brought with them as they migrated to these islands.

European languages

Language is a clear cultural indicator in Europe. Europe is a **patchwork quilt of cultures**, a hotchpotch of ethnic groups. Many of these ethnic groups have their own languages and dialects. These languages give their users a sense of identity and belonging. **A common language can unite people, but languages can divide people too.**

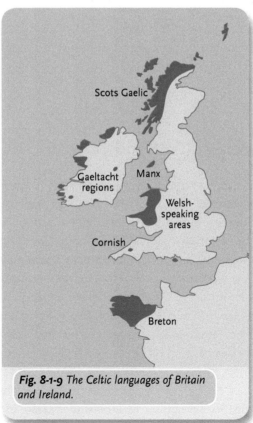

Fig. 8-1-9 *The Celtic languages of Britain and Ireland.*

Geofact
English is the first or native language of some 400 million people.

Definition
HOTCHPOTCH: A mixture, a jumble.

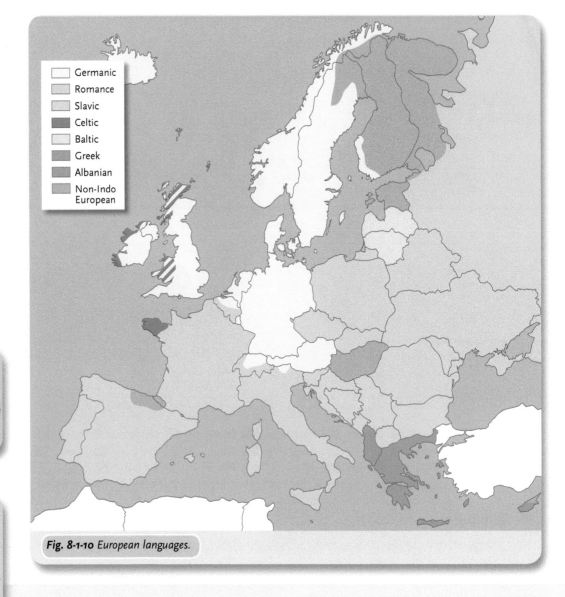

Germanic
Romance
Slavic
Celtic
Baltic
Greek
Albanian
Non-Indo European

Fig. 8-1-10 *European languages.*

Link

Language is a **divisive force** in Belgium. See *Today's World 1*, pages 263–4.

Geofact

The Basque, Finnish and Magyar languages are older than the Indo-European languages of Europe.

CASE STUDY

CS

Polish – a strong cultural indicator and a unifying force

Polish, a Slavic language, is spoken by about 40 million people in Poland today. For centuries, the Poles were overrun by powerful neighbours such as Russia, German states and the Austrian empire. Throughout its history, Poland has been invaded, carved into chunks, put back together and carved up again. Yet Poles have retained their Polishness, their sense of identity.

To preserve that identity through their turbulent history, Poles clung to their language and their Catholic religion. In spite of the fact that the Polish language was not allowed to be taught in schools or used in government administration or law courts by Russian overlords, Polish survived because it became a symbol of cultural resistance to foreign rule. Polish poems, songs and legends were retold in every village in Poland for centuries. Polish therefore united the Polish people. Poland became an independent state in 1919, lost its independence to the Nazis in 1939, regained it again in 1945, lost it again to Communist USSR, regained its independence in 1991 and became a member of the EU in 2004. Today, Polish is a strong language with a thriving literature.

Link

Revise *Today's World 1*, page 384, for the challenges faced by the Irish language. Do you see any parallels between the challenges faced by Polish and Irish?

CASE STUDY

French – a strong cultural indicator in France

The French language is possibly the most important indicator of French culture. France has one official language – French. At the time of the French Revolution of 1789, only 3 million of the 25 million people in France spoke Parisian French. France was a Tower of Babel, with many regional languages and dialects. The Revolutionaries made French the symbol of national unity and laws were passed that French would be the only language tolerated in public life and in schools in France.

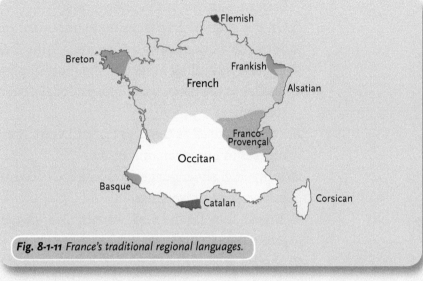

Fig. 8-1-11 *France's traditional regional languages.*

Definition

FRANGLAIS: New words that combine English and French words, such as *le weekend*.

These laws pushed the boundaries of French outwards to the provinces of France. Today, French is the first language of 88% of the population of France. National identity is closely associated with the French language. The purity of the language is protected by the Académie Française, where its 40 members decide which new words will be included in the language. The Toubon Law of 1994 makes the use of French mandatory in all spheres of public life in France.

The government has also discouraged borrowings from English and the use of Franglais. This campaign has had mixed success. In fact, Franglais looks like it is here to stay. Teenagers are importing American slang via the North African districts in French cities, where hip hop is all the rage and street fashion is borrowed from the Bronx. Even ministers now host *un chat on le web*. Learning English has become fashionable because in a globalised world where English is increasingly used, the French realise that the real losers would be themselves. They realise that learning English does not make people less French.

Regional languages in France

While regional languages have declined over the last 200 years, they are still important. Regional languages and dialects such as Breton, Catalan, Corsican, Alsatian, Basque, Provençal and Flemish are still in use. Arabic is also spoken by many North Africans. None of those languages has official status. However, since 1995, regional languages can now be taught in primary and secondary schools. In all cases, this is voluntary for pupils.

THE INFLUENCE OF THE MASS MEDIA ON EUROPEAN LANGUAGES

English, while it does not have the largest number of speakers, is more widely spoken than any other language in the world today. This is the case for two reasons:

- At its peak, the British empire included vast regions in South Asia, Africa, North America, Australia and New Zealand.
- In addition, American English is the language of the US, the economic superpower of the modern world.

Activity

Find out about the Occitan language on the internet.

Mass media, especially television and the internet, have a major role in the spread of English. American television series are part of many Europeans' lives today and CNN broadcasts around the globe. A substantial number of international sports channels use English commentaries.

English is important in many areas:

- On the internet, English is more important than any other language.
- Social networking sites are generally American.
- English is rivalling French as the most important language in the EU.
- English is the language of international aviation for pilots and air traffic controllers.
- English is used as the language of instruction in many post-graduate courses in European universities.
- Many English-language textbooks are used in medical and science courses in European universities.
- English is by far the most important language among translators at international conferences.
- English is studied as a foreign language in schools in the 25 states of the EU that do not use English as their native language. It is more widely studied than any other European language.
- American movies account for up to 80% of the films shown in European cinemas and on TV screens. While some are dubbed, people watch them to improve their English.
- English language pop songs are widely aired on radio stations in EU countries.
- Presenters and scorekeepers use English and French on that great annual song-fest, Eurovision.

However, the EU favours linguistic diversity. The EU had 23 official languages in 2012. We have already seen that the French in particular are very conscious of the need to protect their language against the growing importance of English and Franglais.

The Germans are also becoming aware of the increasing use of Denglish – a mixture of Deutsch and English – in everyday speech.

Geofact
English is widely used in Disneyland Paris.

THE SURVIVAL OF MINORITY LANGUAGES

Minority languages such as Scots Gaelic, Irish and Welsh are under threat. However, they can survive if they are supported by the local population, the state and the media. We will now examine how minority languages such as Welsh and Irish fare in a world that is increasingly dominated by English media.

The Welsh language

Welsh is a Celtic language and has been spoken in Wales for 2,500 years. Welsh has been under threat from English – the language of rule – for centuries. Welsh is strongest in the north-western areas of Wales, where up to 80% of the population speak Welsh. In the urban south-east, an area that includes Cardiff, less than 20% speak the language.

Today, approximately 611,000 people are able to speak Welsh. At least 340,000 of those use Welsh as their first language – many times greater than those who speak Irish as their first language. People who visit Wales are struck by the positive attitude that people of all ages have to the Welsh language.

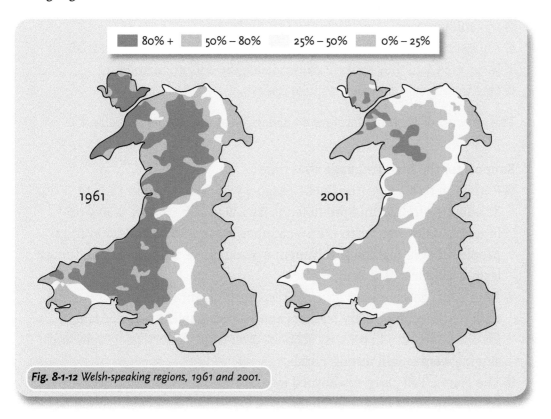

Fig. 8-1-12 *Welsh-speaking regions, 1961 and 2001.*

Support for Welsh

◼ The Welsh Education Act of 1993 put Welsh on an equal status with English in everyday life. The public sector has a duty to treat Welsh and English on an equal basis. Welsh people can use Welsh in court if they wish.

◼ The Welsh Language Measure of 2011 gives the Welsh language official status in Wales. All official documents in Wales are now available in English and Welsh.

◼ The Welsh Language Board encourages Welsh in everyday life. The board encourages bilingualism in homes where one partner speaks Welsh. The board encourages adult language classes and supports the Welsh language in theatre, in literature and in the media.

◼ Welsh is a compulsory subject for all pupils in Wales between the ages of 5 and 16. More than 25% of the pupils in Wales attend schools where the medium of instruction is Welsh. Welsh is taught in all secondary schools either as a first or a second language.

◼ *Eisteddfods* (Welsh cultural festivals) are held annually in August. These are celebrations of Welsh culture, including drama, literature, art and music. The Welsh language is used in these festivals.

Welsh is used widely in local radio, in local newspapers and in some TV stations. Plaid Cymru, the Welsh nationalist party, actively supports Welsh as an expression of Welsh identity.

The future of Welsh as a minority language seems reasonably secure.

An Ghaeilge – a minority language
The 2011 census revealed the following facts:
- 1.77 million people said they could speak Irish.
- Almost one-third of 10- to 19-year-olds said they could not speak Irish.
- Just 77,185 said they spoke it daily outside the education system.
- One in four said they never spoke Irish.

The survival of Irish is therefore a challenge for the people of Ireland.

Support for the Irish language over time
- Connradh na Gaeilge (the Gaelic League) was established in 1893 to de-anglicise Ireland and promote the language. It had more than 600 branches. However, when the 26 counties became independent in 1922, people believed that the government would restore the language and most league branches died away.
- After 1922, governments gave the responsibility for the restoration of the Irish language to primary teachers and to their pupils. Irish was taught for one hour a day in primary schools. Over time, history, geography and singing were taught through Irish.
- The Fianna Fáil party, established in 1926, strongly supported the restoration of the language. In the Irish Constitution of 1937, Éamon de Valera established Irish as the first official language of the state. Mr de Valera supported Pádraig Mac Piarais in his belief that a nation's language is central to its identity.
- Responsibility for the restoration of Irish was also placed on second-level teachers and on their pupils. Students who answered subjects *as*

Geofact
In the 2011 Irish census, 514,000 people said they spoke a foreign language at home, with Polish being the most common.

Pádraig Mac Piarais said, *'Tír gan teanga, tír gan anam.'* How do you respond to this? See also page 218.

Posters dated 1949 which encouraged Irish people to cease buying publications imported from Britain.

Gaeilge received a bonus of 10% on a sliding scale in Junior and Leaving Cert exams, a situation that still applies. During the years 1934 to 1973, students who failed Irish in the Inter and Leaving Cert exams failed the whole examination. That put a great deal of pressure on both students and teachers of Irish.

The results of this policy
In spite of these efforts, Irish outside the Gaeltacht generally remained in the classroom. For the first time, the number of full-time speakers in the Gaeltacht dropped below 100,000 in the 1960s. The Language Freedom Movement of the 1960s wanted to eliminate the compulsory nature of Irish in schools.

Recent efforts
Great efforts are being made to maintain and restore the language in modern times. Raidió na Gaeltachta and TG4 provide support to the language. Thousands of students spend a few weeks in the Gaeltacht every summer. A number of voluntary bodies promote the language. Many schools have a *seachtain na Gaeilge* every year. The teaching of Irish is more focused on the spoken language, with 40% of the marks assigned to the *scrúdú béil*, a sensible move. *Gaelscoileanna* teach 50,000 students – more than 7% of the student population. Parents send their pupils to *Gaelscoileanna* voluntarily. There are now calls for an Irish-speaking university.

The future of the language is in the hands of the Irish people. Governments can support the language, but only the people can restore it.

Geofact
Many of the new Irish from different cultures are astonished that Irish people allowed the Irish language to decline.

TG4's Máire Treasa Ní Dhubhghaill and Síle Ní Bhraonain with comedian and Irish language enthusiast Des Bishop at the launch of Abair Leat! (Have Your Say!). Abair Leat! is the world's first social network exclusively dedicated to a minority language.

CASE STUDY

The Gaeltacht areas – distinctive cultural regions today?

A view of the Great Blasket, with the ruins of the past.

Undoubtedly, the Gaeltacht areas were distinctive cultural regions in the past. The way of life practised by the Irish-speaking inhabitants of the Blasket Islands was unique. The language of the island was handed down in its purity from generation to generation and was studied by many language scholars. This way of life was recorded by writers such as Muiris Ó Súilleabháin in *Fiche bliain ag fás* (1933) and by Tomás Ó Criomhthain in *An t-Oileánach* (1929). The last inhabitants finally left the island in the 1950s.

'I have written minutely of much that we did, for it was my wish that somewhere there should be a memorial of it all, and I have done my best to set down the character of the people about me so that some record of us might live after us, for the like of us will never be again.' – the final words of *An t-Oileánach*

The influence of the modern world has come to bear on the Gaeltacht in recent decades. These influences include:

- English-language television stations
- English-medium textbooks in schools
- the English-medium culture of pop songs and popular entertainment
- the internet.

Raidió na Gaeltachta and TG4 are helping to counteract the influence of English to some extent. However, many people from the Gaeltacht areas commute to work outside the Gaeltacht every day. The long-term future of Gaeltacht culture will continue to be at risk.

Tomás Ó Criomhthain – author of *An t-Oileánach*.

Link

An Gaeltacht, *Today's World 1*, pages 262–3 and pages 384–5.

The Gaeltacht areas still retain many distinctive cultural characteristics. The most important characteristic is, of course, the use of Irish in everyday speech by many people in the Gaeltacht areas.

The Irish language

Irish, as it is spoken in the Gaeltacht, has three main regional dialects – in Munster, Connacht and Donegal. While students in Ireland learn what is known as standard Irish, the dialects of the Gaeltacht areas have their own local characteristics and accents.

Examples of regional variations:

How are you?

Munster: *Conas taoi?*

Connacht: *Ce'n chaoi a bhfuil tú?*

Donegal: *Goidé mar atá tú?*

■ Munster Irish tends to stress the second syllable of a word, e.g. *bio-**rán***, while in Connacht the first syllable is frequently stressed, e.g. ***bio**-rán*.

■ Munster users are more likely to say **bhíomar**, while Connacht users say **bhí muid**.

■ Donegal speakers use *cha* where other dialects use *ní*.

It is generally believed that Munster Irish is spoken much more slowly than Connacht Irish. Donegal Irish has some similarities with Scottish Gaelic.

Donegal Irish is widely spoken in the Rosses and in Gweedore. In Connacht, South Connemara and the Aran Islands have strong Gaeltachtaí. Ballyvourney, Ring and the Irish-speaking area west of An Daingean/Dingle are Gaeltacht areas in Munster. Examiners who correct Leaving Cert papers written through Irish read the dialects of the main Gaeltacht areas during corrections. The Connemara dialect is mostly used in the TG4 series *Ros na Rún*, the storyline of which is set in the Gaeltacht.

Language borrowings in the Gaeltacht

One of the strengths of any living language is its ability to borrow words from other languages. That is one of the great strengths of English. The Irish language as spoken in the Gaeltacht borrows many words from English. These include *mo bhycicle, an computer, an t-internet, an microwave, mo wardrobe* and *tá mo mhála istigh sa bhút*.

Fíor-Ghaeilge: Deirtear go bhfuil fíor-Ghaeilge á labhairt go fóill in Inis Meán in Oileáin Árainn. (It is said that the real traditional Irish is still spoken in Inis Meán in the Aran Islands.)

Bheadh na fataí bainte, nite, bruite, ite ag Connachtach a fhad is a bheadh práta á rá ag Muimhneach!

Geofact

Donegal Irish is spoken by Enya and Máire Ní Bhraonáin, na Casadaigh and Mairéad Ní Mhaonaigh!

Activity

Check out the people mentioned in the geofact on the internet.

CASE STUDY

Sean-nós singing and dancing – distinctive cultural features of the Gaeltacht

Sean-nós singing and dancing are associated with the Gaeltacht, particularly south Connemara. The key features of sean-nós singing include the following:

- It is sung in Irish and is unaccompanied.
- It has no dynamic (soft/loud).
- vocal ornamentation is used to express emotion.
- A drone effect is achieved by an emphasis on the consonants and on nasalisation.
- The melody may vary from one verse to the next.

Sean-nós dance is a solo form of dance. The footwork is low to the ground, has improvised steps, free arm movement and a battering step. The dancer improvises steps based on the music that is played. The emphasis is on spontaneous expression. When it is well done, the music and the dancer are in total harmony. The steps are the visible expression of the music. Personal style is highly prized in sean-nós.

Sean-nós singing and dancing have long since emerged from their Gaeltacht origins and are seen and heard wherever Irish people gather at *seisiúin*.

Emma O'Sullivan performing a sean-nós dance.

Activity

Check out sean-nós singing and dancing on the internet.

Questions

1. Find out the meaning of the word 'nasalisation'.
2. Explain the term *seisiúin*.

RELIGION – A CULTURAL INDICATOR

Religion is a powerful cultural force in many parts of the globe. It is a strong indicator of the culture of individual regions. When visitors enter a foreign city, it is likely that they will see places of religious worship, a number of which are prominent buildings. People practise their religion very visibly in many countries. Religion also influences people's daily lives.

World religions

The world's major religions came into being in Asia. Three important religions began in the Middle East. The Jewish religion began in the area around Jerusalem. Christianity began in the same region, while Islam developed in the area now known as Saudi Arabia. Buddhism and Hinduism came into being in India. Christianity is widely distributed across the globe.

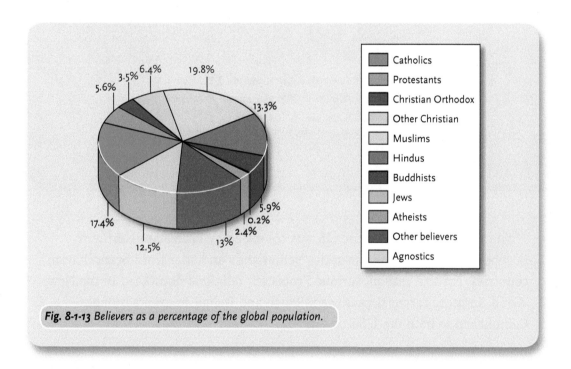

Fig. 8-1-13 *Believers as a percentage of the global population.*

The distribution of Christianity today

Christianity, in its various forms, is widely distributed across the globe. During the Middle Ages, the heartland of Christianity was in Europe. However, when the European discoveries of the New World took place in 1492, Europeans began to migrate to the American continents. Spanish and Portuguese colonists brought the Catholic religion to Central and South America. In fact, one reason why Spain and Portugal wanted to colonise this region was that missionaries wished to convert native people to Catholicism. After the soldiers, who committed terrible acts of atrocity against native people, came the priests. Catholicism became the religion of most of the people of Latin America. Churches were built in the European style all over Latin America.

Link
Religions in Brazil, *Today's World 1*, page 366.

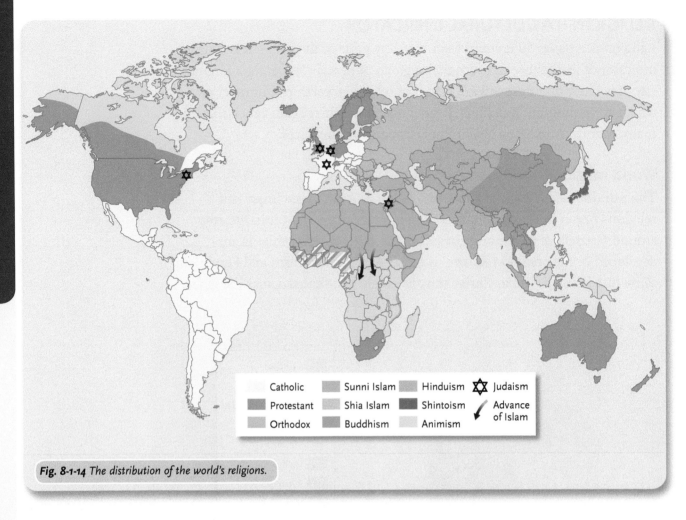

Fig. 8-1-14 *The distribution of the world's religions.*

The area now known as the US was colonised by Protestant Northern Europeans from England, from the Netherlands and later from Scandinavian countries. For that reason, various Protestant religions flourished in the New World. In more recent times, Irish, Polish and Italian migrants brought Catholicism to both the US and Canada.

Geofact

As many as 6,000 Irish missionaries – priests, nuns and brothers – worked abroad in the 1960s.

Activity

Find out the meaning of the word 'animism' on the internet.

The interior of a Catholic church in Santa Barbara, California. The sanctuaries of Catholic churches are very similar all over the world.

Missionary activity

Christian religions have actively sought converts. In the 19th century, as the scramble for Africa by European countries took place, missionaries from France, Belgium, Britain and Portugal brought Christian religions to Africa. Belgian missionaries toiled in the region known as the Belgian Congo, now the Democratic Republic of Congo. Anglican missionaries from England won converts in East Africa where British colonies were established.

Irish missionaries still work in mission fields, from Japan and the Philippines to Africa and Latin America.

The spread of Islam

Islam has spread far from its cultural hearth in Saudi Arabia. After the death of Muhammad in 632, his followers spread Islam by the use of the sword. Within a century, the region around the Persian Gulf had become Islamic.

Islamic armies later conquered North Africa and spread into Spain and later into southern France. The Islamic advance into Europe was halted at the Battle of Tours in 733. In Eastern Europe, the Ottoman empire advanced as far as Vienna before its armies were repulsed in battle in the 16th century.

A mosque in Hamburg, Germany.

Questions

Look at Fig. 8-1-14 on page 230 and answer the following questions.
1. Why is Catholicism very strong in Latin America?
2. Name three Islamic countries in North Africa and three Islamic countries in the Middle East.
3. What is the main religion in India?
4. What is the religion of Scandinavia?

Islam in Europe today

Muslims have been migrating to Europe for several decades. We have already seen that North African Islamic migrants live in France. Germany has several million Turkish Muslims, while Muslims from Pakistan and Bangladesh live in British cities. It is believed that more than 40,000 Muslims are living in Ireland, who are mostly recent immigrants. Many of them came as asylum seekers from repressive regimes.

Link

The ban on the wearing of the niqab, page 63.

Definition

A **SECULAR COUNTRY** is one that is strictly neutral where matters of religion are concerned.

The influence of religion on politics

Religion has a more important influence on politics in some countries than in others. This influence has varied over time and from region to region. This particularly applies to public education systems. In secular countries, religious emblems are not allowed in state schools, offices and courts.

In secular countries, divorce and abortion are allowed. Euthanasia is legal in the Netherlands, Belgium and Luxembourg. Assisted suicide is legal in Switzerland and in three US states. In France, the wearing of the niqab by Muslim women in public has been banned. In France, the practice of religion is a private matter.

Church–state relationships in Ireland

The Southern Irish state of 26 counties was founded after the Anglo-Irish Treaty of 1921. Because the overwhelming majority of the people of the state were Catholics, the culture of the new state reflected the influence of the Catholic Church. Later history suggests that the Southern Irish state became a **Catholic state for a mainly Catholic people.**

The Eucharistic Congress, 1932

The Eucharistic Congress of 1932 highlighted the close relationship between Church and state in Ireland. This was a religious celebration that commemorated the 1,500th anniversary of St Patrick coming to Ireland. The Congress was a great success, with 1 million people attending mass in the Phoenix Park. The fact that the great majority of the Cabinet were devout Catholics also helped to throw the weight of the government behind the success of the Congress.

The Congress asserted the identity of the Irish Free State as a leading Catholic nation. Efforts were made to present Ireland as being at the centre of a spiritual empire with thousands of missionaries abroad. This was presented as morally superior to the British empire.

The Irish constitution of 1937 – Bunreacht na hÉireann

Bunreacht na hÉireann was largely the work of Éamon de Valera, then leader of the government. He was strongly influenced by Catholic teaching on education and Catholic marriage. The new Constitution included the following articles:

■ The Catholic Church was accorded a special position as 'the guardian of the faith professed by the great majority of the citizens of the state'. Other religions were recognised.
■ The institution of marriage was guarded with 'special care'.

Éamon de Valera.

■ Divorce was not permitted.
■ Abortion was not allowed.

In 1973, the special position of the Catholic Church was removed after a referendum.

The Mother and Child Scheme

The Mother and Child Scheme, the brainchild of Dr Noel Browne, proposed free health services for all mothers and children under 16. Catholics bishops opposed the scheme because they feared that doctors might encourage the use of birth control and abortion.

CASE STUDY

Dr Noel Browne.

The Cabinet was not prepared to face down the Catholic Church and Dr Browne was forced to resign. The government collapsed shortly afterwards.

The Irish Times commented on the matter: 'The most serious revelation, however, is that the Catholic Church would seem to be the effective government of the country.'

Church–state relations in recent times

The Catholic Church has never since wielded the influence that it had at the time of the Mother and Child Scheme. Ireland has become increasingly **secular** in recent decades. Attendance at mass has declined, as have religious vocations. Artificial means of contraception were legalised in 1979. Civil divorce was passed by a narrow majority in 1995 following a second referendum. The Catholic Church has been rocked by a series of scandals in recent years, which has caused its influence to decline.

Abortion remains illegal in the Republic of Ireland except where there is a real and substantial risk to the life of the mother. This includes the risk of suicide.

If a woman decides to have an abortion, it is her legal right to leave Ireland to do so. This is the position at the time of printing in early 2013.

Geofact

The Vatican is the world's only Christian theocracy. It is governed by the Pope.

Activity

Check out the Eucharistic Congress of 1932 and 2012 on the internet. Click on images for photos of both events. What similarities and contrasts do you notice?

CASE STUDY

The influence of religion on politics in the Islamic region

Some countries with large Muslim majorities have governments that follow Islamic laws and enforce them on the population. This makes life difficult for people of other religions in those countries.

Why does Islam reject secularism?

Islam requires its followers to surrender themselves to God. Islam is opposed to secularism because secular countries allow practices that are unlawful in the Koran and in God's revelation. **Sharia, or the law of God**, is binding for Muslims.

Link

The Islamic region, *Today's World 1*, page 266.

Geofact

A secular country is one where the Church and Church teachings have no influence on politics.

Definition

THEOCRACY: A government operated by religious authorities or rulers guided by religious teaching.

CASE STUDY

Islamic theocracies

Several countries that have large Muslim majorities are **theocracies** to a greater or lesser degree. These include Iran, Saudi Arabia, Sudan, Yemen, the United Arab Emirates, Pakistan and Malaysia. On the other hand, a number of countries that have a mainly Islamic population are secular, such as Turkey and Morocco.

Many laws in **theocracies** are loosely based on Sharia law:

■ Homosexuality between consenting adults is illegal in some countries.

■ Women's dress codes and roles are also dictated by Sharia law.

■ Adultery is strictly forbidden.

■ The consumption of alcohol and pork is banned in several Islamic countries.

■ Blasphemy laws are punishable by death or imprisonment in some countries.

Muslims Against Crusades (MAC) protest outside the French embassy in London over the introduction of a French ban on the facial veil.

Pakistan's blasphemy laws allow the death penalty or heavy fines for anyone insulting Islam, the Koran or the Prophet Muhammad. Pakistani Christians live in fear of being arrested under the laws, which critics say are often misused to settle personal scores or family feuds. Two senior political figures in Pakistan were assassinated in 2011 when they called for a relaxation of the blasphemy laws.

Definition

A **MADRASSA** is a school used for teaching Islamic theology and religious law.

Young boys study the Koran at a madrassa in Karachi, Pakistan.

Islamic fundamentalists want a country to be ruled on strict Sharia laws and they totally reject modern values. The Taliban who ruled in Afghanistan in the 1990s applied Sharia laws strictly. Girls were forbidden to attend school and had to completely cover themselves in public. In the 1990s, a civil war occurred in Algeria between the government and forces who

wished to create a theocracy in Algeria. This led to the deaths of 200,000 people, some of them girls in primary schools killed by fundamentalists because their parents sent them to school.

Definition

A **FUNDAMENTALIST** is a person who follows a set of beliefs very strictly and literally.

RELIGIOUS CONFLICT

Religion can be a divisive force. European history is full of examples of religious conflict. The Reformation divided Europe along religious lines in the 16th century. Many wars were fought by Catholic and Protestant forces in Europe for generations after the Reformation. German lands in particular were ravaged by those wars.

We will now examine two case studies in India and Nigeria, where religious differences have led to conflict.

CASE STUDY

Religious conflict in the Indian subcontinent

Mahatma Gandhi had been waging a peaceful campaign for Indian independence from Britain for many years. In 1945, the British government decided to quit the Indian subcontinent. However, there were major religious and ethnic differences between Hindus and Muslims in the region. The Muslims distrusted the idea of an independent united India because they believed that the Hindus – the majority group – would not share power with them.

On 16 August 1946, Muslim leaders called for a Direct Action Day in Kolkata, a city where Hindu and Muslim populations were intermingled. However, 6,000 people were killed in violence on that day.

After this, any hope of a united India was lost. The British decided that the partition of India was the only viable solution, despite Gandhi's objections. In 1947, the last viceroy, Lord Mountbatten, proposed two states:

■ India, where more than 80% of the population was Hindu
■ East and West Pakistan, which were overwhelmingly Muslim.

Muslim leaders favoured this solution. The border was drawn up by a commission led by a British lawyer, Cyril Radcliffe.

In a very short time, the border was established and partition was a done deal. However, many Hindus and Muslims found themselves on the wrong side of the new borders. Millions of Hindus who found themselves in the new Pakistan fled into India. Many Muslims in the new India fled into one of the two Pakistans. Up to 1 million people were killed in the violence that accompanied this migration. Only Gandhi's fast until death put a stop to it.

Gandhi himself was assassinated in 1948. East Pakistan became the independent Bangladesh in 1971. Tensions between Pakistan and India have simmered for decades. Both Pakistan and India have nuclear warheads.

Question

Check out the life and influence of Mahatma Gandhi on the internet.

Mahatma Gandhi, one of the most famous people of the 20th century.

Fig. 8-1-15 *India and East and West Pakistan at the time of independence in 1947.*

CASE STUDY

Sharia law in Nigeria

Nigeria has a federal government. The majority of the people in the northern states are Muslim, while the south is mostly Christian. Tensions have existed for decades between the two regions. Several aspects of Sharia law are applied in many states in northern Nigeria. This is the religious law and moral code of Islam, as laid down in the Koran. Sharia law lays down strict behaviour between the sexes. A woman found guilty of a sexual offence such as adultery may be punished by stoning or flogging. Theft may incur the amputation of a hand.

In 2002, worldwide attention was drawn to Nigeria because a woman accused of adultery, Amina Lawal, was sentenced to death by stoning in the state of Katsina in northern Nigeria. This sentence was handed down by an Islamic court in Katsina despite the fact that the Nigerian federal court found the death penalty for adultery to be unconstitutional. Ms Lawal was later released after her sentence was overturned.

In recent years, religious tensions continue to simmer in Nigeria. Boko Haram, an extremist Islamic group, want all of Nigeria to be ruled in accordance with Sharia law. They have targeted Christian churches on symbolic days such as Christmas Day. Many people have been killed in explosions while attending religious ceremonies. The group has attacked the UN headquarters in Nigeria.

Economics also come into the tension between Muslims and Christians. The people of northern Muslim states are much poorer than those in the south, with up to 70% unemployment. Northern Muslims suspect that the federal government in the south is corrupt and that oil money is pocketed by corrupt officials in the largely Christian south. The government cannot provide large areas of Nigeria with electricity or clean water in spite of the massive taxes from oil revenues. In addition to religious tensions, ethnic tensions between many of the country's 250 ethnic groups continue to claim lives.

'Each day, Nigerians are forced to accept new depths of crudity and violence as the norm,' wrote columnist Okey Ndibe at the end of December 2011 in the *Daily Sun* newspaper. 'We are in danger of becoming a country where the slaughter of hundreds, even thousands, of defenceless citizens is deemed a normal fact of life.'

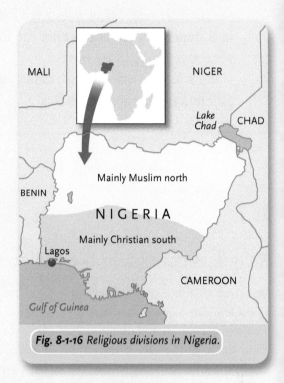

Fig. 8-1-16 *Religious divisions in Nigeria.*

Link

Religious conflict in Northern Ireland, pages 250–2.

Question

Explain how religion influenced political events in the Indian subcontinent at the time of independence in 1947.

EVERYDAY EXPRESSIONS OF CULTURE

People express their culture and identity in many ways through their language, religion, costume, folk stories, music, dance and sport. These give people a sense of identity and of belonging. Culture gives people a sense of their uniqueness as a group.

CASE STUDY

Everyday culture and identity in Ireland

Music and dance

Music and dance are important expressions of Irish culture in everyday life. Irish jigs, reels and hornpipes are unique. Irish traditional music is heard on radio and television (especially TG4) and in other places of entertainment. It has been played in venues throughout the world, from the US to China and Japan, by groups such as the Chieftains, Planxty and Stockton's Wing.

Thousands of Irish children learn the tin whistle, concertina, *bosca ceoil* and fiddle. Parents take great pride as they see the traditions of Irish music passed on to the next generation.

The Gaeltacht areas in particular have enriched Irish culture, with sean-nós dancing and singing. When a sean-nós dancer is in harmony with the music, her/his dancing is the physical expression of the music. Sean-nós singing is sung without accompaniment and often expresses a lament for fishermen lost at sea and other local topics.

Festivals such as the Willie Clancy Summer School in Miltown Malbay give musicians an opportunity to display their talents before local people and tourists. Most festivals have an important tutorial aspect. Young musicians sit at the feet of the masters and learn their skills. Many of the festivals also attract large numbers of foreign tourists who have an interest in Irish music and dance.

Triúr cailín dea-ghléasta ag damhsa.

CASE STUDY

OPTION 8 – CULTURE AND IDENTITY

Fleadh Ceoil na hÉireann is a major celebration of Irish culture and is attended by thousands annually. Competitors from Ireland and abroad perform either individually or as groups for much-coveted All-Ireland titles in singing, dancing and instruments.

Sport

People express their sense of Irish identity through sport, especially through the national games of hurling, Gaelic football and camogie. The GAA, established in 1884, is possibly the greatest **amateur sporting organisation** in the world. Apart from a small number of administrative staff in Croke Park, the organisation depends on thousands of volunteers who train teams both at underage and senior levels.

The GAA is an important social outlet for many people and championship matches arouse intense interest and rivalry between parishes and inter-county teams. Teams represent their own parish or county and therefore are territorial.

All-Ireland finals in Croke Park are great cultural occasions when

Michael Flatley and the Riverdance group have brought Irish music and dancing to the world.

the best of GAA sporting talent is showcased. Finals are followed closely by Irish expatriates all over the world on TV. They provide Irish people living abroad with an important link with home. In fact, from Sydney to Seoul, the GAA is important to Irish exiles and much of their social life revolves around GAA activities. The Asian Gaelic Games tournaments have been held since 1996 and more than 50 teams now take part. This indicates how important the GAA is to the sense of identity of the Irish abroad.

Rugby, soccer, cricket and other international sports are played in Ireland and arouse great enthusiasm and a sense of pride in the success of Irish national and provincial teams.

Religion

The practice of religion is also an important aspect of Irish culture. The great majority of the people of the Republic of Ireland are baptised Catholics. In earlier centuries, most Irish people remained loyal to Rome, partly as a means of resisting British rule and British culture. Young men were educated in France and Spain to serve as priests in Ireland. Mass rocks date from Elizabethan times in the 16th century. These mass rocks were in remote places where mass could be celebrated. Attendance at mass gave Irish communities a sense of solidarity and strengthened their resistance to British rule.

The All-Ireland Hurling Final in September 2012 between Kilkenny and Galway.

238

A mass rock on the Beara peninsula in Co. Cork.

Activity

Examine Fig. 5·5·2 on page 94. Locate the mass rock at O 075 846.

Definition

SHROVE: The weeks before Lent, ending on Shrove Tuesday.

The practice of religion is an important aspect of the social calendar of many Catholics, even today. Until recently, mass attendance on Sunday was among the highest in the Catholic world. Twice only in the 20th century, **1 million people** came together, both times in Phoenix Park – to celebrate the 1932 Eucharistic Congress and to greet Pope John Paul II in 1979.

Traditionally, young Catholic couples married during Shrove, as weddings did not occur during Lent. People even now abstain from items such as cigarettes, chocolate and alcohol during Lent. Catholics get their throats blessed on St Blaise's Day.

Knock, Co. Mayo, is a famous Marian shrine that thousands of pilgrims visit every year. Croagh Patrick is Ireland's holy mountain and climbing the Reek is very popular, especially on the last Sunday in July.

Many family events such as First Communion and Confirmation centre around religious activities. Catholics' birth and death revolve around the Church. Funeral masses are attended by large numbers of family and friends.

Today, Catholic culture is not as significant as it was even 30 years ago for many reasons that include abuse scandals. However, churches are packed for midnight mass at Christmas and Easter.

The Church of Ireland and the Islamic community are small but significant groups in Ireland. For the Islamic community in particular, religion is central to their culture.

Leaving Cert Exam Questions

1   Examine the impact of colonisation and migration on racial patterns. (80 marks)

2   Examine how migration can impact on racial patterns. (80 marks)

3   Examine **two** of the challenges created by international migration. (80 marks)

4   Discuss the role of migration in any European region you have studied. (80 marks)

5   Examine the impact of colonisation on racial distribution. (80 marks)

6   'Religion can be a divisive as well as a unifying force.' Discuss with reference to examples that you have studied. (80 marks)

7   'The influence of religion on politics varies from time to time and from region to region.' Discuss this statement with reference to examples you have studied. (80 marks)

8   Examine the significance of **either** language **or** religion as a cultural indicator. (80 marks)

9   Examine the importance of language as a cultural indicator. (80 marks)

10 'The Gaeltacht areas are distinctive cultural regions.' Discuss. (80 marks)

11 Multiculturalism is common in the modern world. Examine how multiculturalism may lead to conflict or may be a unifying force. (80 marks)

12 'Conflicts can occur between national governments and cultural groups.' Discuss. (80 marks)

13 Discuss how people express their culture and identity in everyday life. (80 marks)

Nationality and the nation state

Nationality and the nation state are political entities placed on the physical and cultural landscape. Because many states contain different cultural groups, complex issues and conflicts arise.

Learning objectives

After studying this chapter, you should be able to understand:

- the meaning of the words 'nationality' and 'nation state'
- the various types of political boundaries
- that many states have cultural minorities
- that many groups, such as the Kurds and the Basques, wish to have their own states
- that conflict sometimes occurs between cultural minorities and the states in which they find themselves.

NATIONALITY AND THE NATION STATE

What is a nation?

A nation or a national group is a community of people with a sense of common identity. People with a common identity share a common history that binds them together. They may share the same language, customs and religion (but not always). The French and the Danes are examples of nations or national groups.

What is a state?

A state is an independent political entity with a sovereign territory within clearly defined boundaries. These boundaries are recognised by other states. In Ireland, a border marks the boundary between the Republic of Ireland and Northern Ireland.

What is a nation state?

A nation state is an ideal that rarely exists, where people of only one cultural group are governed in their own state. Iceland and Japan are examples of such a state. In reality, most states have some cultural minorities.

PHYSICAL AND POLITICAL BOUNDARIES

A boundary is the demarcation line that separates countries from each other. It can be a physical boundary or an imaginary line, such as a line of latitude.

Physical boundaries

■ **Mountains:** The Pyrenees form the boundary between France and Spain; the Alps between Italy and France; and the Andes between Chile and Argentina.

■ **Rivers and lakes:** The Rhine forms part of the boundary between France and Germany. Lake Geneva forms part of the boundary between France and Switzerland. The Great Lakes form part of the boundary between the US and Canada.

■ **Seas:** The English Channel separates France from the UK. The eastern border of the Republic of Ireland is separated from Britain by the Irish Sea.

Fig. 8-2-1 *The political boundaries of Europe.*

Questions

1. Name the sea boundary that separates the Republic of Ireland from the UK.
2. What physical feature forms the boundary between France and Spain?
3. Name two sea straits that form boundaries between countries in Europe.
4. Name the river that forms part of the boundary between France and Germany.
5. Name the river that forms the boundary between Romania and Bulgaria.
6. Why are boundaries of little relevance today in Western Europe?

The Pyrenees are an effective physical boundary between France and Spain.

Geofact
Internal boundaries within the EU are far less important today than in the past. A key aim of the EU is the free movement of goods, capital and people between member states. As the EU has become more integrated, barriers and checks at boundary crossings between member states have all but disappeared. Internal boundaries are obsolete in the EU today.

The effectiveness of physical boundaries

In the past, countries sought natural barriers such as mountains that offered protection from an attack by their neighbours. Boundaries are effective if they are not disputed by neighbouring countries.

Some physical boundaries are/were effective, others are not. The **English Channel** and the Strait of Dover were an effective natural boundary for Britain against Nazi aggression during World War II. Britain's island position protected it from Nazi occupation.

Today, with Europe at peace for many decades, Britain no longer fears for its security from Europe. The Channel Tunnel links Britain with mainland Europe. Today in the EU, what matters are transport links rather than barriers and boundaries.

Mountains are effective barriers but only if they are high. Switzerland, a country guarded by the Alps and Jura Mountains, was only one of five European countries whose neutrality was not violated during World War II. Switzerland emerged unscathed even though it lay between Germany and Italy, who were allied together. Switzerland was well prepared to repel invasion behind its mountain defences.

High mountains divide cultural groups and are therefore more likely to be accepted as natural boundaries by rulers. The Pyrenees divide France and Spain effectively. The boundary of the Alps between French and Italian cultures is not in dispute.

Geofact
Boundaries today offer far less security to a country than in the past. Modern warfare is now largely conducted by air forces that can fly into enemy territory. This was evident during World War II and the Vietnam War. The attack on the Twin Towers in 9/11 took place from within the US by terrorists who had migrated to the US.

Rivers are not effective barriers. Unlike mountains, riverbanks are natural meeting places for trade. People living on opposite banks can share the same culture. The Rhine forms part of the border between France and Germany and the people of Alsace in France speak a German dialect, which helps to explain why Alsace was occupied by Germany twice since 1871.

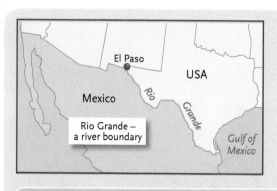

The Rio Grande
This river forms part of the boundary between Mexico and the US. However, over the years, meanders and seasonal flooding cause the river channel to change course. The result is that small sections of the boundary do not follow the course of the river.

Fig. 8-2-2 *The Rio Grande boundary between Mexico and the US.*

Political boundaries – boundaries based on political decisions

These include the following:

- The 49th parallel between the US and Canada, an agreed boundary that is not in dispute
- The 38th parallel between North and South Korea, a boundary that has divided people of the same culture since the end of the Korean War. This boundary separates communist North Korea from free market South Korea
- Colonial boundaries in Africa created by colonial powers.

The weaknesses of some politically agreed boundaries are clear in an examination of African boundaries and of the boundary between North and South in Ireland.

Geofact

Southern Sudan became Africa's newest state in 2011.

African boundaries

Many African boundaries are relatively ineffective. They were drawn up between colonial powers without any reference to local tribal peoples. Some boundaries are simply straight lines on the map. In many instances, they do not follow physical features that create natural barriers between peoples and cultures. When colonies received their independence in the 1960s, a number of new countries experienced terrible civil wars between tribal groups. These

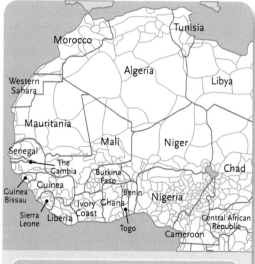

Fig. 8-2-3 *The political map of West and North-west Africa. The boundaries in blue do not at all coincide with the tribal groups, shown in a light brown colour.*

included Nigeria, the Congo, Rwanda and in recent years, Sudan. Civil wars plunged these countries into chaos, led to terrible loss of life and slowed the development of those countries for years.

Israel's Separation Wall in the West Bank.

Activity
Find out about the Separation Wall and why the Israelis built it.

CASE STUDY

The boundary between Northern Ireland and the Republic of Ireland – an effective political boundary?

Ireland has two major cultural groups, Nationalists and Unionists. Unionists are concentrated in north-east Ulster. As the 20th century dawned, Nationalists outnumbered Unionists by more than three to one in the island of Ireland as a whole.

Under British rule, Ireland was ruled as one colony. However, extreme Nationalists – Republicans – in the South organised the 1916 Rising in their aspiration for political independence for Ireland. Unionists did not wish to be ruled by a Dublin government that would be overwhelmingly Catholic. Unionists believed the Pope would interfere in Irish political affairs.

The Government of Ireland Act, 1920
This is also known as the Partition Act. Under this Act, the Unionists of Ulster received six counties in Ulster. The Unionists would have autonomy in local affairs such as education and policing. However, they would remain part of the UK.

The Treaty of Ireland Act of 1921 gave independence to a 26-county Southern Irish state. Ireland had effectively been **partitioned**.

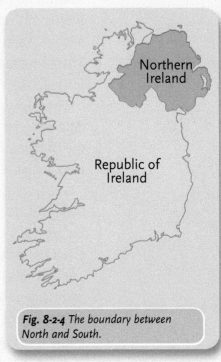

Fig. 8-2-4 *The boundary between North and South.*

CASE STUDY

The border

The border between North and South is a **subsequent boundary**, i.e. a boundary that is drawn up after cultural groups have settled in a region. The border is made up of county boundaries that were drawn up in the 13th century. The border bears little relationship to physical features or cultural groups. Two hundred roads cross the border and it even runs through some farms. The border is an unsatisfactory boundary because it does a poor job of dividing Unionists and Nationalists. A large Nationalist minority (now more than 600,000) lives north of the border, where they suffered discrimination for decades after

1920. Unionists in Donegal, Cavan and Monaghan found themselves in the South with prospects that were quite daunting for many of them. While many people from the Unionist tradition have remained in the South, several families have emigrated to Britain over time.

The smuggling of cigarettes, cattle, laundered goods and other goods across the border has been a problem for customs officers on both sides of the border. In addition, the border was porous in terms of security. Many times during the Troubles that began in the 1970s, militant Republicans crossed the border from the South to commit acts of violence in the North.

Question
Examine the effectiveness of the political boundary between North and South.

Link
Cultural regions: Northern Ireland, *Today's World 1*, page 267.

CULTURAL GROUPS WITHIN STATES

The Basques

Many minority cultural groups live within states. Examples include the Nationalist minority in Northern Ireland and the Catalans and Basques in Spain. We will now examine the fortunes of the Basque cultural group in Spain. The Basques are a unique cultural group who live on each side of the Western Pyrenees between France and Spain. The great majority of Basque people live in Spain. The Basques have their own language and traditions. Their language, Euskara, is older than the Romance languages of Italian, Spanish, Catalan and French.

The Basques lived in the mountains and valleys of the Western Pyrenees long before the growth of the Roman empire. The Romans never conquered the Basques. Thus, their language and culture survived. The Basques call their region Euskadi.

Geofact
Basques live in France as far as Bayonne.

Political hostilities with Spain

Before the Spanish Civil War (1936–39), the Republican government had given the Basque people greater control, or autonomy, over their local affairs. The Nationalists called in General Franco to overthrow the Republican government because they feared a break-up of Spain. General Franco had no patience with regional autonomy for the Basques or Catalans. During the civil war, the Basque people suffered severely. The town of Guernica was flattened by Hitler's Luftwaffe, which was called in by Franco in his efforts to win the civil war, with great loss of life.

Link
The Islamic minority in France, page 63.

The repression of Basque culture

After Franco's victory, Basque leaders crossed the border into France. Franco banned the Basque flag, Basque regional holidays, the speaking of the Basque language in public places and the teaching of Basque in school. As some Basques reacted with violence against these measures, imprisonment and executions of Basque people became commonplace.

The Basques after Franco

Franco died in 1975. The new king, Juan Carlos, released Basque political prisoners. The Basque region was granted a large measure of political autonomy that fell far short of independence. An extremist Basque separatist group, ETA, used violence against the Spanish government in Madrid to achieve its aim of Basque independence. This led to the violent deaths of more than 800 people over the years.

However, the co-operation of the Spanish and French governments succeeded in the arrest of many ETA leaders, hundreds of whom were still in jail in 2012. The low support in the Basque region for their campaign of violence also weakened ETA.

On 20 October 2011, ETA declared a 'definitive end' to its 'armed activity'. The years ahead are likely to see a political resolution to the question of Basque political aspirations.

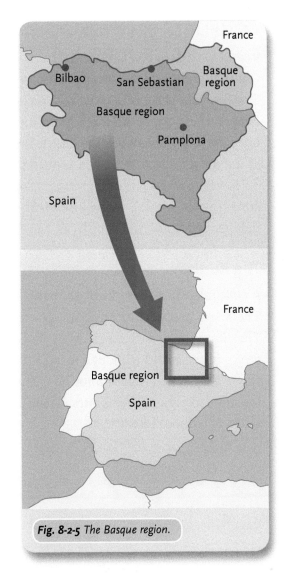

Fig. 8-2-5 *The Basque region.*

A sign in the Basque language in the Basque territory.

CONFLICTS BETWEEN POLITICAL STRUCTURES AND CULTURAL GROUPS

Cultural groups have a strong sense of cultural identity. The Czechs and the Slovaks were part of the state of Czechoslovakia for much of the 20th century. However, in 1992, both cultural groups chose to go their separate ways and to form two separate states, the Czech Republic and Slovakia. This was known as the Velvet Revolution. The break-up was achieved peacefully.

However, many cultural groups resort to violence to achieve their political aims. In this context, we will examine **conflict in the Kurdish struggle for independence** and **the conflict in Northern Ireland**.

The Kurds

A cultural group spread across many states

The Kurds are a distinct cultural group of 25 million people in Western Asia. They have no state of their own. Indeed, they may be the largest cultural group in the world without a state. Kurds live in Turkey, Syria, Iran and Iraq, where they are sizeable minorities. They have their own language and are Muslims like their neighbours. Their language helps to maintain their strong sense of cultural identity.

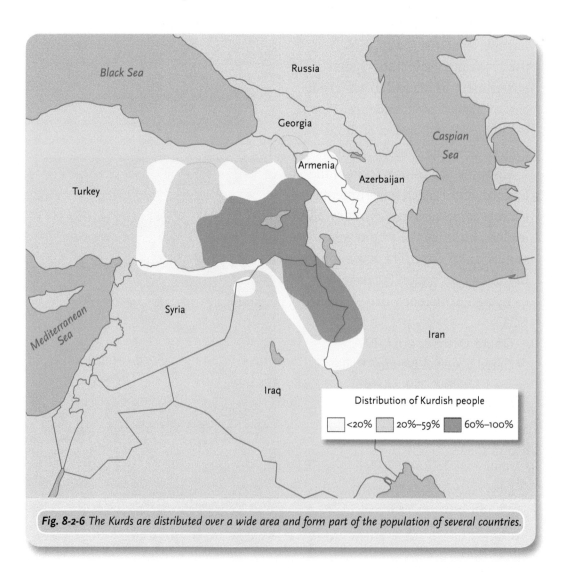

Fig. 8-2-6 *The Kurds are distributed over a wide area and form part of the population of several countries.*

It has been said of the Kurds that no country wants them in their territory and yet no country wants to give them a state of their own. This is because none of the states in the region wants to surrender territory to a new Kurdish state. Before 1919, the Kurds were part of the large Ottoman (Turkish) empire ruled from the city then known as Constantinople. However, at the Paris Peace Conference, when the Ottoman empire was broken up, the Kurds did not receive their own state.

Turkish Prime Minister, Recep Tayyip Erdogan, and President of the Kurdistan Region of Iraq, Massoud Barzani, shake hands before their meeting in Istanbul, Turkey 19 April 2012.

The Kurds in Turkey

More Kurds live in Turkey than in any other country. The Kurds have had a difficult relationship with the Turkish government. Turkey continues to deny that they are a separate cultural group and Kurds are referred to as Mountain Turks. Kurds who spoke their own language were committing a crime by doing so until 1991.

During the 1990s, militant Kurdish separatists, the PKK, conducted a campaign of violence against Turkey. This was severely repressed by Turkey, which razed hundreds of Kurdish villages and tortured and killed Kurdish leaders. Many Kurds fled across the border into Iran and Iraq, where they launched attacks against Turkish forces.

What do the Turkish Kurds want today?

Kurds are aware that, in the immediate future, an independent Kurdish state is beyond their reach. Their **wish list** includes the following:

- regional autonomy for the Kurdish people in Turkey
- education through the medium of the Kurdish language
- an amnesty for PKK prisoners and an end to repressive laws that crowd the jails with Kurdish political prisoners.

Since Turkey became a candidate country to join the EU, the EU has taken a great interest in Turkey's treatment of the Kurds. Turkey has softened its policy towards Kurds in recent years.

In the meantime, the Kurdish problem continues and is likely to remain a source of tension in Turkey and neighbouring states for the foreseeable future.

The conflict in Northern Ireland – a conflict based on religious differences between cultural groups

Why did conflict occur in Northern Ireland?

Northern Ireland is composed of two cultural groups, which are divided by religion: Unionists, who are Protestant, and Nationalists, who are Catholic. Religion has divided the people of Northern Ireland for 400 years. In 1920, when Nationalists all over Ireland were fighting for national independence, Unionists were alarmed. They did not want to be ruled by a Catholic government in Dublin. The Unionists wanted to maintain strong political links with Britain. The Government of Ireland Act gave them what they wanted: Unionists in the six counties of Ulster were given the state of Northern Ireland with control of its internal affairs. This state remained part of Britain. Therefore, the Nationalists who lived in the six counties found themselves being ruled from Belfast when in fact they wished to be part of the southern Nationalist state.

Stormont Castle, the seat of government in Northern Ireland.

Life for the Nationalist minority in Northern Ireland

Nationalists were distrusted by the Unionists of the North. The North became **a Protestant state for a Protestant people** – a fact Britain chose to ignore. Nationalists were discriminated against in housing, jobs, promotion prospects and political representation. The redrawing of political constituencies in a process known as gerrymandering meant that Nationalists were under-represented in politics. The Unionist party ruled Northern Ireland for decade after decade to the advantage of the Protestant community.

The civil rights movement – late 1960s

After more than 40 years of discrimination, the Nationalist minority began to seek basic rights that had been denied them for so long. A series of civil rights marches led to clashes between Unionist and Nationalist communities. The Royal Ulster Constabulary (RUC) was not up to the task of protecting the marchers.

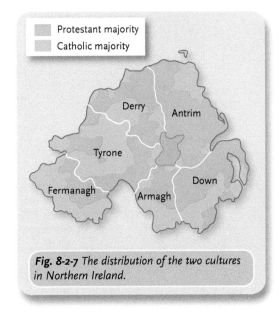

Protestant majority
Catholic majority

Fig. 8-2-7 *The distribution of the two cultures in Northern Ireland.*

The descent into violence

The British army was brought to Northern Ireland to restore peace. The Provisional IRA (Irish Republican Army), known as the Provos, emerged from the Nationalist community. The Provos were Republicans whose agenda was to drive the British out of Northern Ireland and establish a 32-county state. Loyalist (Unionist) paramilitaries opposed them. Soon, violence became commonplace and was to last for the next 25 years. As many as 3,500 people lost their lives.

Direct rule

The Unionist government of Northern Ireland responded with internment without trial to quell violence. This was a conspicuous failure because it aroused strong resentment in the Nationalist community. The British government introduced direct rule from Westminster.

Sinn Féin

The Provos waged a propaganda war to swing public opinion at home and abroad. Republican prisoners began a campaign of hunger strikes and other protests. Bobby Sands, who died as a result of a hunger strike, became widely known across the world. His hunger strike put huge pressure on the British government to find a political solution to Northern Ireland.

Violence in the British mainland

Nationalist paramilitaries brought the campaign of violence to Britain. The Canary Wharf bombings in London and the Brighton bombing when the British Conservative Cabinet was targeted rocked communities in Britain and Ireland. The Provos proved that they could penetrate the tightest British security.

Link
The boundary between North and South, pages 245–6.

Link
The Northern Ireland region, *Today's World 1*, page 267.

Definition
POWER SHARING: Both Unionist and Nationalist parties form the government.

A mural on a gable-end wall in a Protestant area of Belfast.

A political solution

Nevertheless, by the mid-1990s, Republican paramilitaries had realised that a military victory was beyond their reach. John Hume worked behind the scenes with Gerry Adams, leader of Sinn Féin, to reach a political solution in Northern Ireland. The IRA ceasefire was followed by the Good Friday Agreement, to be established in 1998. Under this agreement, the British and Irish governments helped to broker a power-sharing deal across the political divide in the North.

In the years that followed, militant organisations in the North put their weapons beyond use. The Police Service of Northern Ireland (PSNI)

A memorial to IRA dead in West Belfast in 2008.

became the new police force. Sinn Féin recognised the PSNI in 2007 and encouraged Nationalists to co-operate with and join the PSNI.

The power-sharing executive, with the Democratic Unionist Party (DUP) and Sinn Féin sharing power, has seen the continued **devolution**, or transfer, of powers from Westminster to Stormont, the seat of government in the North.

The Titanic Quarter in Belfast. The ghosts of the past are receding as a new Belfast emerges.

 # Leaving Cert Exam Questions

1. 'Cultural groups and national borders do not always coincide.' Discuss. (80 marks)

2. Many states have different cultural/ethnic groups within their borders. Examine how these groups relate to one another with reference to examples you have studied. (80 marks)

3. 'Conflicts exist between political structures and cultural groups.' Discuss this statement with reference to examples you have studied. (80 marks)

4. Examine the effects of political boundaries on cultural groups. (80 marks)

5. Examine, with reference to examples you have studied, the relative effectiveness of boundaries on **both** features of the physical landscape and political decisions. (80 marks)

Cultural identity in the modern state

You are required to examine a case study of a European region that draws together issues of race, nationality and identity that have been examined throughout Option 8. We will examine Switzerland, a case study suggested in the syllabus.

Learning objectives

After studying this chapter, you should be able to understand:

- that Switzerland has considerable cultural diversity but has successfully created a sense of national identity

- that the Swiss nation developed over time

- that the Swiss have strong cultural traditions

- that inward migration has political consequences in Switzerland today.

SWITZERLAND – A SENSE OF IDENTITY

Switzerland is not a linguistic or religious unit. It has four languages (German, French, Italian and Romansch) and two religions (Protestantism and Catholicism), which each have many followers in Switzerland. However, the Swiss people are a nation in spite of these differences because they have a shared sense of identity. Temperamentally, the Swiss are seen as rugged, disciplined and with a strong work ethos.

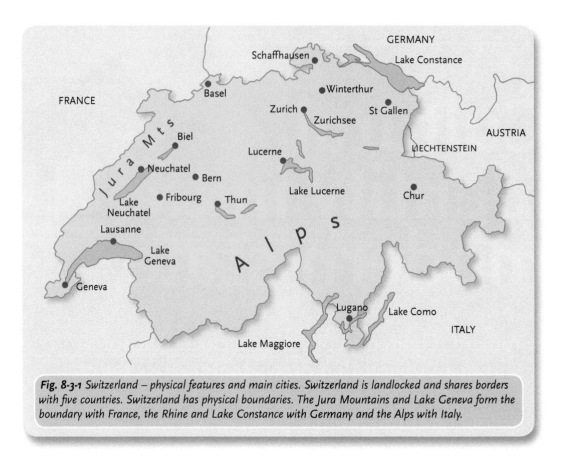

Fig. 8-3-1 *Switzerland – physical features and main cities. Switzerland is landlocked and shares borders with five countries. Switzerland has physical boundaries. The Jura Mountains and Lake Geneva form the boundary with France, the Rhine and Lake Constance with Germany and the Alps with Italy.*

Geofact
38%: The percentage of Swiss people who are Protestant.
44%: The percentage of Swiss people who are Catholic.

WHAT IS THE SECRET OF THEIR SUCCESS IN NATION-BUILDING?

The answer lies in their shared history, their political system, their neutrality abroad and their tolerance of cultural differences.

Swiss history

Swiss cantons, or counties, began to join together as early as the 13th century. In 1291, the Swiss Confederation was formed by three cantons that came together for their common protection. Over several centuries, other cantons joined the confederation until the total number of cantons reached 26 in the 19th century.

However, throughout these centuries, bitter religious wars were fought between Catholics and Protestants, especially during the Reformation in the 16th century. Even as recently as the 1840s, religious conflict threatened to destroy the confederation.

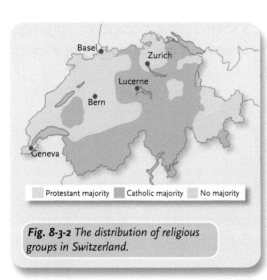

Protestant majority   Catholic majority   No majority

Fig. 8-3-2 *The distribution of religious groups in Switzerland.*

Nevertheless, in 1848, the cantons came together to establish the Federal Constitution. This divided powers between the national government in Bern and the cantons.

The 600th anniversary of the confederation was celebrated in 1891. After this date, Swiss people began to forge a real sense of identity and became proud of being Swiss.

The Swiss political system

As already stated, the Swiss political system is federal. The national government controls coinage, postal services, foreign affairs, the national army and the national budget. The Swiss federal government meets in Bern.

Each canton has its own constitution, parliament, government, courts and educational system. The people have real political power with strong democratic foundations. Referendums are held regularly on many matters of national and local interest. For instance, after a referendum, women were granted the right to vote in canton elections in 1959 and in federal elections only as recently as 1971. The Swiss have a strong loyalty to the cantons in which they live. The Swiss are quite conservative.

Definition

FEDERAL SYSTEM:
Political powers are split between the federal (national) and local governments. The US, Germany and Belgium have federal systems of government.

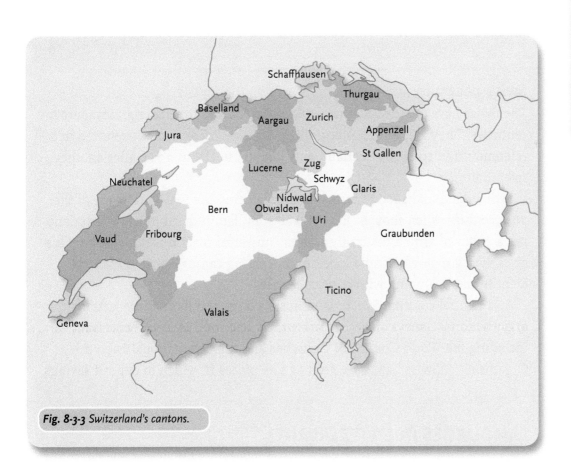

Fig. 8-3-3 *Switzerland's cantons.*

Memorial to William Tell in a Swiss town.

The power of legend
The Swiss, in common with many other countries, celebrate their hero – William Tell. According to legend, William Tell helped to free Swiss cantons from Austrian rule. Tell refused to accept Austrian rule and was seized by the bailiff, Hermann Gessler. As a punishment, he was ordered to shoot an apple from his son's head. Tell split the apple in two and later killed Gessler.

Whether Tell existed or not is a matter of debate. The legend of William Tell serves as a way of embodying Swiss independence in a single heroic figure.

Question

Do you think the Swiss were wise not to join the EU in 1992? Explain your answer.

Swiss neutrality

The Swiss have guarded their mountainous country from foreign invaders for centuries. They are not members of the EU – membership was rejected in a referendum in 1992. Switzerland only joined the UN in 2002 after another referendum.

Switzerland managed to remain neutral during the two world wars of the 20th century, when most of Europe was engulfed in the conflict. Switzerland has a policy of armed neutrality and has universal male military service. This gives young men who come together in training camps a strong sense of identity and belonging with their colleagues.

As a neutral country, Switzerland hosts a large number of international organisations. Geneva alone has more than 200 international organisations, including the World Council of Churches and the International Labour Organisation. Swiss banks are seen as safe places in which to deposit savings.

LANGUAGES IN SWITZERLAND

Four languages are spoken in Switzerland. German is the most widely spoken, followed by French. Italian is spoken in the province of Ticino. Romansch, a language derived from Latin, is a minority language in the south-east. Many Swiss are bilingual or even trilingual and official documents of the federal government are published in each language. The Swiss honour cultural differences.

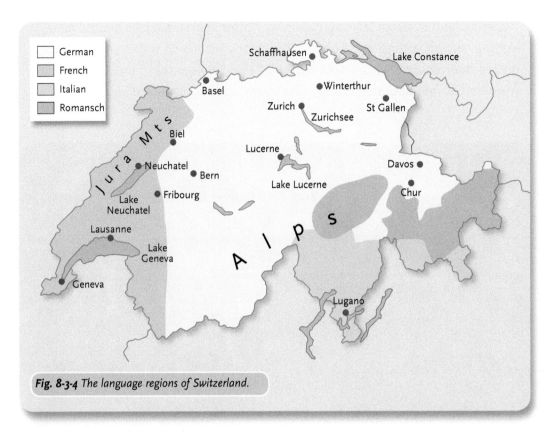

Fig. 8-3-4 *The language regions of Switzerland.*

CULTURAL ACTIVITIES

As a people who are cut off by mountains from their neighbours, the Swiss have developed distinct traditions in sport, festivals and music.

Sport

The Alpine region has distinct sports, including:

- *schwingen*, an Alpine type of wrestling
- *waffenlauf*, a long-distance race
- cow fights in agricultural valleys
- curling, a game played on ice by two teams.

Activity

Check out on the internet the activities listed on the left.

Swiss alphorn players. The Swiss are a very rugged people, proud of their ability to survive harsh winters in the mountains.

Switzerland is also a leading nation in winter sports, such as skiing, ice skating, snowboarding and bobsledding. Many resorts in the country have hosted international winter sports events. The Swiss excel in these events and winners become national heroes. The country has a respected soccer team.

Swiss cowherds in traditional costume bringing the cows down from the high mountain pastures for the winter in the town of Lenk.

Festivals

The Swiss love festivals. The country unites to celebrate their national day on 1 August every year. Many rural areas have their own local festivals. Cows are important farm animals and are honoured in spring and autumn every year for their importance to the rural economy.

Carnivals are held before Lent. These include parades by local bands in traditional costumes, masked parades and street dancing.

The Swiss also host international festivals, including:

- the Lucerne Festival of classical music
- the Montreux Jazz Festival
- the International Jazz Festival in Bern
- the Locarno Film Festival
- music festivals in Bern and St Gallen.

THE CHALLENGES POSED BY INWARD MIGRATION

The Swiss did well in the 20th century. The country avoided two world wars and standards of living were among the highest in the world. In the later decades of the 20th century, inward migrants have been needed to fill job vacancies, especially in lower-paid jobs. These mainly came from Mediterranean countries such as Italy, Turkey and Greece.

In recent years, asylum seekers from the war-torn Balkans and from Sub-Saharan Africa have sought asylum in Switzerland. Many have received refugee status. Therefore, Switzerland now has several racial and cultural minorities.

The SVP (Swiss People's Party) – a right-wing party

The presence of foreign cultures has led to the increasing popularity of the SVP, a right-wing party. This party has an anti-immigration stance and blames immigrants for much of the country's crime. The SVP is adept at persuading people that the increasing number of immigrants is a threat to Swiss cultural identity. The SVP has gained up to 29% of the national vote in elections in recent years. The SVP has succeeded in banning minarets from Muslim mosques, through a referendum. The Swiss have a high tolerance of cultural differences between the local Swiss cultures, but many of them have yet to extend that tolerance to races and cultures that have recently come in from abroad.

Therefore, in spite of its prosperity, Switzerland has not escaped much of the turbulence of the modern world.

Leaving Cert Exam Questions

1   'Cultural identity is defined by many diverse factors.' Discuss this statement with reference to **one** case study of a European region you have studied. (80 marks)

Today's World 3
OPTION 9

The atmosphere–ocean environment

9.1

The atmosphere–ocean environment

The atmosphere and oceans are linked systems. The atmosphere affects the oceans, for example when winds drive the surface ocean currents. The oceans in turn influence the atmosphere because of their ability to store huge quantities of heat and moisture. The atmosphere and oceans have physical characteristics that can be observed and recorded.

Learning objectives

After studying this chapter, you should be able to understand:

■ the composition and structure of the atmosphere and oceans

■ how to measure atmospheric and oceanic data.

THE ATMOSPHERE

The atmosphere is the envelope of colourless, odourless and tasteless gases that surrounds Earth.

The atmosphere:

■ absorbs energy from the sun to give us heat

■ transports heat energy from the tropics towards the polar regions, thus moderating temperatures

■ filters out harmful ultraviolet rays through its ozone layer

■ protects us from the cold vacuum of outer space

■ protects us from space debris such as meteorites

■ provides conditions that are suitable to support life.

Composition of the atmosphere

The atmosphere is composed mainly of nitrogen (78%) and oxygen (21%). Other gases present in minute quantities include radon, ozone, water vapour, carbon dioxide and methane.

Carbon dioxide and methane are greenhouse gases that regulate the temperature of the atmosphere.

Not all these gases are good gases. Radon, produced by the decay of uranium, can cause cancer.

Geofact

The water cycle, which constantly recycles Earth's water supplies, could not exist without the atmosphere.

The atmosphere also contains some solids. These include volcanic ash, dust, salt and ice particles.

Structure of the atmosphere

The atmosphere is divided into four main **layers**. As you move upwards through the layers, atmospheric pressure decreases rapidly with height and the air temperature also changes. At the upper end of the atmosphere there is no clear boundary, as the gases get thinner and thinner and drift off into space.

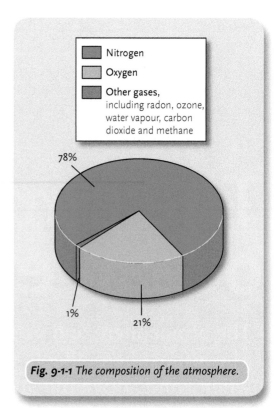

Nitrogen

Oxygen

Other gases, including radon, ozone, water vapour, carbon dioxide and methane

78%

1%

21%

Fig. 9-1-1 *The composition of the atmosphere.*

Geofact
50% of air is found in the lowest 6 km of atmosphere.

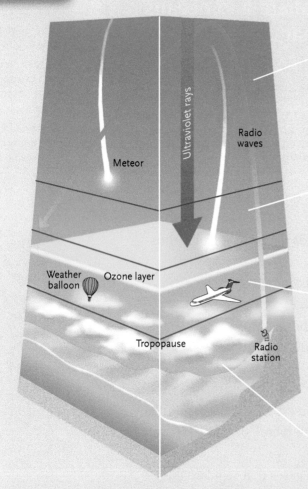

Ultraviolet rays

Radio waves

Meteor

Weather balloon

Ozone layer

Tropopause

Radio station

Fig. 9-1-2 *The layers of the atmosphere are separated from one another by pauses.*

Thermosphere
- The thermosphere extends to a height of about 600 km above Earth.
- Temperature increases with altitude and can reach 2,000°C at the top. Even so, you wouldn't feel warm because it is almost a vacuum.
- The aurora borealis (northern lights) occur in the thermosphere.
- The International Space Station orbits here.

Mesosphere
- The mesosphere does not contain clouds, dust or ozone.
- Temperatures decrease with altitude to about −90°C.
- Meteors burn up here (shooting stars).
- It has the strongest winds in the atmosphere (up to 3,000 km/hr).

Stratosphere
- The stratosphere is a cloudless layer of thin, dry air.
- It contains about 20% of the atmosphere's gases.
- The temperature increases with altitude because the ozone layer absorbs sunlight.
- The ozone layer also absorbs harmful ultraviolet rays from the sun.
- It is a very calm layer of the atmosphere.

Troposphere
- The troposphere varies in height from 8 km at the poles to about 18 km at the equator.
- It contains about 75% of the atmosphere's gases.
- It is normally warmest at ground level, with temperature dropping by about 7°C for every 1,000 m increase in altitude.
- It contains most of the atmosphere's water vapour and pollution.
- The tropopause acts like an invisible barrier, so most weather processes occur within the troposphere.

Measuring atmospheric conditions

Atmospheric conditions are observed and measured in order to try to find a pattern or trend. This will assist in forecasting what may happen in the future, i.e. getting an accurate weather forecast.

Among the conditions that can be measured are:

- atmospheric pressure
- temperature
- humidity
- wind speed and direction.

Atmospheric condition	Instrument	How it operates
Atmospheric pressure is measured by a **barometer** or a **barograph** (a barometer that produces a printout).		Changes in atmospheric pressure cause a bellows-like vacuum chamber (at centre) to expand or contract.
The unit of measurement is **millibars** (mb) or **hectopascals** (hPa).		As the pressure varies, a series of levers and gears, linked to the vacuum chamber, move the recording arm. The tip of the recording arm has an inkwell.
		A recording sheet is mounted on a cylinder. The cylinder, powered by a spring, revolves slowly (once per week).
		The atmospheric pressure is inked onto the recording sheet.
Temperature is measured by a **thermometer**.	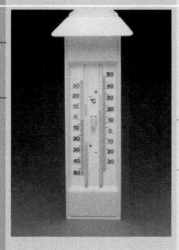	It consists of a U-shaped glass tube with temperature scales set along each arm of the U. One is for showing the maximum temperature and the other for the minimum temperature.
The thermometer shown is a **Six's maximum and minimum thermometer**.		
The unit of measurement is degrees Celsius (°C) or Fahrenheit (°F).		The tip of the mercury column in either arm indicates the current temperature.
		The maximum and minimum temperatures are indicated by a metal pin in each arm, since these have been pushed up as the temperature rose or fell.

Table 9-1-1 Measuring atmospheric conditions.

Geofact
Humans breathe the equivalent of 13 kg of air each day, compared to eating 2.4 kg of food and drinking 1 kg of liquid.

Geofact
Some scientists call the **tropopause** a cold trap. It is the point where rising water vapour cannot go higher because it changes into ice and is trapped. If there was no cold trap, Earth would lose all its water!

Atmospheric condition	Instrument	How it operates
Relative humidity is measured by a **hygrometer** or **wet-bulb** and **dry-bulb thermometers** (shown). The unit of measurement is a **percentage** (the amount of water in the air relative to the amount the air can hold when saturated).		The bulb of one thermometer is wrapped in muslin that is kept moist. This is the wet-bulb thermometer and it measures the temperature of saturated air. The dry-bulb thermometer is an ordinary thermometer that measures the actual air temperature. Both the air temperature and the difference between the wet and dry temperature readings are noted. Relative humidity is calculated using these figures and a humidity table.
Wind speed is measured with a **cup anemometer**. **Wind direction** is measured by a **wind vane**. The unit of speed of wind is **kilometres per hour** (km/hr). Wind direction is indicated by **compass directions** (indicating the direction the wind is blowing from).	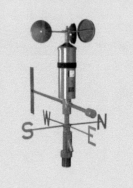	The cup shapes catch the wind, causing them to rotate. An electrical device records the revolutions of the cups and calculates the wind speed. This is then shown in a display window. An arrow is fixed to an upright rod so that it is able to rotate freely. The heavier end of the arrow always points into the wind, with the lighter end pointing to the direction the wind is coming from. The direction of this arm is noted on the cardinal points of the compass that are usually shown on the wind vane.

Table 9-1-1 continued Measuring atmospheric conditions.

Question

List three atmospheric conditions and describe how each is measured.

Geofact

Less than 3% of the water on Earth is freshwater. Only half of this is available to living organisms at any one time. The remainder is taken up by icecaps and water vapour.

THE OCEANS

Oceans cover over 70% of the Earth's surface and contain over 97% of the world's water as seawater. Most of it is contained in the three great oceans of the world – the Pacific, Atlantic and Indian oceans. The Pacific Ocean is by far the largest, containing over half the water on Earth.

Characteristics of the oceans

The oceans have a layered structure. This is mainly as a result of differences in:

- salinity
- temperature
- density and pressure.

Salinity

Salinity refers to the salt content of the oceans and is measured in **parts per thousand** (ppt). While the average salinity of the oceans is 35 ppt, it varies with location and conditions. Most of this salt is common table salt (sodium chloride).

■ Salinity is highest in sea areas such as the Mediterranean Sea and Red Sea, often reaching 40 ppt. These are enclosed sea areas whose waters do not mix freely with the main oceans. Evaporation rates are greater due to the high temperatures and precipitation levels are low.

■ Salinity is lower in regions that have high levels of precipitation (equatorial climate). It is also low in low latitude seas where the saltwater is diluted by melting ice and continued precipitation. Seas that receive substantial run-off from precipitation falling on the land also may have low salinity. For example, the Baltic Sea has an average salinity of 10 ppt.

■ The level of ocean salinity increases below depths of about 1 km, as the water becomes colder and denser.

Temperature

Temperature varies with the depth of the ocean, the temperature decreasing with depth. Thus, the ocean is divided into three vertical temperature zones.

■ The top layer is the warmest layer. It varies from almost 40°C on the surface of shallow coastal waters near the equator to the nearly freezing waters of the arctic.

■ The second temperature layer is known as the thermocline layer. Here the water temperature drops as the depth increases, since the sun's penetration drops too.

■ The deep water layer is coldest, with water almost reaching freezing point.

Density

Density of seawater refers to its weight relative to its volume.

■ Seawater becomes dense as temperature decreases and depth increases.

■ Seawater becomes more dense as salinity increases.

■ Less dense seawater floats on top of more dense seawater.

■ Since the deepest areas of the ocean have the coldest and most saline water, they also have the water with the greatest density.

■ With the weight of all the overlying seawater, **pressure** is greatest in deeper waters.

Question

Describe how the structure of the oceans varies, referring to:
■ Salinity
■ Temperature
■ Density and pressure

Link

The variations in salinity, temperature and pressure cause seawater to move within the oceans. This is the basis of understanding ocean currents. See **Oceanic circulation**, pages 299–302.

Vertical structure of the oceans

As a result of differences in salinity, temperature, density and pressure, the oceans have a layered structure. Four different layers or **zones** have been identified.

Geofact

Some squid and fish that live in the twilight zone use their bodies to make light.

Question

Describe the vertical structure of a typical ocean.

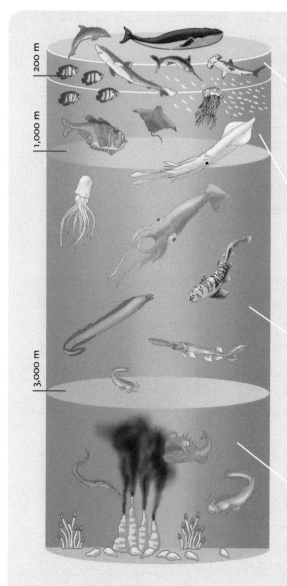

Sunlight zone
- This is the top layer, nearest the surface.
- It extends to a depth of about 200 m and is easily penetrated by sunlight.
- The sunlight supports photosynthesis. As a result, more than 90% of all marine life is found in this zone.

Twilight zone
- It extends to a depth of about 1,000 m.
- Only a small amount of light can penetrate the water at this depth.
- Plants do not grow here.
- Only animals that have adapted to little light survive here.

Midnight zone
- It extends to a depth of about 3,000 m.
- About 90% of the ocean is in this zone.
- It is entirely dark and the temperature is close to freezing.
- Just 1% of all marine life is found here.

The abyss
- This zone reaches the ocean floor.
- It is pitch black and pressure can reach 1 tonne per square centimetre.
- The deepest sections, called **trenches**, are associated with subduction zones (see *Today's World* 1, page 14).

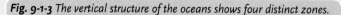

Fig. 9-1-3 *The vertical structure of the oceans shows four distinct zones.*

9.2
Solar energy and global temperatures

Solar energy is distributed unevenly over the surface of the Earth. It is transferred and redistributed through circulation patterns in the atmosphere and the oceans.

Learning objectives

After studying this chapter, you should be able to understand:

- the energy budget
- how the Earth is heated unevenly
- global temperature patterns.

THE ENERGY BUDGET

The sun is the Earth's main source of energy. Earth receives this incoming energy as solar radiation (or **insolation**). Just 50% of total solar radiation is absorbed by the surface of the Earth.

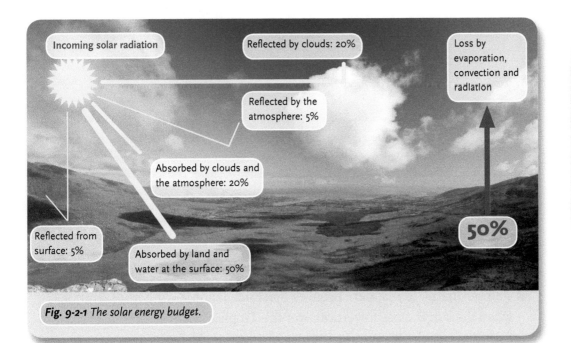

Incoming solar radiation

Reflected by clouds: 20%

Loss by evaporation, convection and radiation

Reflected by the atmosphere: 5%

Absorbed by clouds and the atmosphere: 20%

Reflected from surface: 5%

Absorbed by land and water at the surface: 50%

50%

Fig. 9-2-1 *The solar energy budget.*

Definition

INSOLATION is the amount of solar radiation (energy) that reaches a given area (incoming **solar radiation**).

For Earth's temperature to be stable over long periods of time, the gains of incoming energy and the losses of outgoing energy have to be equal. Thus, there is an overall balance between the energy that Earth receives and the energy that is lost from Earth into space. This flow of incoming and outgoing energy is known as Earth's **energy budget**.

UNEVEN HEATING OF THE EARTH

The sun does not heat the Earth evenly. There are several factors that influence the amount of insolation that is received at a particular place and time. They include the following:

- curvature of Earth and latitude
- altitude
- land and sea masses
- prevailing winds
- ocean currents.

Curvature of Earth and latitude

Earth is shaped like a sphere, so its surface curves away from the sun.

- Places near the equator receive direct insolation onto a small surface area. The insolation has a relatively small amount of atmosphere to pass through, so there is only a little energy loss by being absorbed or reflected.
- Towards the poles, the surface area to be heated increases, as does the amount of atmosphere to pass through. Thus, these regions receive much less insolation.

As a result, temperature decreases as one moves from lower latitude (equatorial) regions towards high latitude (polar) regions.

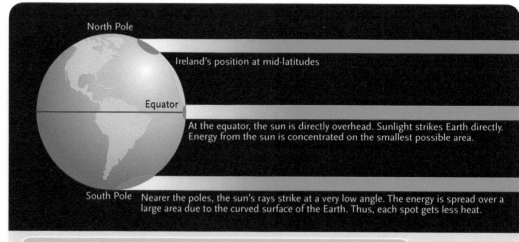

North Pole

Ireland's position at mid-latitudes

Equator

At the equator, the sun is directly overhead. Sunlight strikes Earth directly. Energy from the sun is concentrated on the smallest possible area.

South Pole Nearer the poles, the sun's rays strike at a very low angle. The energy is spread over a large area due to the curved surface of the Earth. Thus, each spot gets less heat.

Fig. 9-2-2 *The influence of latitude and the curvature of Earth on heat distribution.*

Earth orbits the sun with its axis at an angle of 23.5°. As a result, the amount of solar radiation that a region receives varies through the seasons.

- The Northern Hemisphere receives most insolation during midsummer, when the sun is close to vertical over the Tropic of Cancer and Earth's axis is tilted towards the sun.

Question

Explain the terms 'insolation' and 'energy budget'.

Question

List three factors that influence the amount of insolation received.

- In winter, the axis is tilted away from the sun and insolation hits the Northern Hemisphere at a lower angle. The sun's rays spread their heat over a larger area.

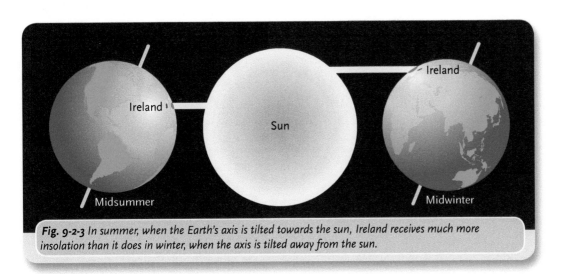

Fig. 9-2-3 *In summer, when the Earth's axis is tilted towards the sun, Ireland receives much more insolation than it does in winter, when the axis is tilted away from the sun.*

Altitude

The atmosphere is not heated directly by the sun, but mostly by heat that is radiated from the surface of the Earth. As a result, air is warmer near the ground because it is closer to its source of heat.

Temperature decreases when there is an increase in altitude. On average, there is a drop of 7°C with every increase of 1,000 metres in altitude. This decrease in temperature is called the **lapse rate**.

- Air expands and becomes less dense at higher altitudes. As a result, it loses some of its ability to hold heat.
- There is an increase in cloud cover in higher altitudes. This reduces the amount of insolation.
- Wind travels faster in less dense air, so it is much windier, and thus colder, in higher altitudes.

Question

Explain the influence of altitude on temperature.

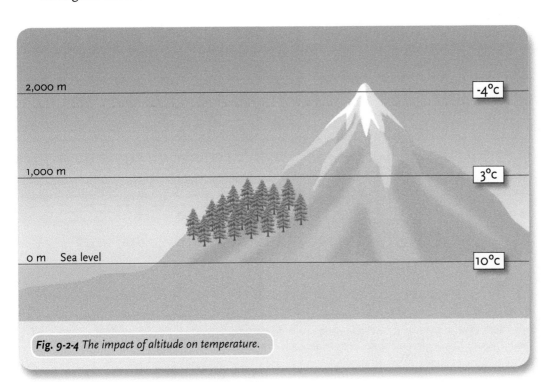

Fig. 9-2-4 *The impact of altitude on temperature.*

Kilimanjaro is almost 6,000 metres in height and is regarded as the highest freestanding mountain in the world. Even though it lies within 3° latitude of the equator, its summit is snow-capped throughout the year.

Land and sea masses

Land and sea masses differ in their ability to absorb, transfer and radiate heat.

- Seawater takes much longer to heat than land, but once it is warmed up, it retains the heat for a lot longer and takes longer to cool down. Thus, the sea acts as a huge heat reservoir.
- Land absorbs heat more rapidly than the sea but also loses it more rapidly. This means the further away from the sea you are, the warmer the summers will be, but the winters will be cooler too.
- Coastal regions have a smaller temperature range than regions at the centre of continental masses. Thus, coastal regions have a more moderate climate, which means people are less likely to feel intense cold in winter and intense heat in summer.

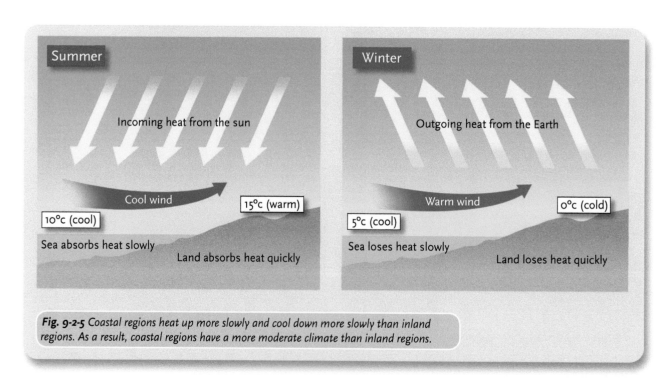

Fig. 9-2-5 *Coastal regions heat up more slowly and cool down more slowly than inland regions. As a result, coastal regions have a more moderate climate than inland regions.*

Prevailing winds

Wind is the movement of air from areas of high pressure to areas of low pressure. The direction of the prevailing winds has a major effect on temperature. This is because the temperature of a wind is determined by the characteristics of the region where it originated.

In Ireland, the prevailing winds are the **south-westerlies**. These travel over the Atlantic Ocean, where they are warmed by the North Atlantic Drift.

- Ireland and Britain have warmer winters than one might expect, given their latitude.
- In summer these south-westerlies are cooler than a corresponding land wind.

Occasionally there is a 'blast from the north'. This brings very cold weather from the arctic and is characterised by icy winds, snow and frost.

Ocean currents

Water in the ocean moves in paths called **currents** and these can be either warm or cold. The temperature of the water affects the temperature of the air above it. If the water is warm, it heats the air above it. If the water is cold, it cools the air above it.

- **Warm currents** travel away from the equator and they raise the air temperature of the land masses they flow by. The warm North Atlantic Drift is responsible for the mild winters in Ireland.
- **Cold currents** carry water towards the equator and reduce the temperature of coastal regions that they flow by. The Labrador Current is partly responsible for the cold winter temperatures of the American north-east.

GLOBAL TEMPERATURE PATTERNS

Looking at temperature maps of the Earth we see that temperature patterns vary not just according to latitude and season, but by hemisphere.

- The highest temperatures occur in tropical and subtropical regions close to the equator. Annual temperature ranges tend to be small.
- High latitude locations have much lower annual temperatures. However, the seasonal temperature range is large.
- In summer, continental regions are much warmer than coastal regions on the same latitude.
- In winter, coastal regions are warmer than continental regions on the same latitude.
- There is a seasonal contrast between the Northern Hemisphere, with its large land masses, and the Southern Hemisphere, with its smaller land masses.

Definition

A **PREVAILING WIND** is one that blows for the most part from a single direction.

Link

Atmospheric circulation, page 287.

Link

Oceanic circulation, page 299.

Question

Shannon has an average January temperature of 6°C. New York, which lies 1,300 km closer to the equator, has an average January temperature of –1°C. Explain one reason for this.

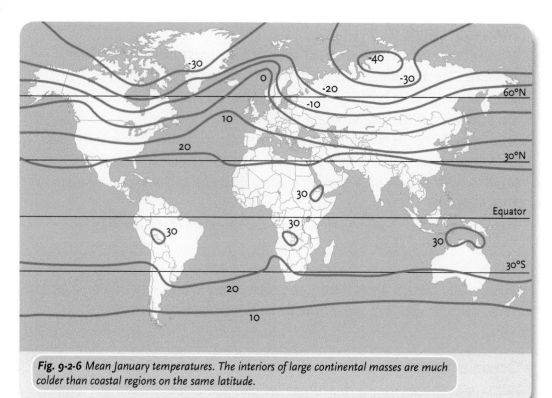

Fig. 9-2-6 *Mean January temperatures. The interiors of large continental masses are much colder than coastal regions on the same latitude.*

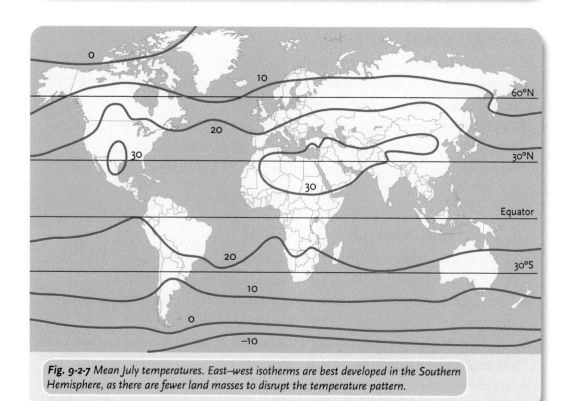

Fig. 9-2-7 *Mean July temperatures. East–west isotherms are best developed in the Southern Hemisphere, as there are fewer land masses to disrupt the temperature pattern.*

Leaving Cert Exam Question

I Explain why temperatures vary greatly over the surface of the Earth. (80 marks)

9.3

Moisture in the atmosphere

Exchanges of water between oceans and the atmosphere vary greatly over the surface of the Earth and give rise to distinctive weather and climate regimes.

MOISTURE IN THE ATMOSPHERE

Less than 3% of Earth's water is fresh. Two-thirds of it is in solid form, found in icecaps and glaciers. Because it is frozen, it is not available for use.

That leaves about 1% of all the Earth's water in a form that is useable to humans and land animals. This freshwater is found in lakes, rivers, streams and ponds and in the ground.

A small fraction of the freshwater is held in the atmosphere as water vapour. It holds enough moisture to give every place on Earth about 25 mm (1 inch) of rainfall.

A typical molecule of water stays in the atmosphere for an average of only eight days. The atmosphere must therefore replace and **recycle** its store of moisture regularly.

Learning objectives

After studying this chapter, you should be able to understand:

- the hydrological cycle
- cloud type and classification
- the occurrence and distribution of precipitation.

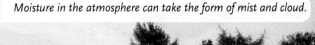

Moisture in the atmosphere can take the form of mist and cloud.

THE HYDROLOGICAL CYCLE

The hydrological cycle is also called the **water cycle**. It is a model that describes the transfer and storage of water between the three main reservoirs – oceans, land and atmosphere.

It is called a cycle because it is a continuous process and has no beginning or end. As water goes through this cycle, it can be a solid (ice), a liquid (water) or a gas (water vapour).

Energy from the sun is absorbed by the water, which heats it and causes **evaporation**.

■ This is the process where water changes directly from a liquid to a vapour. The water is evaporated from seas, lakes and rivers.

■ The rate of evaporation varies. The warmer and drier the air is, the greater the rate of evaporation.

■ Transpiration is a similar process, where water is evaporated from vegetation.

■ Warm air currents rise up from Earth's surface, lifting the water vapour into the atmosphere.

As the moist air rises through the atmosphere, it cools and the water vapour turns into tiny droplets of water or ice crystals. This process is called **condensation**. We see these tiny droplets and crystals as clouds.

■ The prevailing winds then blow the clouds over the land. The clouds may be forced to rise and as they do, the air is cooled further.

■ The amount of water vapour in the air is called humidity. When humidity increases to the extent that the air cannot hold any more water vapour, the air is said to be **saturated**.

■ Humidity is now 100% and any further cooling will overload the atmosphere with moisture.

Following further cooling, the cloud droplets become so big that the swirling atmospheric winds can no longer hold them up. The droplets then fall from the sky as **precipitation**. Depending on atmospheric conditions, precipitation can be in the form of rain, snow, hail or sleet.

■ Rain occurs when water droplets become too heavy to remain in the cloud and, as a result, fall toward the surface as drops of rain.

■ When tiny individual ice crystals collide within a cloud, they become frozen together and eventually fall as snow.

■ Precipitation also occurs as sleet (small frozen raindrops) or hail (large frozen raindrops) if the atmosphere is very cold.

Following precipitation, water takes a number of routes to complete the water cycle.

■ Once precipitation hits the ground, some of it may be **re-evaporated**.

■ Much of the water will become surface **run-off** that finds its way into rivers and lakes as it flows back into the ocean.

Definition
EVAPOTRANSPIRATION
is the term for the combined processes of evaporation and transpiration.

Question
Explain the part played by each of the following in the water cycle:
■ Evaporation
■ Condensation
■ Precipitation
■ Run-off
■ Infiltration

■ Some of the precipitation will be absorbed into the ground. This is called **infiltration**. Large amounts of water are stored in the ground as Earth's **groundwater** supply.

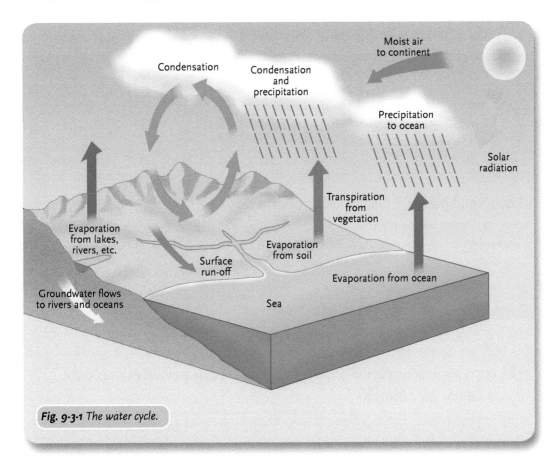

Fig. 9-3-1 *The water cycle.*

Geofact
Other forms of precipitation include dew, frost, fog and mist.

CLOUDS

Clouds are visible masses of water droplets or solid ice crystals that float in the lowest part of Earth's atmosphere (the troposphere).

Clouds form when the atmosphere becomes saturated following cooling. Water vapour condenses into tiny droplets of water or ice crystals. These are so small and light that they can float in the air. Water vapour then comes in contact with dust particles in the air to create clouds.

The cooling occurs when air is forced to rise. Air rises or lifts for three reasons:

■ **Relief lifting** occurs when air is forced to rise when it meets a barrier such as a mountain range.

■ **Frontal lifting** occurs when two air masses meet and the warmer air mass is forced up over the colder air mass.

■ **Convectional lifting** occurs when a body of air close to the ground is heated and begins to rise.

Geofact
You have probably walked through a cloud before – fog is an example of a cloud that is close to the Earth's surface.

Link
For more detail, see **Rainfall** on page 282.

Classifying clouds

Clouds are classified according to their **height**, **shape** and **appearance**.

Latin words or combinations of them are used to describe the different types of cloud.

The first part of a cloud's name describes height.

Prefix	Height
Cirro	High level (above 6,000 metres)
Alto	Medium level (2,000–6,000 metres)
Strato	Low level (below 2,000 metres)

Table 9-3-1

The second part of the name describes shape.

Latin word	Meaning
Cirrus/cirro-	Curl of hair (thin and wispy)
Stratus/strato-	Layered
Cumulus/cumulo-	Heap or pile (lumpy/cotton wool)

Table 9-3-2

The term **nimbus** or **nimbo-** is added to indicate that a cloud can produce precipitation. For example:

Cirrostratus	A high-level, layered cloud
Nimbostratus	A low-level, rain-bearing cloud
Cumulonimbus	A heaped, rain-bearing cloud

Table 9-3-3

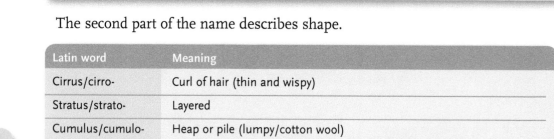

Question

Give the meaning of each of the following terms:
- Cirrus
- Alto
- Stratus
- Cumulus
- Nimbus

Cirrus are high-level clouds that are composed of ice crystals. They appear as white delicate wisps or streaks. The long streaks or feathery ends have the common name of 'mares' tails'. Cirrus clouds are associated with dry conditions.

Altocumulus are middle-level clouds that are composed of tiny water droplets. Altocumulus clouds usually form in groups and are about 1 km thick. They are greyish-white in colour. These clouds sometimes have shadows or dark areas and can sometimes signal that bad weather is approaching.

Clouds have an impact on incoming solar radiation (see Fig. 9-2-1 on page 271). They are also the source of precipitation. Finally, they are a good indicator of approaching weather.

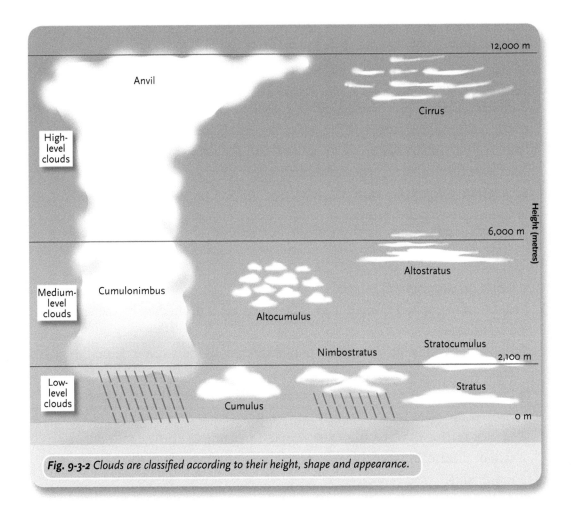

Fig. 9-3-2 Clouds are classified according to their height, shape and appearance.

Question
What are clouds?

Stratus are low-level clouds that are composed of tiny water droplets. They are greyish in colour and often cover the entire sky. They resemble fog that does not reach the ground. Usually no precipitation falls from stratus clouds, but sometimes they may bring drizzle.

Cumulonimbus clouds stretch from near the ground to 12,000 metres up in the air. They consist of both water droplets and ice crystals. They are more like tall towers than regular cumulus clouds. The wedge at the upper end is called the anvil. They are associated with thunderstorms.

PRECIPITATION

Precipitation occurs when water is released from clouds in the form of rain, sleet, snow or hail.

For precipitation to occur, the following conditions must apply:
- the air must be saturated with water vapour and
- the saturated air must be cooled, usually by rising.

Rainfall

Rain occurs when tiny cloud droplets collide to form bigger droplets. This continues until the droplet is too heavy for the air to support it. The droplet then begins to fall, colliding with more cloud droplets as it gains in size. There are three distinct types of rainfall:
- relief (or orographic) rainfall
- frontal (or cyclonic) rainfall
- convectional rainfall.

1. Relief (or orographic) rainfall

Relief (or orographic) rainfall is so called because it is affected by the shape of the landscape.
- Prevailing winds blow warm air that is laden with moisture in from the oceans.
- If the air meets a natural barrier such as hills or mountains, it is forced to rise. As the air is forced up, further cooling occurs.
- Clouds form and when the water droplets become too heavy, they fall as rain or drizzle. Most of this occurs on the windward side of the hills or mountains.
- As the air descends on the leeward (sheltered) side of the mountain, it becomes warmer and is able to retain any remaining moisture. The leeward side receives very little rainfall and is called a **rain shadow**.

Relief rain is common in the mountainous regions that stretch along much of the west coast of Ireland from Kerry to Donegal. These are among the wettest regions in Ireland. The lowlands of the east of Ireland lie in the rain shadow of these mountains.

Geofact

Millions of cloud droplets are required to produce a single raindrop.

Question

Explain how relief rainfall occurs.

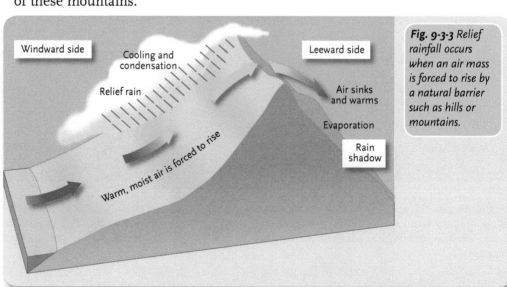

Windward side

Cooling and condensation

Relief rain

Warm, moist air is forced to rise

Leeward side

Air sinks and warms

Evaporation

Rain shadow

Fig. 9-3-3 *Relief rainfall occurs when an air mass is forced to rise by a natural barrier such as hills or mountains.*

2. Frontal (or cyclonic) rainfall

Frontal (or cyclonic) rainfall is so called because it is associated with weather fronts and the movement of depressions.

■ Two air masses, one a warm air mass and one a cold air mass, meet at a front.

■ At a warm front, the **lighter warm air is forced to rise** over the heavier cold air.

■ At a cold front, the **heavier cold air mass cuts under** the lighter warm air, forcing it to rise.

■ In both cases, the warm air is cooled and condensation takes place.

■ A variety of clouds form and when the water droplets become too heavy, rain falls over a wide area. It can take the form of showers or heavy rainfall.

Most of the rain that falls over the Atlantic Ocean, Ireland and other parts of Western Europe is frontal rainfall and is associated with the passage of depressions across the Atlantic.

Question

Explain how frontal rainfall occurs.

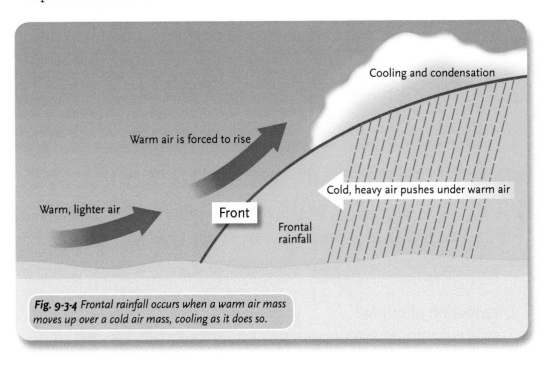

Fig. 9-3-4 *Frontal rainfall occurs when a warm air mass moves up over a cold air mass, cooling as it does so.*

3. Convectional rainfall

Convectional rainfall is so called because it is caused by the vertical rise (convection) of heated air.

■ Earth's surface is heated by the energy from the sun.

■ The air above the ground then absorbs some of this heat, becoming hotter as the day goes on.

■ The heated air causes moisture from the ground, rivers and lakes to **evaporate**.

■ As the air is further heated, it expands, becomes lighter than the air surrounding it and rises.

■ This warm, moist air then begins to cool, resulting in saturation, followed by **condensation**.

■ Convection tends to produce towering cumulonimbus clouds, which produce heavy rain and possible **thunder and lightning**, generally in the afternoon.

Convectional rain is common in areas where the ground is heated by the hot sun, such as the tropics. This is why those areas, including the Amazon and Congo basins, experience heavy rainfall most afternoons.

Convectional rain can also fall in Ireland on long, hot summer days. It takes the form of short, heavy thundershowers that are separated by periods of sunshine.

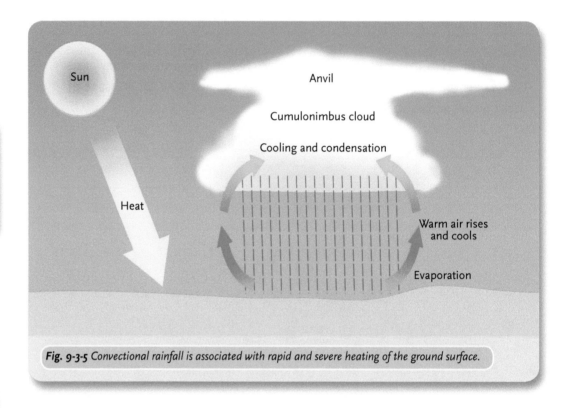

Fig. 9-3-5 *Convectional rainfall is associated with rapid and severe heating of the ground surface.*

Distribution of rainfall

Rainfall is distributed very unevenly over the Earth's surface, from less than 100 mm annually to a maximum of more than 3,600 mm annually, depending on location.

This is due to a variety of factors that are active in the global climate system, including global winds, ocean currents and varying temperatures.

Equatorial regions have the highest precipitation, receiving over 2,000 mm annually.

■ Their low latitude means that these regions receive constant solar heating. This encourages convection lifting of air.

■ Global circulation patterns cause northern and southern air masses to converge here and moist tropical air is forced upwards.

Mid-latitude regions have large amounts of precipitation, but decreasing from west to east.

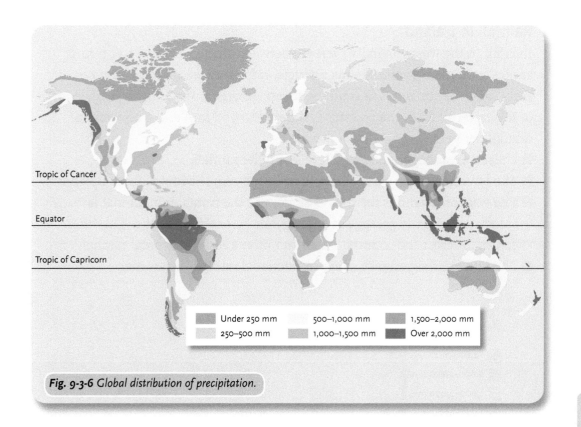

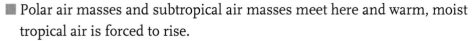

Tropic of Cancer

Equator

Tropic of Capricorn

| Under 250 mm | 500–1,000 mm | 1,500–2,000 mm |
| 250–500 mm | 1,000–1,500 mm | Over 2,000 mm |

Fig. 9-3-6 *Global distribution of precipitation.*

Question

List the factors that affect the global distribution of rainfall.

- Polar air masses and subtropical air masses meet here and warm, moist tropical air is forced to rise.
- These air masses generally move from west to east, causing levels of precipitation to decrease as the distance from the ocean increases.

West coast subtropical regions tend to be dry and many have **desert** conditions.

- Due to global wind patterns, these areas are dominated by descending air rather than rising air.
- Many deserts are onshore of cold ocean currents.
- They are impacted by a rain shadow effect.

Continental interiors tend to be drier.

- They are far removed from the main sources of moisture, such as the oceans.
- Moist ocean air masses are blocked by mountain ranges.
- Any moisture that was in the air has almost completely disappeared by the time it reaches these areas.

Polar regions have low levels of precipitation.

- Cold polar and arctic air masses dominate these regions.
- Cold air is unable to hold as much water vapour as warm air.

Satellite image of Africa and the Arabian Peninsula. Arid areas, such as the Sahara Desert and Arabian Desert (background), are shown in light brown. Tropical rainforest and grassland areas are shown in dark green.

Rainfall in Ireland

Rainfall in the west generally averages between 1,000 mm and 1,400 mm annually. In many mountainous districts, rainfall exceeds 2,000 mm per year. Some summits in the south-west receive over 3,000 mm annually. Most of the eastern half of the country gets between 750 mm and 1,000 mm of rainfall per year.

- Upland areas experience high levels of relief rainfall.
- The lowlands of the east of Ireland lie in the rain shadow of these uplands.
- The west of Ireland is the first to encounter the frontal rainfall that is associated with the passage of depressions across the Atlantic. They then continue across the country. These conditions result in frontal rainfall.
- The Midlands experience some convectional rainfall in summer.

Question

Give two reasons why the western seaboard receives more rainfall than the Midlands and east.

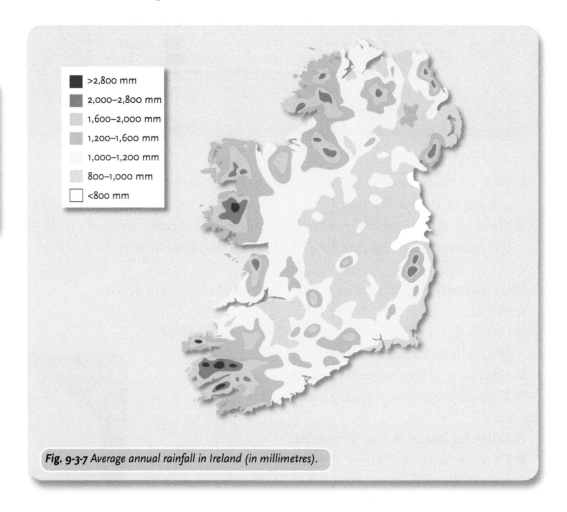

Fig. 9-3-7 *Average annual rainfall in Ireland (in millimetres).*

Legend:
- >2,800 mm
- 2,000–2,800 mm
- 1,600–2,000 mm
- 1,200–1,600 mm
- 1,000–1,200 mm
- 800–1,000 mm
- <800 mm

Leaving Cert Exam Questions

1   Examine the exchange of water between the oceans and the atmosphere. (80 marks)

2   'Exchanges of water between ocean and atmosphere vary over the surface of the Earth and this gives rise to distinctive weather conditions.' Discuss this statement with reference to examples you have studied. (80 marks)

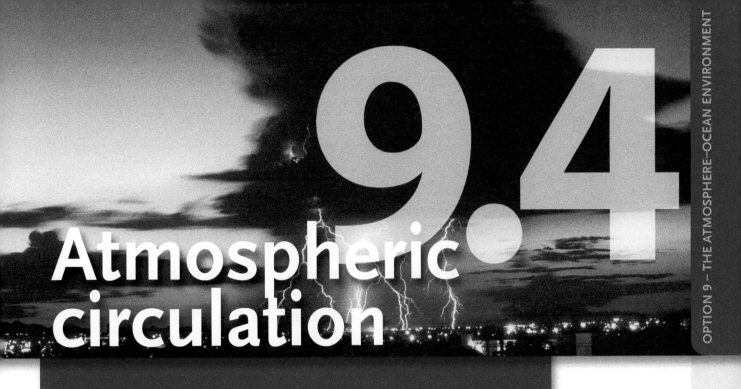

9.4

Atmospheric circulation

Circulation in the atmosphere affects weather and climate patterns on a variety of levels.

ATMOSPHERIC CIRCULATION

Atmospheric circulation refers to the general movement of air in the lower and upper atmosphere. This movement of air is called **wind**.

Winds transfer heat around the world, helping to reduce temperatures in equatorial regions while raising them in polar regions. Winds also affect ocean currents and precipitation. Thus, wind has a major influence on much of our weather.

Winds circulate on two scales:
- ■ global winds
- ■ local winds.

GLOBAL WIND PATTERNS

Global winds blow in a pattern where the surface winds of each hemisphere are divided into belts. These global wind belts are the result of two main factors:
- ■ uneven heating of Earth's surface, which creates **high and low pressure belts**
- ■ the rotation of the Earth on its axis, which results in the **Coriolis effect**.

High and low pressure belts

Winds form because the sun heats different parts of Earth unequally. Places close to the equator get much more heat than places near the poles.
- ■ When air is heated at the equator, it expands, becomes lighter and rises. This creates an area of **low** atmospheric pressure.

Learning objectives

After studying this chapter, you should be able to understand:

- ■ the pattern of global winds

- ■ large-scale weather systems, including mid-latitude depressions and cyclones

- ■ local weather systems, including land and sea breezes, valley and mountain winds and thunderstorms.

■ When air cools, it becomes heavier and descends. This presses down on the surface of the Earth, creating an area of **high** atmospheric pressure at the poles.

■ The difference in pressure causes the air to move. (Think of air escaping from a balloon.)

■ The air returns along the surface from polar highs to equatorial lows. The upper-level return of air from the equator to the poles completes the **circulation cell**.

If the Earth did not rotate, atmospheric circulation would be very simple. The air would rise along the equatorial regions and sink at the poles, resulting in one single circulation cell in each hemisphere.

Question

Explain the following terms:
■ Atmospheric circulation
■ Global wind patterns

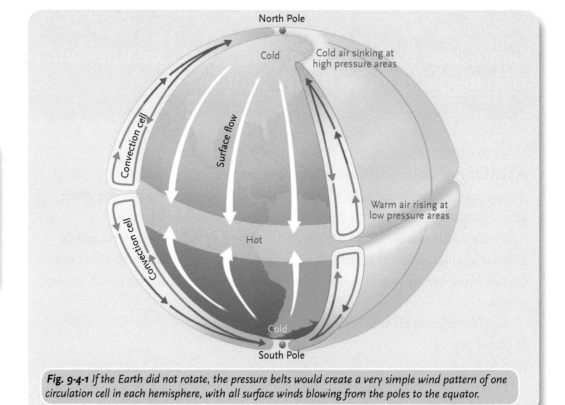

Fig. 9-4-1 *If the Earth did not rotate, the pressure belts would create a very simple wind pattern of one circulation cell in each hemisphere, with all surface winds blowing from the poles to the equator.*

Geofact

One of the misunderstandings associated with the Coriolis effect is that it causes water going down the drain of a sink to rotate.

The Coriolis effect

The Earth spins on its axis from west to east. Above its surface, air is moving freely from high pressure belts to low pressure belts. Because of the spinning of the planet, any moving object above its surface tends to drift sideways from its original path. As a result:

■ air is deflected to the right of its path in the Northern Hemisphere
■ air is deflected to the left of its path in the Southern Hemisphere.

This is the **Coriolis effect** – the impact of Earth's rotation on the direction of the winds.

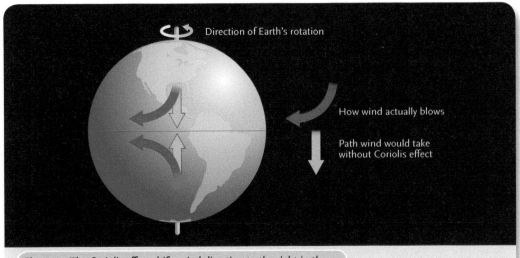

Fig. 9-4-2 *The Coriolis effect shifts wind direction to the right in the Northern Hemisphere and to the left in the Southern Hemisphere.*

Circulation cells

Global wind patterns are affected not just because the Earth spins on its axis, but also because its axis is tilted and there is more land in the Northern Hemisphere than in the Southern Hemisphere.

As a result, instead of a single-cell circulation, the global model consists of **three circulation cells** in each hemisphere. These three cells are the:

- **Hadley cell**
- **Polar cell**
- **Ferrel cell**.

The cells in each hemisphere mirror each other, so we will only look at the circulation cells of the Northern Hemisphere.

Link

Ocean currents are driven by the movement of wind across the waters of the oceans. Thus, the Coriolis effect also affects the movement of the ocean's currents (see page 275).

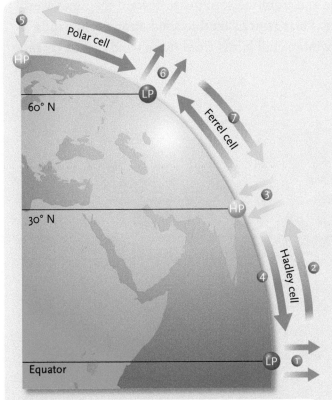

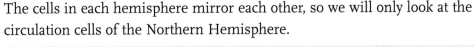

Fig. 9-4-3 *There are three circulation cells in each hemisphere.*

The **Hadley cell** circulates between the equator and 30°N.
1. Air is heated and rises up into the atmosphere at or near the equator. As it does so, it creates a belt of low pressure (LP).
2. The warm air flows toward the poles above the surface of the Earth, cooling as it does so.
3. The air is now cooler and heavier. It begins to press downwards and descend. This creates a belt of high pressure (HP) at about 30°N.
4. The air now flows back towards the equator as surface winds. The Hadley cell is now complete.

The **Polar cell** circulates between 60°N and the North Pole.
5. The extremely cold air in polar regions sinks, forming an area of high pressure (HP). The air now flows back towards the equator as surface winds.
6. At about 60°N, they converge with winds in the Ferrel cell. Air rises here to create an area of low pressure (LP). The air then returns towards the North Pole to complete the Polar cell.

The **Ferrel cell**, a third wind system, now develops between the Hadley cell and polar cell.
7. Air moves along the surface from the high pressure (HP) belt at 30°N towards the low pressure (LP) belt at 60°N, where it rises. It then returns in the upper atmosphere to complete the cell.

Prevailing surface winds

When the Coriolis effect is applied to the circulation cells, three main surface wind belts develop in each hemisphere:

- the trade winds
- the westerlies
- the polar winds.

1. Trade winds

The **trade winds** are prevailing surface winds over the tropical ocean. They blow from the subtropical HP belts to the equatorial LP belt. They blow from the north-east (towards the south-west) in the Northern Hemisphere and from the south-east (towards the north-west) in the Southern Hemisphere. They are constant, steady winds. They are called the trade winds because sailing ships depended on them to drive their ships between Europe and the New World.

2. The westerlies

The **westerlies** blow from the subtropical HP belts towards the poles. More exactly, they are known as the south-westerlies in the Northern Hemisphere and the north-westerlies in the Southern Hemisphere because of their direction of origin. They do not blow as regularly as the trade winds. They are usually quite strong and may be associated with storm conditions.

3. Polar winds

The **polar winds** blow southwards from the HP belt towards the subpolar low (about 60° latitude). They blow from the north-east (toward the south-west) in the Northern Hemisphere and from the south-east (toward the north-west) in the Southern Hemisphere. Polar regions tend to send strong cold winds towards the equator. In the winter, chill blasts from these winds reach far into the middle latitudes.

Geofacts

The **doldrums** is the name given to the low pressure area where the two trade wind circulations meet. The region lies very close to the equator and is characterised by very light winds.

The **horse latitudes** is the name given to the area of high pressure lying about 30° to 35° north (and south) of the equator. It is a region of subsiding dry air and high pressure that result in weak winds.

The **polar front** is the name given to the low pressure area at about 60° north (and south) of the equator, where warmer tropical air meets colder polar air. Depressions originate at the polar front. These can bring wet, cloudy and windy conditions.

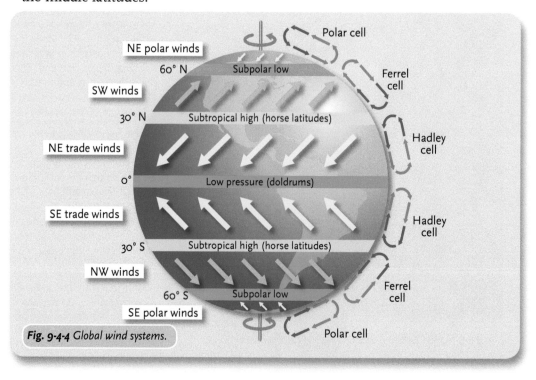

Fig. 9-4-4 *Global wind systems.*

LARGE-SCALE WEATHER SYSTEMS IN THE MID-LATITUDES

The mid-latitudes lie between the tropics and polar regions in both hemispheres. We will deal with the Northern Hemisphere only.

Mid-latitude weather systems are influenced by the movement of warm air from tropical regions and cold air from polar regions. They include:

■ **depressions**
■ **anticyclones**.

Mid-latitude depressions

Depressions, also known as a cyclones or **lows**, are low pressure systems in the atmosphere with pressure decreasing towards the centre. Depressions can have a life cycle of two to five days and can be up to 1,500 km in diameter. They are very common at about 60° latitude. Hence, they have a major influence on the climate of Ireland.

Depressions bring **unsettled**, **changeable** weather with **windy** and **cloudy** conditions as well as periods of rain and snow in winter.

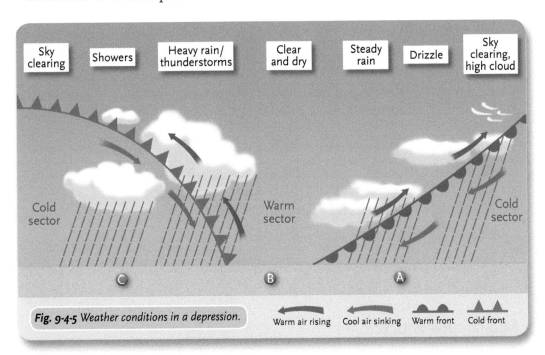

Fig. 9-4-5 *Weather conditions in a depression.*

Warm air rising   Cool air sinking   Warm front   Cold front

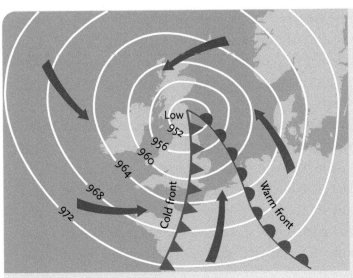

Fig. 9-4-6 *Characteristics of a low or depression.*

Link

Depressions and anticyclones, *Today's World 1*, pages 245–7.

Question

Explain the following terms:
■ Warm front
■ Cold front
■ Depression

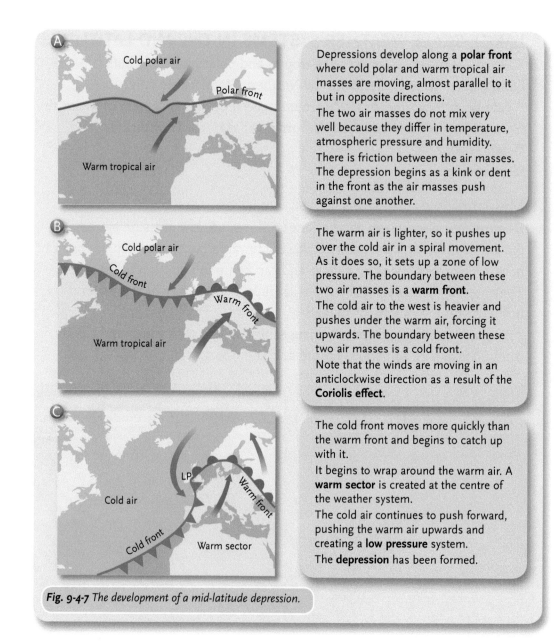

A Depressions develop along a **polar front** where cold polar and warm tropical air masses are moving, almost parallel to it but in opposite directions.

The two air masses do not mix very well because they differ in temperature, atmospheric pressure and humidity.

There is friction between the air masses. The depression begins as a kink or dent in the front as the air masses push against one another.

B The warm air is lighter, so it pushes up over the cold air in a spiral movement. As it does so, it sets up a zone of low pressure. The boundary between these two air masses is a **warm front**.

The cold air to the west is heavier and pushes under the warm air, forcing it upwards. The boundary between these two air masses is a cold front.

Note that the winds are moving in an anticlockwise direction as a result of the **Coriolis effect**.

C The cold front moves more quickly than the warm front and begins to catch up with it.

It begins to wrap around the warm air. A **warm sector** is created at the centre of the weather system.

The cold air continues to push forward, pushing the warm air upwards and creating a **low pressure** system.

The **depression** has been formed.

Fig. 9-4-7 *The development of a mid-latitude depression.*

Mid-latitude anticyclones

An anticyclone, or **high**, is a single mass of sinking air that creates a zone of high pressure on the Earth's surface. The roughly circular closed isobar at its central region indicates the area of highest pressure.

Anticyclones are much larger than depressions and can be up to 3,000 km in diameter. They are slow moving and may remain stationary over a region for many days and even weeks.

Winds blow outwards from the centre of the anticyclone. They blow in a clockwise direction in the Northern Hemisphere.

Since the air is sinking, it is becoming warmer. Evaporation, rather than precipitation, is taking place. Clouds do not form, leading to **clear skies** and **dry** conditions. Anticyclones are typically relatively slow-moving features. The air sinks gently, so winds are generally light if conditions are not calm.

While the weather conditions associated with anticyclones are regarded as settled, they vary with the seasons.

- **Summer anticyclones** can bring **long sunny days** and warm temperatures. The weather is normally **dry**, although very hot temperatures can trigger the occasional afternoon thunderstorm. The cooling of the ground at night can lead to morning mist.
- **Winter anticyclones** can bring overnight air or **ground frosts**. The clear skies allow heat to be lost from the surface of the Earth by radiation and the temperature falls steadily. Falling temperatures can also encourage fog to form overnight.

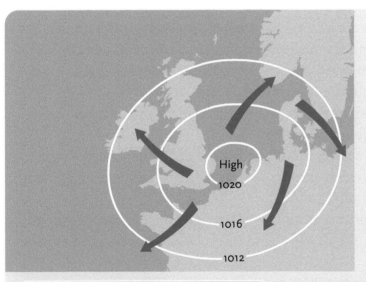

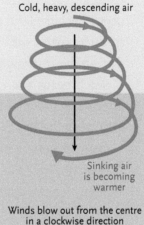

Cold, heavy, descending air

Sinking air is becoming warmer

Winds blow out from the centre in a clockwise direction

Fig. 9-4-8 Characteristics of an anticyclone, or high.

Questions

1. Explain the term 'anticyclone'.
2. List three characteristics of an anticyclone.

The image shows the clear skies associated with an anticyclone over the southern parts of Ireland and Britain as well as much of Western Europe. Note the depression over the Atlantic (to the west of Spain) that is tracking its way towards Ireland and Britain. Most of the skies of Northern Europe have a covering of cloud.

LOCAL WEATHER SYSTEMS

The movement of air also occurs on a smaller, local scale and produces local variations in climatic conditions. These **local climates** are known as microclimates.

The local weather conditions that result include:

- land and sea breezes
- valley and mountain winds
- thunderstorms.

Land and sea breezes

Land and sea breezes occur in coastal areas during spring and summer. They occur because land and seawater absorb and lose heat at different rates. This in turn creates differences in atmospheric pressure. These changes occur during day and night, so these are **diurnal** (daily) breezes.

Sea breezes are onshore flows of air that reach their maximum in the afternoon and cool the coastal zone.

- During the day the sun heats the land faster than it does the sea. The air over the land is heated, so it expands and rises. This creates a zone of **low pressure** over the land.
- Seawater can absorb great quantities of heat but have only a slight rise in temperature. Thus, the air over the sea is cooler and this creates a zone of high pressure.
- Winds blow from areas of high pressure to areas of low pressure. Cool air is drawn in from the sea to replace the rising air over the land.

Geofact
Sea breezes may bring in humid air, resulting in coastal fog and haze.

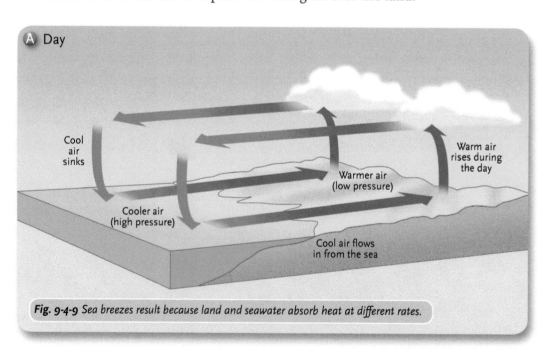

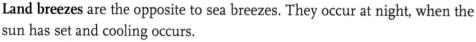
Fig. 9-4-9 *Sea breezes result because land and seawater absorb heat at different rates.*

Land breezes are the opposite to sea breezes. They occur at night, when the sun has set and cooling occurs.

- The sea has absorbed and retained heat from the day's sunshine. It is warmer than the land and loses this heat very slowly. Thus, the air over the sea is relatively warm. This creates a low pressure area of rising air.

- The land loses its heat more quickly than the sea. The air over the land begins to cool and sink, creating an area of high pressure.
- Cool air is drawn out from the land to replace the rising air over the sea. Land breezes have now developed.

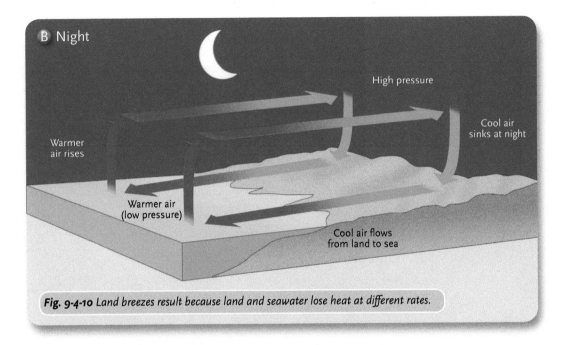

Fig. 9-4-10 *Land breezes result because land and seawater lose heat at different rates.*

Question

List three ways land breezes and sea breezes are different.

Valley and mountain winds

Valley and mountain winds are common in areas that have great variations in **topography**. They are also **diurnal** (day/night) winds and result from variations in atmospheric pressure.

Valley winds occur during the day as the sun heats the valley sides. Valley winds are so called because they flow up the sides of the valley towards the mountains.

- The land surface absorbs heat much more quickly than the air. The land surface then radiates this heat. This heats the air close to the sides of the valley but does not affect the air further away from the mountain slope.

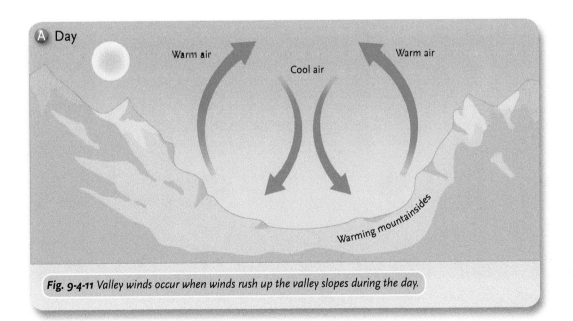

Fig. 9-4-11 *Valley winds occur when winds rush up the valley slopes during the day.*

OPTION 9 – THE ATMOSPHERE–OCEAN ENVIRONMENT

- The warmer air is less dense than the cooler air in the middle of the valley. It rushes up along the sides of the valley, creating winds that blow nearly every afternoon.
- The cooler air above the middle of the valley is heavier and sinks down toward the ground, replacing the rising warm air.

Paragliders make use of the updrafts of air that result from valley winds.

Mountain winds occur at night-time when atmospheric cooling occurs. Mountain winds are so called because they flow down from the mountains into the valley.

- Once the sun goes down, the ground starts to cool rapidly. The air close to the mountain slope is cooled and becomes heavier than the surrounding air.
- The cool air starts sinking first along the mountain slopes and flows down into the valley bottom, causing a mountain breeze.
- The air in the centre of the valley does not cool down as quickly as the ground.
- The cold, heavy air forces the warmer air that it replaces to rise. This completes the circulation cell.

Geofact

Mountain winds are usually stronger than valley winds and can reach speeds as high as 150 km/hr.

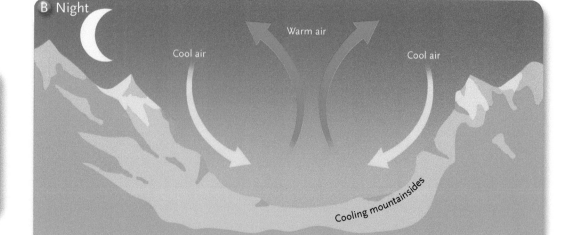

B Night

Warm air

Cool air

Cool air

Cooling mountainsides

Fig. 9-4-12 *Mountain winds occur when winds rush down from the mountains during the night.*

Thunderstorms

A thunderstorm is a local weather system whose main characteristics are **severe downdraft winds**, **heavy rainfall**, **thunder** and **lightning**. Depending on the intensity of the thunderstorm, it can last anywhere from 15 minutes to hours.

There are three stages in the life of a thunderstorm:

■ developing stage – when the storm is strengthening
■ mature stage – when the storm is at its peak
■ dissolving stage – when the storm is dying away.

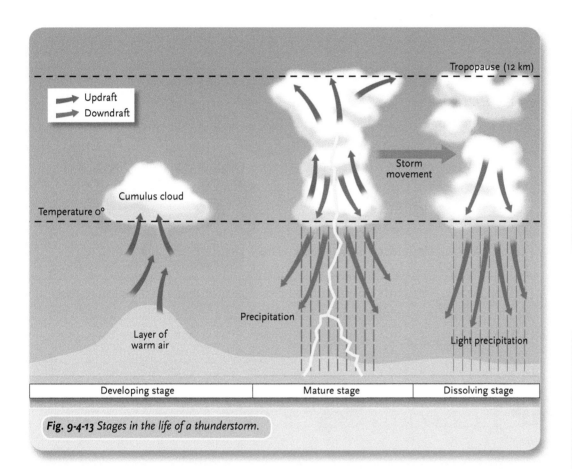

Fig. 9-4-13 Stages in the life of a thunderstorm.

Geofact
Warm, humid conditions are highly favourable for the development of thunderstorms.

Geofact
One large thunderstorm can discharge enough electricity to supply the entire US with electricity for 20 minutes.

The **developing stage** commences when there is intense heating of the air by solar insolation.

■ Warm air is heated, expands and starts to rise in an updraft, like a hot air balloon.
■ As it mixes with the cooler, higher air, the warm air currents are cooled.
■ The water vapour condenses to form large cumulus clouds.
■ At this stage, the clouds are composed primarily of water droplets.
■ The cloud continues to grow, still carried higher into the atmosphere by updrafts.

The **mature stage** commences as the cumulus clouds develop into cumulonimbus clouds that stretch as far as the tropopause, with their distinctive anvil.

■ Tiny droplets of water join together and begin to fall as heavy rain.

Thunderstorm accompanied by lightning.

Geofact

Count the number of seconds between the flash of lightning and the clap of thunder. Divide the number by 5. The answer tells you the distance in miles of the lightning from your position.

- If the atmosphere is cold enough, some of the droplets freeze and begin to fall as hail.
- The falling rain creates a series of downdrafts. These travel even faster than the falling rain.
- The continuous updraft and the new downdrafts cause turbulence as they collide with one another.
- As the water droplets and hail are battered about in the atmosphere, they become charged with electricity. The electric charge builds up until it is discharged as lightning.

The **dissolving stage** commences when the warm updrafts cease and no longer fuel the storm.

- Since warm, moist air can no longer rise, cloud droplets can no longer form.
- The storm dies out with light rain as the cloud disappears from bottom to top.

Leaving Cert Exam Questions

1   Describe and explain the development of patterns of air circulation. In your answer you should refer to at least two of the following:
    - global wind systems
    - land and sea breezes
    - mountain and valley winds. (80 marks)

2   Describe and explain the formation of mid-latitude depressions and anti-cyclones and the weather patterns associated with them. (80 marks)

3   Describe and account for the development of patterns of circulation in either the atmosphere or the oceans. (80 marks)

4   Exchanges of water between ocean and atmosphere vary over the surface of the Earth and this gives rise to distinctive weather conditions. Discuss this statement with reference to examples you have studied. (80 marks)

5   Analyse and explain the interaction between the Earth's atmosphere and oceans. (80 marks)

9.5
Oceanic circulation

Circulation in the oceans affects weather and climate on a variety of scales.

OCEANIC CIRCULATION

Ocean waters are constantly on the move. Any continuous movement of seawater is known as an **ocean current**. These currents are basically rivers in the oceans. There are two types of ocean currents:

■ surface ocean currents
■ deep water ocean currents (see 'Global ocean conveyor belt' on page 301).

Surface ocean currents

These waters make up about 10% of all the water but operate only in the upper 200 metres of the ocean's surface. They are driven by the **wind** and also by **solar heating**.

■ When **wind** blows over the ocean, there is friction between it and the water. This friction causes the surface water to be dragged forward and to move in the direction of the wind. Surface currents roughly follow the wind pattern, so they also come under the influence of the Coriolis effect.

■ **Solar heating** causes water to expand. There is greater heating near the equator, so the water there is about 8 cm higher than it is in the mid-latitudes. This causes a slight slope and water wants to flow down that slope.

The movement of ocean currents is **interrupted by continental land masses**. The result is that as they approach land, surface currents may be split or deflected to flow onwards in a direction that is not related to the global wind pattern.

Learning objectives

After studying this chapter, you should be able to understand:

■ the pattern of surface and deep ocean circulation

■ the pattern and impact of the currents of the North Atlantic.

As a result of all the above factors, surface ocean currents have developed into large circular patterns called **gyres**. Gyres flow in a clockwise direction in the Northern Hemisphere's ocean and anticlockwise in the Southern Hemisphere's ocean because of the Coriolis effect.

Each gyre is made up of warm-water currents and cold-water currents.

■ **Warm surface currents** invariably flow from the tropics towards the higher latitudes.

■ **Cold surface currents** come from higher latitudes and tend to flow towards the equator.

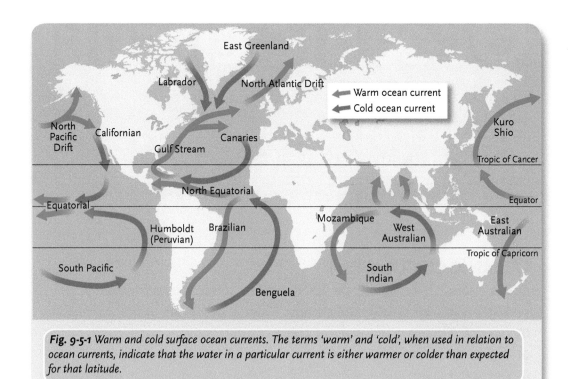

Fig. 9-5-1 *Warm and cold surface ocean currents. The terms 'warm' and 'cold', when used in relation to ocean currents, indicate that the water in a particular current is either warmer or colder than expected for that latitude.*

Impact of ocean currents

Since surface ocean currents transfer large quantities of warm or cold water from one part of the world, they have an impact on climate and weather.

1. Surface currents influence temperatures

Winter temperatures along the coastal regions of north-west Europe are raised because the prevailing westerly winds are warmed as they pass over the North Atlantic Drift. Fiords and ports on the coast of Norway are mostly ice free as a result of its warm waters.

In contrast, the Labrador Current (a mid-depth current) brings cold air and water from polar regions. The coast of Labrador, on the same latitude as Norway, is ice bound for up to five months of the year. The current also brings icebergs into the shipping lanes of the North Atlantic.

2. Surface currents influence precipitation

As air masses pass over the Gulf Stream and North Atlantic Drift, they are warmed and absorb more moisture. Ireland is in the path of these rain-bearing air masses, explaining why we have precipitation throughout the year.

Link

El Niño, pages 310–11. Note the impact of changes in the patterns of ocean currents.

Air masses that pass over the Canaries Current off the coast of Africa are cooled and lose much of their moisture over the ocean. This partially explains the dry conditions that have led to the existence of the coastal section of the Sahara Desert.

Global ocean conveyor belt

There is a large-scale pattern to the way that seawater moves around the world ocean. This pattern is driven by changes in the density of the water. It is known as the global ocean conveyor belt or **thermohaline circulation**. It affects water at the ocean surface and all the way to the deep ocean.

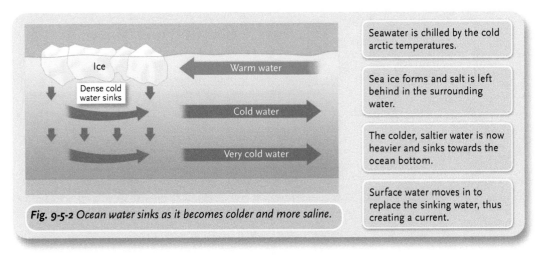

Seawater is chilled by the cold arctic temperatures.

Sea ice forms and salt is left behind in the surrounding water.

The colder, saltier water is now heavier and sinks towards the ocean bottom.

Surface water moves in to replace the sinking water, thus creating a current.

Fig. 9-5-2 *Ocean water sinks as it becomes colder and more saline.*

1 The conveyor belt begins on the surface of the ocean in the arctic. Cold saline water sinks towards the ocean bottom.

2 This deep water moves south, between the continents, past the equator and down to the ends of Africa and South America.

3 As it moves around Antarctica, the conveyor splits into two and each turns northward. One section moves into the Indian Ocean, the other into the Pacific Ocean. These two sections warm up and become less dense as they travel northward toward the equator.

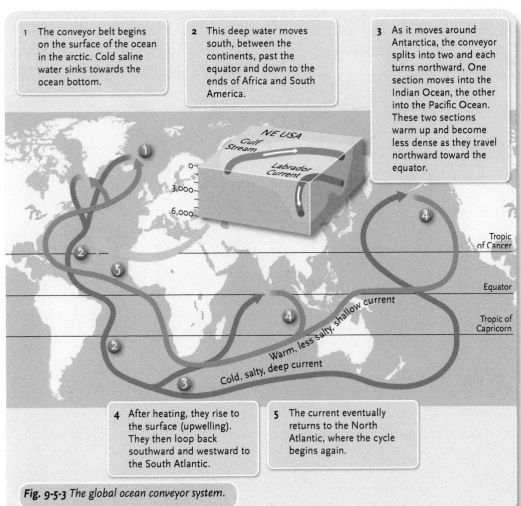

4 After heating, they rise to the surface (upwelling). They then loop back southward and westward to the South Atlantic.

5 The current eventually returns to the North Atlantic, where the cycle begins again.

Fig. 9-5-3 *The global ocean conveyor system.*

Question

The mean January temperature at Shannon Airport is 6°C. The mean January temperature at New York is –6°C, even though New York is about 1,300 km closer to the equator. Why is there such a difference?

Definition

THERMOHALINE CIRCULATION of the ocean refers to the flow of ocean water caused by changes in density as a result of variations in temperature and salinity.

Geofact

It is estimated that water takes about 1,000 years to complete the journey along the global conveyor belt.

Ocean currents of the North Atlantic

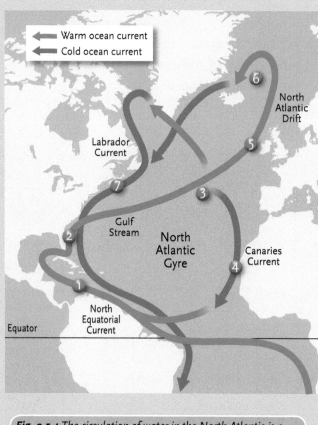

Fig. 9-5-4 *The circulation of water in the North Atlantic is a combination of warm surface currents and cold deep currents.*

1 The circulation in the North Atlantic is set off by the **North Equatorial Drift**. Driven by the NE trade winds, this massive surface current of warm water is driven westward towards the Gulf of Mexico.

2 Now called the **Gulf Stream**, it travels north along the surface of the ocean and up the east coast of America.

3 It then moves out into the Atlantic Ocean. When it reaches the Mid-Atlantic Ridge, it splits into two sections.

4 One branch moves down along the west coast of Africa (the cold **Canaries Current**) to complete a full circulation. This circulation is called the **North Atlantic Gyre**.

5 The second branch, now called the **North Atlantic Drift**, moves in a north-easterly direction, hugging the coasts of Ireland, Scotland and Norway.

6 When it reaches the arctic, it is a cold saline current. This heavy water now sinks towards the bottom of the ocean.

7 It flows southward along the east coast of America as the cold deep-water **Labrador Current**.

Geofact
The Gulf Stream is about 80 km wide and travels at about 6 km per hour. The Gulf Stream moves about 500 times as much water as the Amazon River and all its tributaries.

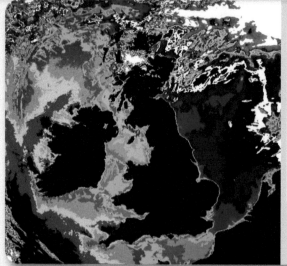

Coloured satellite image depicting the sea surface temperatures around Ireland and Britain. The colours are coded from red (warmest) through yellow and green to blue (coolest). The generally warmer (red and yellow) seas to the west of the British Isles are caused by the influence of the warm Gulf Stream and North Atlantic Drift currents. Note how much colder the English Channel and North Sea are.

Leaving Cert Exam Questions

1   Analyse and explain the interaction between the Earth's atmosphere and oceans. (80 marks)

2   Describe and account for the development of patterns of circulation in either the atmosphere or the oceans. (80 marks)

Climatic environments

The surface of the Earth can be divided into distinctive climatic environments.

WORLD CLIMATES

The world can be divided into six major climatic regions, according to the **Koppen climate classification system**. This system is based on average monthly averages of **temperature** and **precipitation**.

Koppen's system is only a guide to the general climatic regions of the planet. The borders between the regions do not represent instant shifts in climate, but are merely transition zones where climate, and especially weather, can vary.

Learning objectives

After studying this chapter, you should be able to understand:

■ the classification of world climates

■ the distribution and characteristics of the tropical rainforest climate.

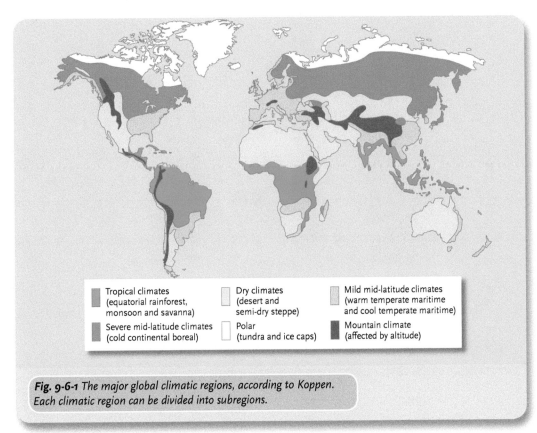

Tropical climates (equatorial rainforest, monsoon and savanna)

Severe mid-latitude climates (cold continental boreal)

Dry climates (desert and semi-dry steppe)

Polar (tundra and ice caps)

Mild mid-latitude climates (warm temperate maritime and cool temperate maritime)

Mountain climate (affected by altitude)

Fig. 9-6-1 *The major global climatic regions, according to Koppen. Each climatic region can be divided into subregions.*

The syllabus requires that you study one distinctive global climate. We will study the equatorial climate.

EQUATORIAL CLIMATE

Equatorial climate is also known as a tropical rainforest climate. It is a climate in which temperatures are very high, humidity levels are high and there is rain throughout the year. The other characteristic is that there is very little seasonal variation in the climate.

Distribution of the equatorial climate

Equatorial climate zones in which tropical rainforests grow are found close to the equator, extending to about 15° of latitude, north and south. There are three belts of equatorial climate that span the globe within these latitudes:

■ **South and Central America:** The largest of the equatorial climate zones is located in the Amazon Basin. Other zones include parts of Panama, Costa Rica and Nicaragua.

■ **Africa:** The largest zones in Africa are found in the Congo Basin and Guinea coast. The island of Madagascar, off the east coast of Africa, also has a large zone of equatorial climate.

■ **Australasia:** The main equatorial climate zones are found in western India, Bangladesh, Malaysia and the islands of Java and Borneo. There is a very small zone in north-eastern Australia.

Geofact
Tropical climates include equatorial climate, monsoon climate and savanna climate.

Questions
1. Which South American country has the greatest land area with equatorial climate?
2. Name the two continents that do not have a land area with equatorial climate.

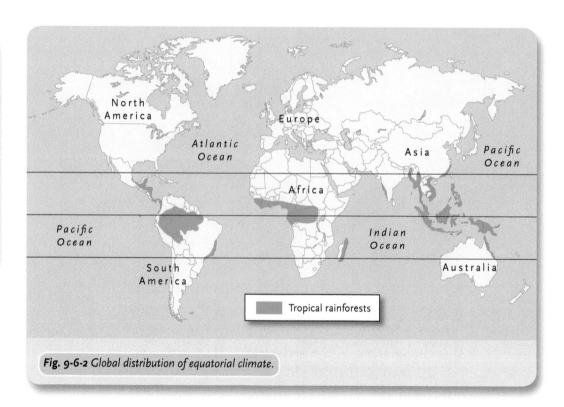

Fig. 9-6-2 *Global distribution of equatorial climate.*

Characteristics of the equatorial climate

On average, the **temperature** of the equatorial climate is about 27°C.
The annual range of temperature (the difference between the average
temperatures of the warmest and coolest months) is very small: hardly more
than 2°C to 3°C. The daily range (the difference between the day and night
temperatures) can be up to 9°C, leading to the description that 'night is the
winter of the equatorial climate'.

■ The low latitude of these zones means that sunlight strikes Earth at a very
high angle. This means that there is more direct sunlight hitting the land
and sea than anywhere else.

■ This intensity is also due to the consistent day length for regions on or near
the equator: about 12 hours a day, 365 days per year.

■ The daily temperature range is due to the sunny mornings and cloudy
afternoons of cooling rain.

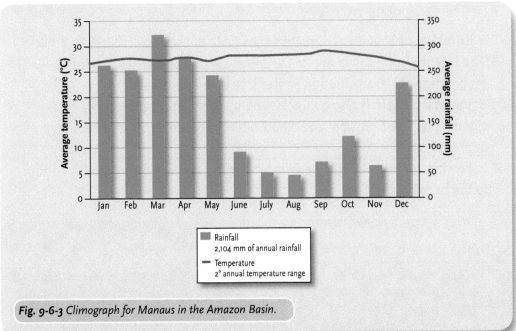

Fig. 9-6-3 *Climograph for Manaus in the Amazon Basin.*

Questions

Examine Fig. 9-6-3 and
answer the following
questions.
1. What is the hottest
   month?
2. What is the coolest
   month?
3. What is the annual
   temperature range?
4. What is the driest
   month?
5. What is the total
   rainfall for the first
   three months of the
   year?

Annual average **precipitation** exceeds 2,000 mm, with some regions
experiencing 3,600 mm. Precipitation is not only abundant, but also
dependable. While rain falls on most days, it is not evenly distributed
throughout the year. Two seasons can be identified: the very rainy season and
the less rainy season (see Fig. 9-6-3). Afternoons are characterised by very
heavy showers. About 50% of the precipitation in the rainforest comes from
its own evaporation.

■ The north-east trade winds and south-east trade winds converge in a low
pressure zone close to the equator (see Fig. 9-6-4). These winds bring with
them a fairly large amount of moisture from over the warm tropical oceans.

■ Solar heating in the region forces the warm air to rise through convection.
The air is cooled as it rises and condensation occurs.

■ Clouds form in the late morning and early afternoon hours and by
mid-afternoon, convectional thunderstorms form and precipitation begins.

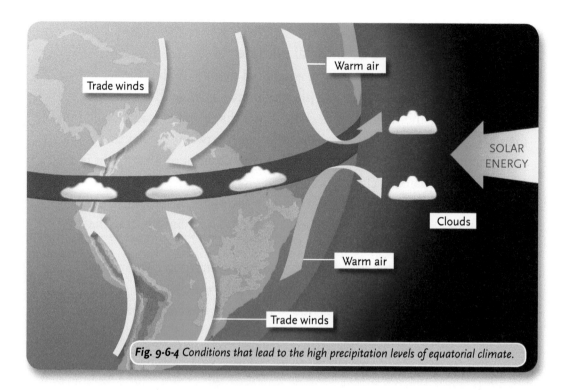

Trade winds

Warm air

SOLAR
ENERGY

Clouds

Warm air

Trade winds

Fig. 9-6-4 *Conditions that lead to the high precipitation levels of equatorial climate.*

The **humidity** of equatorial climate zones does not usually fall below 80%.

■ The intense humidity is due to the moisture that comes from rainfall, evaporation and transpiration (water loss through leaves).

■ Equatorial climate is also characterised by fairly large amounts of cloudiness. The humidity and cloudiness make the equatorial heat very oppressive.

■ Following cooling at night, early morning fog and heavy dew occur, adding to the humidity.

An afternoon tropical rainstorm in the Amazon Basin. Note the dense cloud cover.

Leaving Cert Exam Questions

1   Give an explanatory account of any one global climate you have studied.
    (80 marks)

2   Account for the distinctive nature of one global climate that you have studied.
    (80 marks)

9.7

Climate change

The characteristics of climate have changed over time and space and continue to change today. Some of this change is as a result of natural phenomena, both long term and short term. Other change is as a result of human activity.

Learning objectives

After studying this chapter, you should be able to understand:

■ how climate has changed in the past

■ how climate continues to change today

■ human influences on climate change.

ICE AGES

Ice ages are an example of **long-term natural climate change** that has occurred in the past and may occur again in the future.

Earth has experienced a number of ice ages. The most recent began about 2 million years ago and ended about 10,000 years ago. This is the ice age that shaped much of the Irish landscape.

There are at least two explanations as to what caused the Earth to enter an ice age:

■ the so-called Milankovitch cycle

■ changes within Earth and its atmosphere.

Milankovitch cycle

There are gradual changes in the passage of Earth through space. The changes are sometimes called **stretch**, **tilt** and **wobble**. Each can cause a small reduction in temperature, but when all three combine, the combined reduction in temperature may trigger an ice age. This is called the Milankovitch cycle, named after a Serbian astronomer. As a result, there are variations in the amount of incoming solar radiation (insolation) as well as changes in its seasonal distribution.

It is not a matter of the world suddenly getting colder, however. It's more that it does not get warm enough in the summer. If the amount of summer sunshine drops below a critical value, snow from the past winter does not

Definition

The warm period between ice ages is called an **INTERGLACIAL**.

melt away. As snow continues to accumulate, ice sheets begin to grow and an ice age is more likely to occur.

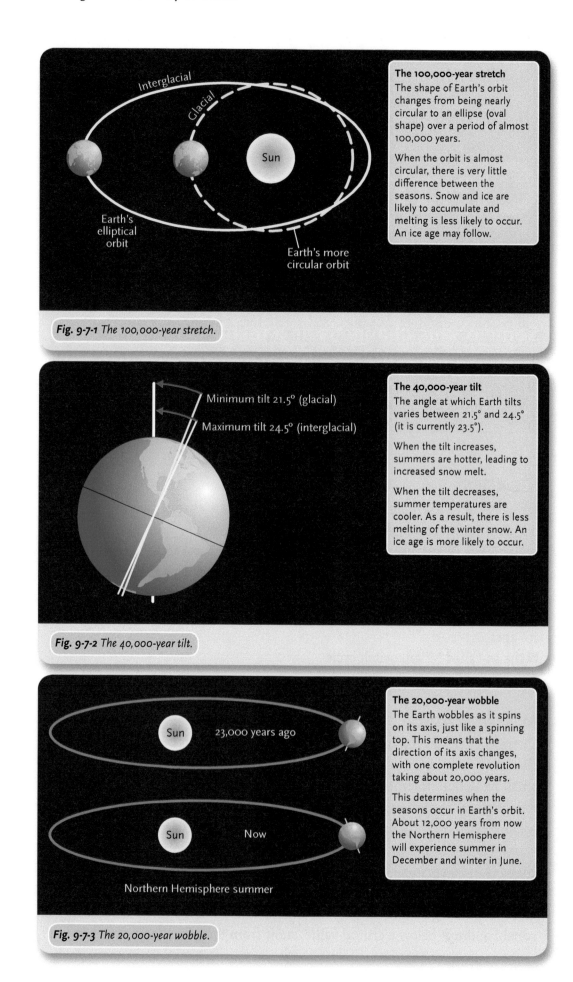

The 100,000-year stretch
The shape of Earth's orbit changes from being nearly circular to an ellipse (oval shape) over a period of almost 100,000 years.

When the orbit is almost circular, there is very little difference between the seasons. Snow and ice are likely to accumulate and melting is less likely to occur. An ice age may follow.

Fig. 9-7-1 *The 100,000-year stretch.*

The 40,000-year tilt
The angle at which Earth tilts varies between 21.5° and 24.5° (it is currently 23.5°).

When the tilt increases, summers are hotter, leading to increased snow melt.

When the tilt decreases, summer temperatures are cooler. As a result, there is less melting of the winter snow. An ice age is more likely to occur.

Fig. 9-7-2 *The 40,000-year tilt.*

The 20,000-year wobble
The Earth wobbles as it spins on its axis, just like a spinning top. This means that the direction of its axis changes, with one complete revolution taking about 20,000 years.

This determines when the seasons occur in Earth's orbit. About 12,000 years from now the Northern Hemisphere will experience summer in December and winter in June.

Fig. 9-7-3 *The 20,000-year wobble.*

Changes within Earth and its atmosphere

The positions of the continents change as a result of continental drift. The presence of large landmasses close to the poles seems to trigger the development of extensive ice sheets. For example, about 250–350 million years ago, the southern portion of Pangaea was at the South Pole. Scientists believe this may have led to an ice age over what are now the southern parts of Africa, South America, India and Australia (see *Today's World 1*, Figure 2.3, page 9).

Continental uplift following plate collision may have been sufficient to start an ice age. The Himalayas resulted from such uplift. They are so high that they divert atmospheric circulation (winds). This in turn can change the pattern of ocean currents, creating colder climates. When the Tibetan Plateau was raised past the snow line, an ice-covered surface of more than 2 million km² resulted. This ice can reflect up to 70% of incoming energy.

Volcanic eruptions release huge amounts of dust, gas and ash into the atmosphere. This can impact global climate by reflecting solar energy back into space. This reduces the amount of solar radiation (insolation) that reaches Earth's surface, causing global cooling.

The so-called Little Ice Age was caused by a 50-year-long series of massive volcanic eruptions in the tropics. These spewed dust, gas and ash into the atmosphere of the Northern Hemisphere. The Little Ice Age began around 1300 and extended through to the mid-1800s. Glaciers advanced in the mountains of Europe and North America. The River Thames and the canals and rivers of the Netherlands often froze over. Advancing glaciers in Iceland extended so far around the island that they closed the harbours to shipping.

Question

Explain two reasons why an ice age might occur again.

The Frost Fair of the Winter of 1683–4 on the River Thames, with Old London Bridge in the Distance.

Geofact

About 400,000 people are believed to have died during the Great Frost that swept across Ireland between 1739 and 1741.

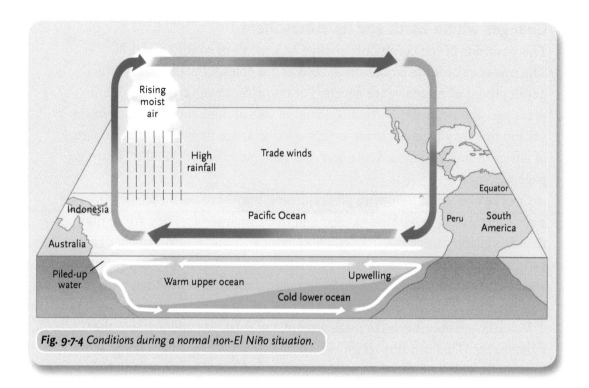

Fig. 9-7-4 *Conditions during a normal non-El Niño situation.*

Questions

1. Explain how El Niño occurs.
2. Describe its effects.

EL NIÑO

El Niño is an example of **short-term natural climate change**. It is a local event that occurs every three to seven years over the waters of the equatorial Pacific Ocean. It can last for up to two years.

In normal non-El Niño conditions, the trade winds blow west across the tropical Pacific Ocean. They push warm surface water ahead of them so that the ocean surface is about 40 cm higher at Indonesia than it is off South America. The air is heated by the warm water below it, thus increasing the likelihood of heavy rainstorms near Indonesia.

In the eastern part, cold, deep water gets pulled up from below to replace the water that was pushed west. This upwelling of cold water leads to cool temperatures off South America. The air becomes too dense to rise and produce clouds. Thus, Peru is relatively dry.

El Niño happens when the trade winds weaken or even reverse direction. This allows the piled-up warmer water from the western Pacific to flow towards the east. This flattens out the sea level and builds up warm surface water off the coast of South America. The clouds and rainstorms associated with warm ocean waters also shift toward the east.

Effects of El Niño

The effects of El Niño are felt not just in the regions where it occurs, but across the world.

- Rains that normally would fall over the tropical rainforests of Indonesia now start falling over the deserts of Peru. This leads to large-scale destructive flooding and landslides, which in turn damage roads, bridges and property.
- Plankton that lives in the cold waters off the coast of Peru cannot survive in warm waters. This upsets the food chain, and the anchovies that feed off

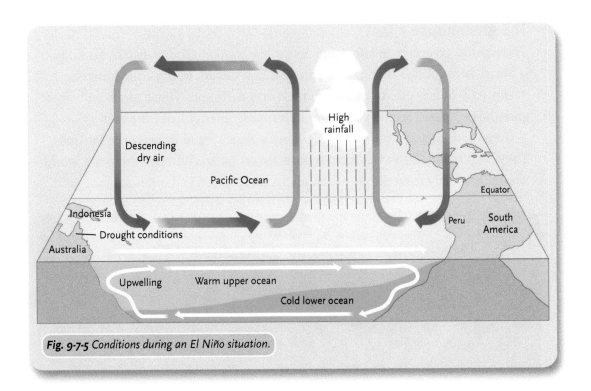

Fig. 9-7-5 *Conditions during an El Niño situation.*

them are forced to move to other, colder waters. Fishing for, processing and exporting anchovies are major industries in Peru and have been damaged as a result.

■ Regions in the west Pacific (including Australia and Indonesia) are affected by drought. This can sometimes lead to devastating bush and forest fires in Australia. Fires can cause millions of dollars worth of damage to property.

■ The eastward movement of the atmospheric heat source changes the global atmospheric circulation. This in turn disrupts weather patterns in regions that are far removed from the tropical Pacific.

■ The west coast of Mexico and the US sees more hurricanes hitting landfall during El Niño – but there is a reduction in the number of Atlantic hurricanes.

■ There is a link between a strong El Niño and weather over Central and Western Europe (including Ireland). It may lead to heavier than normal spring rainfall and summer heat waves.

GLOBAL WARMING

'Global warming' is the term used to describe the gradual increase in temperature of the Earth's atmosphere and oceans. It is an example of **climate change influenced by human activities**. These activities have led to an increase in the **greenhouse effect**.

Global warming does not mean we will all have warmer weather in the future. As the planet heats, climate patterns will change. There will be more extreme and unpredictable weather across the world – some places will be hotter, some colder; some wetter, others drier.

Geofact
Earth has warmed by an average of nearly 1°C in the past century.

Geofact
The 17 warmest years on record have all occurred since 1995.

The greenhouse effect

The **natural greenhouse effect** acts like a big blanket around Earth, keeping it warm. Most of it is due to water vapour and clouds in the atmosphere. About 10% of it is due to carbon dioxide and methane. These gases, known as **greenhouse gases**, are very efficient at trapping energy from the sun.

Greenhouse gases are vital in the Earth's atmosphere in certain quantities. They help make life as we know it possible on Earth. Without them the world would be mostly frozen. But too much of these gases is dangerous too.

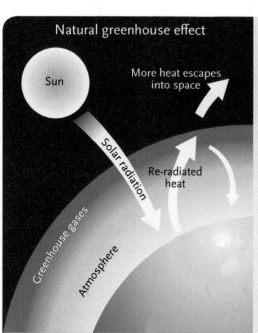
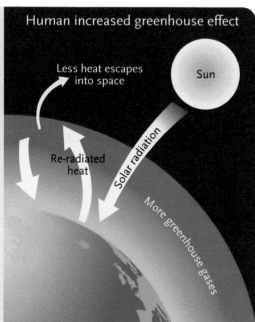

Fig. 9-7-6 *As the amount of greenhouse gases in the atmosphere increases, they trap an increasing amount of solar radiation, leading to an increase in the temperature of the atmosphere.*

The **human increased greenhouse effect** occurs when there is an increase in the amount of greenhouse gases in the atmosphere. This means that more heat gets trapped, causing the temperature of the Earth to rise, resulting in **global warming**.

The increase in **carbon dioxide** in the atmosphere is due to:

■ The burning of fossil fuels. These include coal, oil and gas that are burned for heat, transportation and the generation of electricity.

■ Deforestation and slash-and-burn farming practices. Trees absorb carbon dioxide and deforestation limits the size of this carbon store. Burning the trees adds to the carbon dioxide in the atmosphere.

The increase in **methane** in the atmosphere is due to:

■ The increase in rice production. Paddy fields are the world's greatest source of methane gas.

■ The increase in numbers of cattle. Cattle flatulence and waste put about 100 million tonnes of methane into the atmosphere each year.

Geofact

Without the greenhouse effect, Earth's temperature would be about −18°C.

Geofact

Methane is over 20 to 30 times more effective in trapping heat in the atmosphere than carbon dioxide.

Questions

1. What is the greenhouse effect?
2. How is it influenced by human activities?

Effects of global warming

Global warming affects the weather patterns on Earth, causing **climate change**.

Sea levels will rise. This will happen as ice caps continue to melt and warmer ocean water expands.

■ There will be large-scale **flooding** in low-lying regions. Much of the world's best farmland is low lying, as are many of the world's largest cities. In Bangladesh alone, there are 15 million people living within 1 metre of sea level. An increase of 30 cm in sea level would lead to the flooding of 175,000 hectares of Ireland's coastal zone, including large urban areas.

■ There will be a loss of polar bear and seal habitats and knock-on effects on local people. Canadian Inuit village life is being transformed as rising temperatures are thinning the ice and leading to a loss of hunting and polar bears.

■ The rate of coastal **erosion** will increase. A 1 metre rise in sea level would generally cause soft shorelines to erode inland by between 50 and 200 metres.

Climate models will change. According to experts, the following changes might happen:

■ **Violent storm activity will increase** as temperatures rise and more water evaporates from the oceans. The frequency of hurricanes, typhoons and tornadoes may decrease, but their severity will increase.

■ **Climate belts may shift.** Temperate climate belts would move to higher latitudes and vegetation belts would follow. Ireland's climate might change from a cool temperate climate to a warm temperate climate. This would see a change in farming patterns, with maize and vines replacing grass and barley as the dominant crops.

■ **Ocean currents** may be interrupted. This would have severe impacts, such as those that already result from El Niño (see pages 310–11).

Geofact

Scientists have estimated that sea levels can be expected to rise by 25–40 centimetres by the year 2100.

Flooding in low-lying coastal areas of Bangladesh.

The area of the Arctic that is covered by ice all year round has been decreasing by about 10% per decade. There is less ice to reflect the heat from the sun's rays, so the oceans absorb the heat instead.

Leaving Cert Exam Questions

1   The characteristics of climate can change over time and space. Discuss this statement with reference to examples you have studied. (80 marks)

2   Climate change is a cause of global concern. Discuss. (80 marks)

3   Explore one argument in support of and one argument against the idea that major global climate change is currently underway. (80 marks)

4   Describe and explain why the characteristics of climate change over time. (80 marks)

Climate and economic development

9.8

Climate characteristics have an influence on economic development, in particular on agriculture, domestic water supply, desertification and tourism.

INFLUENCE OF CLIMATE ON AGRICULTURE

Agriculture is especially influenced by two aspects of climate:

■ the amount and seasonal distribution of rainfall

■ temperature.

Ireland

Ireland enjoys a cool temperate maritime climate, due mainly to its proximity to the Atlantic Ocean and the presence of the North Atlantic Drift. It is a climate that could be described as moist, **mild** and **changeable**.

Most of the eastern half of Ireland receives between 750 mm and 1,000 mm of rainfall per year. Rainfall in the west averages between 1,000 mm and 1,250 mm. In mountainous regions, mostly in the west, rainfall exceeds 2,000 mm per year. The wettest months everywhere are December and January. April and June are generally the driest months.

Summers are generally warm, with temperatures averaging 12°C to 16°C. Winters are mild, with average temperatures ranging from 4°C to 7°C. There are regional variations in temperature, with inland areas being cooler in winter and warmer in summer than coastal areas. The south-east has the greatest amount of sunshine.

The well-distributed rainfall makes Ireland one of the finest **grass-producing** regions in the world. Almost 90% of agricultural land is devoted to grass, hay, silage and rough grazing. The mild temperatures mean that there is a long growing season and cattle can be kept on the land for seven to eight months of the year. These characteristics support the **dairy and beef** industries in Munster and the Mid-West.

Learning objectives

After studying this chapter, you should be able to understand:

■ how climate has influenced economic development in agriculture, domestic water supply, desertification and tourism.

Link

Today's World 1, pages 279–80 and 293–4.

Soils in the east and south-east are well-drained brown earths. With mild spring weather and drier, sunny summers, they are suited to **arable** farming. **Barley** is the most popular cereal crop grown by farmers and is used for the malting, seed and feed industries in the country. **Wheat** and oats are the other important cereal crops.

The wetter regions of the country, mostly along the western seaboard, have podzol and peat soils that have been heavily leached by rainfall. This, combined with heavier rainfall and lower temperatures, restricts agriculture. **Sheep farming** is important and an increasing area of upland is being given over to the planting of **coniferous forests**, which grow rapidly in the damp climate. Sitka spruce matures in Ireland in about 33 years.

Climate change may lead to some summer drought in the east and south-east of the country. This will create problems for pasture-based farming (dairy and beef) but may lead to the introduction of new crops, such as soya beans.

RAINFALL AND DOMESTIC WATER SUPPLY

Ireland has one of the highest water availability rates in Europe. The heavy and well-distributed rainfall pattern supplies plenty of water for both domestic and industrial needs. Water usage in Ireland is significantly higher than elsewhere in Europe. Average water leakage levels of almost 30% in Ireland are also well above international standards.

Atlantic weather systems are the dominant influence on Irish weather. Rain-bearing winds hit the west coast first, often in conjunction with weather fronts. The west is therefore generally wetter than the east, as can be seen in the map of Ireland's rainfall distribution (see Fig. 9-3-7 on page 286).

About 80% of domestic water in Ireland is taken from **surface water** sources. This is particularly so for public water supplies. Following extraction, the water has to be treated to make it fit for human consumption (see the following case study).

The remainder of Ireland's drinking water originates from **groundwater** and **springs**. Group water schemes and small private supplies tend to be slightly more reliant on these sources. Water from these sources has considerable benefits. It is generally of good quality and does not need treatment prior to use. Groundwater can come to the surface naturally as springs, although most is extracted by drilling wells.

While we receive enough water from rainfall to meet the needs of the population, there is an imbalance in the demand for water. The eastern part of the country is more densely populated than the west. It also has a relatively smaller supply of rainwater. Climate change will probably result in less precipitation in the east. When the country undergoes a dry spell, water levels drop and it may be necessary to put rationing in place, for example hose pipe bans. These shortages are predicted to increase in severity in the coming decades, with the Dublin Region Water Supply facing the most significant challenges.

Geofact
The average domestic daily water usage per capita in Ireland is 160 litres.

Geofact
The main water-using sector is industry (72%), followed by domestic use (18%) and agriculture (10%).

Question
How might climate change affect
(i) agriculture and
(ii) domestic water supply in Ireland?

For now, public water mains and treatment plants are administered and maintained by the various local authorities. A new body, **Irish Water**, is to be established as a subsidiary of Bord Gáis. It will gradually assume the operation of water services from the local authorities on a phased basis. It is expected that this will not be completed before 2017. This change in policy may also lead to the introduction of water charges and water metering.

CASE STUDY

Dublin Region Water Supply

The largest water scheme involves the provision of more than 520 million litres of water per day to the Dublin Region Water Supply, covering seven local authorities. The two main sources of surface water are the River Liffey (including Blessington Lake) and the River Vartry.

At present there is less than 2% spare capacity between supply and demand. This is regarded as insufficient, since a hot spell can drive up demand by as much as 40 million litres per day. Burst pipes in a bad cold spell can lose as much as 20 million litres per day.

Studies have been underway since 2004 in relation to the development of a potential new water supply source for Dublin Region Water Supply. In total, 10 potential new options were evaluated.

The recommended option involves the extraction of water from the northern end of **Lough Derg on the Shannon**. The plan is to extract about 350 million litres per day – approximately 3% of the river's average discharge.

The raw water would be extracted over 10 months (with no extraction during summer low water) and pumped into large-scale storage lakes in **cutaway bogs** in Co. Offaly. The water would then

Blessington Lake, Co. Wicklow, is an artificial lake/reservoir, covering 2,500 hectares. It was created in the 1930s to supply water to Dublin. Poulaphouca Dam also supplies hydroelectric power to the national grid.

be treated before being pumped to the east. Supplies would be made available not only to the Dublin Region Water Supply, but also to local authorities in the Mid East and Midland regions.

Concerns have been expressed about the proposal. The ESB warned that it would seek compensation if the extraction of water from Lough Derg resulted in a loss of electricity generation capacity at Ardnacrusha. Concerns have also been raised about the possible negative effect it would have on Lough Derg and the lower River Shannon. These relate to the

impact on the navigational flow, fish life and ecology. Negative impact could in turn hit angling and boating, which are major tourist attractions for Killaloe and surrounding villages.

Geofact
The Vartry scheme was constructed in the 1860s by Dublin Corporation and remains in service over 130 years later.

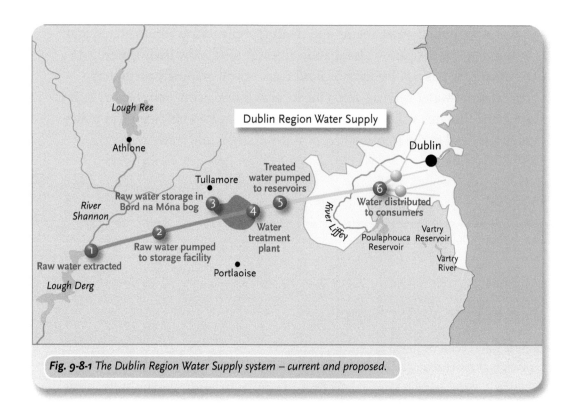

Fig. 9-8-1 *The Dublin Region Water Supply system – current and proposed.*

IMPACT OF DROUGHT AND DESERTIFICATION ON ECONOMIC DEVELOPMENT

The Sahel is a belt of semi-arid land about 3 million km² in area that runs for 4,000 km east to west across Africa. It is the transitional zone between the arid Sahara Desert to the north and the slightly tropical areas of Central Africa to the south. It occupies parts of several countries, including Mali, Burkina Faso, Chad and Sudan.

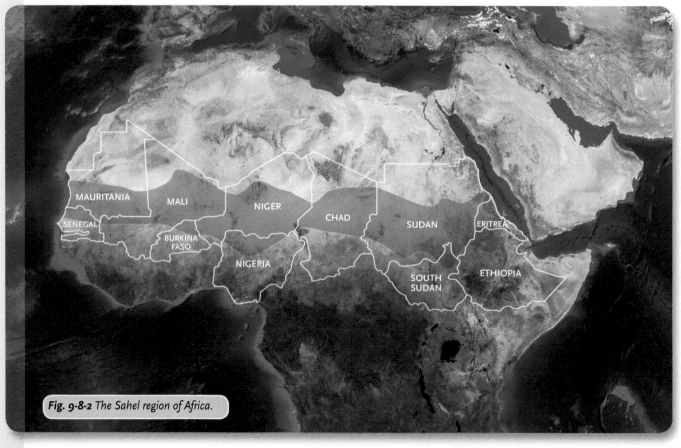

Fig. 9-8-2 *The Sahel region of Africa.*

There is rapid population growth in the region. The growth rate is about 3% per annum, resulting in a doubling of the population approximately every 22 years. Thus, most parts of the Sahel are now overpopulated.

In the latter part of the 20th century, desert conditions advanced southwards into the Sahel by between 5 km and 10 km per year. This spread of desert conditions is known as **desertification**.

Desertification does not just refer to the expansion of existing deserts. It also refers to the formation of areas where soil fertility and vegetation cover have been damaged.

Desertification results from a combination of **climate change** (drought) and **human activities** (overgrazing, overcropping and deforestation).

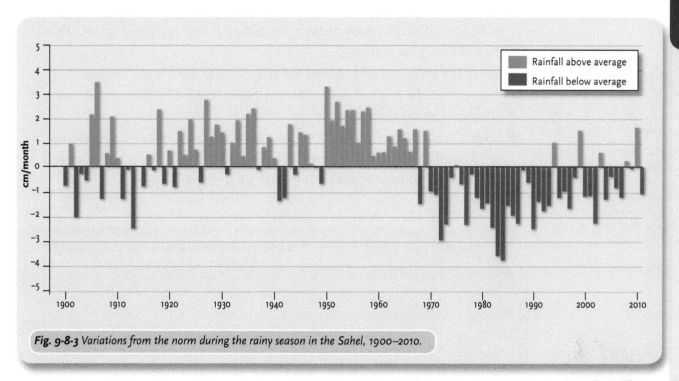

Fig. 9-8-3 *Variations from the norm during the rainy season in the Sahel, 1900–2010.*

- **Climate change:** The climate in the Sahel swings between extreme heat and more temperate conditions, with rain only falling in four or five months of the year, usually between May and October when the growing season gets underway. However, over the past 40 years, rainfall has dramatically decreased and has also become less reliable.

- **Overgrazing:** The ownership of livestock, particularly cattle, was seen as a symbol of wealth and social status in many of the tribes in the Sahel. At the same time, the number of farmers in the region was growing. The increase in cattle and goat numbers led to increased competition for land among **nomadic herders**. The land was grazed beyond the point where it could renew itself.

- **Overcropping:** The population of the region has grown rapidly since 1960, leading to an increased demand for food. Herding was gradually replaced by the growing of **food crops**. As a result, the area devoted to crops has trebled in the past 50 years. With overcropping, fertility declines and yields decrease rapidly.

Link
Desertification in the Sahel, page 176–9.

Definition
DESERTIFICATION is the spread of desert conditions into new lands, turning productive land to wasteland through overuse and mismanagement.

- **Deforestation:** Deforestation is the large-scale clearing of forest and then using the land for a non-forest purpose. Forests are cleared in order to provide extra land for agriculture by the **slash-and-burn** method. They are also cut to provide wood for house construction and especially fuel for cooking and heating.

Economic impacts

The economic impacts of drought and desertification include the following.

- The decrease in production creates a **cycle of poverty** in the affected countries.
- The loss of agricultural production has a negative impact on **employment** and **GDP** as well as personal loss of income. The primary sector employs up to 60% of the active population in the Sahel. It also produces up to 40% of the GDP of these countries.
- There is a serious threat to **food security**. This in turn leads to huge increases in the price of food, creating difficulties for families and leading to hunger, famine and malnutrition.
- Large numbers of **refugees** have fled the Sahel, moving to refugee camps in neighbouring regions. Refugees lose their capacity for self-reliance as well as putting economic strain on the destination regions.

Definition
CYCLE OF POVERTY:
The set of factors by which poverty, once started, is likely to continue unless there is outside involvement.

Village homesteads in the Sahel. The area is vulnerable to drought and soil erosion, leading to desertification.

CLIMATE AND TOURISM

Climate is probably the most important influence on the choice of tourism destinations, whether it is beach destinations in the summer or winter sports.

The eastern and southern coasts of Spain (the Spanish costas) are the most popular tourism destinations in Europe, with the **Mediterranean climate** making them particularly attractive.

Tourism in the costas

Most of the visitors come from Northern Europe. Over 80% of them base their holidays on a 'push-and-pull' effect. They are attracted by the hot, dry, sunny weather of the Mediterranean.

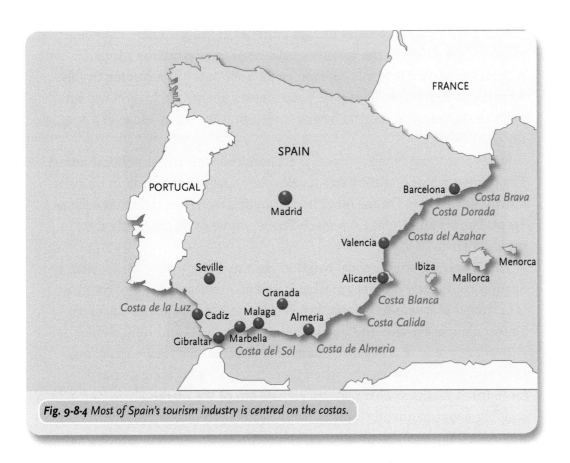

Fig. 9-8-4 Most of Spain's tourism industry is centred on the costas.

The costas have a **warm temperate** (Mediterranean) climate. Summers are hot and dry, with average temperatures ranging from 28°C to 35°C. Winter temperatures average 15°C, attracting many retired people in the off season. The Costa del Sol receives almost 3,000 hours of sunshine per annum. The region experiences very little rainfall during the summer months.

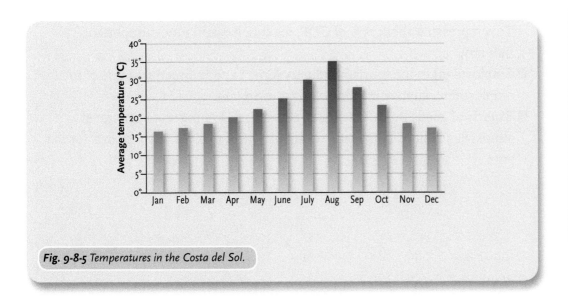

Fig. 9-8-5 Temperatures in the Costa del Sol.

Questions

Examine Fig. 9-8-5 and answer the following questions.
1. Name the hottest month and its temperature.
2. What is the average temperature for June, July and August?
3. What is the annual temperature range?

Economic impacts

Tourism is a labour-intensive service industry. Direct employment occurs in areas such as accommodation, restaurants, transportation, amusements and the retail trade. Indirect employment is generated in areas such as food production, construction and infrastructure.

Tourism dominates Spain's **foreign currency** earnings. These have offset up to 75% of the deficit in the country's balance of trade since the 1960s.

Spanish tourism is highly seasonal, with 40% of tourists coming in July, August and September. This puts pressures on energy production and on water resources, with tourists having three times the water usage of a Spanish city dweller.

Spanish tourism is highly open to economic **downturns** or **political unrest**. The current global recession has resulted in a gradual reduction in tourism activity since 2009. On the other hand, political unrest in countries such as Egypt, Tunisia and Greece has made Spain a more attractive destination in the short term.

The Spanish tourism model **needs to change**. The demand for tourism in Spain is completely different to what it was just 10 years ago. The country is in danger of losing its competitive edge to newer, cheaper destinations. Tourist choices are also diversifying to include cultural and rural elements.

Tourism can have a **negative economic impact** on the local population. Land and property values rise when there is ongoing building demand for tourism facilities. This may price locals out of the market. However, a building boom frequently leads to overinvestment in accommodation. This may eventually lead to a drop in the value of accommodation, creating new problems.

Another problem is that some of this tourism revenue does not contribute to the Spanish economy. Tourists arrive as part of an inclusive tour, using foreign-owned airlines. A significant proportion of the total holiday price paid by tourists may not go to Spain.

Spain's tourism industry is still flourishing, although it showed reductions in all areas in 2012. Nevertheless, early reports suggest that:

- The total contribution of tourism to Spanish **GDP** in 2012 was €150 billion. This represents about 15% of GDP, making it Spain's most important industry.
- **Employment** in the tourism industry (direct and indirect) was 13% of total employment, supporting almost 2,250,000 jobs.
- **Exports** of goods by tourists (gifts, souvenirs, clothing, etc.) generated almost €45 billion. This made up about 15% of total Spanish exports for the year.

Question

List three benefits of tourism to the Spanish economy.

Tourism development at Fuengirola near Malaga on the Costa del Sol.

Leaving Cert Exam Questions

1   Examine the influence of climate on economic development, referring to examples you have studied. (80 marks)

2   Examine the impact of rainfall on agriculture and on domestic water supplies. (80 marks)

3   Examine the impact of climate on the development of tourism in any region you have studied. (80 marks)

4   Climate characteristics have an influence on economic development. Discuss this statement with reference to agriculture. (80 marks)

5   Climate influences economic development. Discuss this statement with reference to examples you have studied. (80 marks)